MEMOIRS OF THE FUTURE

MEMOIRS OF THE FUTURE

W. WARREN WAGAR

Global Publications
Binghamton, New York
2001

Copyright © 2001 by W. Warren Wagar

All rights reserved. No portion of this publication may be duplicated in any way without the expressed written consent of the publisher, except in the form of brief excerpts or quotations for review purposes.

Library of Congress Cataloging-in-Publication Data

Wagar, W. Warren.
 Memoirs of the future / W. Warren Wagar.
     p. cm.
Includes bibliographical references (p.   ) and index.
  ISBN 1-58684-133-5 (pbk. : alk. paper)
  1. Wagar, W. Warren. 2. Futurologists--United States--Biography. 3. Forecasting. 4. Twentieth century--Forecasts. 5. Twenty-first century--Forecasts. I. Title.
  CB158 .W33 2001
  303.49'092--dc21

ISBN 1-58684-133-5

Published and Distributed by:
Global Publications, Binghamton University
State University of New York at Binghamton
LNG 99, Binghamton University
Binghamton, New York, USA 13902-6000
Phone: (607) 777-4495 or 777-6104; Fax: (607) 777-6132
Email: pmorewed@binghamton.edu
http://ssips.binghamton.edu

DEDICATED

with hope and love
to the next generation

CHRISTINA
ELIZABETH
SARAH
ROB
SIMON
JULIA
ERIC
CHRISTOPHER
CASSANDRA
MARK
CYPRESS
MATTHEW
BRIDGET

TABLE OF CONTENTS

PROLEGOMENON ix

CHAPTER 1: Early Days 1

CHAPTER 2: The Institutional Circle 13

CHAPTER 3: Growing Up 27

CHAPTER 4: Manifesto! 43

CHAPTER 5: All's Wells 55

CHAPTER 6: Cosmopolis Revisited 69

CHAPTER 7: Revolution! 83

CHAPTER 8: Believing in Progress 103

CHAPTER 9: High Church 115

CHAPTER 10: Apocalypses 133

CHAPTER 11: Paths to the Future 139

CHAPTER 12: The Human Comedy 155

CHAPTER 13: Paradigms 169

CHAPTER 14: Second Edition 179

CHAPTER 15: The World Party 191

CHAPTER 16: Doomscapes 209
    1. Too Little for Too Many, Too Much for Too Few 210
    2. Oilholics Anonymous 211
    3. Zealotry 212
    4. Warming and Cooling 213
    5. The End of War? 214
    6. Too Clever by Half 216

CHAPTER 17: The Service of Being 221

CHAPTER 18: Rhythms of Reason 229

REFERENCES 243

INDEX 255

PROLEGOMENON

I once had the privilege of presenting the actress Jane Fonda to an auditorium overflowing with inflamed peace-lovers. The day was May 4, 1970, the place was the campus of the University of New Mexico in Albuquerque. A student group had asked Fonda to speak about the U.S. invasion of Cambodia, just then in progress. Some of the crowd spilled over onto the stage, including a Beat poet possibly under the influence of one or more psychochemicals. Loud cheers and applause greeted our arrival. I had an introduction memorized, but suddenly it made no sense. The only person who needed an introduction was myself. I clapped a microphone around Fonda's slender neck and sat down without a word. She spoke, without notes, for an hour. Once or twice the poet, in his exalted stupor, wandered within range of her and I had to steer him gently in another direction, but otherwise my evening's work was over. After Fonda finished, members of the crowd were inspired to storm the University president's house. One intrepid peacenik expressed his outrage by climbing up on the roof and urinating down the president's chimney.

Everyone who lived through that era nostalgically (and not quite accurately) known as the Sixties has a favorite Sixties moment. This was mine.

As I write, it is thirty years later and I am still the only person on stage who needs an introduction. The usual requirement for attempting an autobiography is to be someone that everyone already knows about. This is a requirement I cannot fill. W. Warren Wagar is a household name known throughout the world — but only in a minuscule number of households. If I have the effrontery to write these *Memoirs*, it is not because I imagine for a moment that most of my readers will be drawn to its pages by curiosity about the author. My only excuse is that I may be a fair sample of that odd sort of person who, in the second half of the 20th Century, spent a life-time thinking and writing about the future of humankind. Why did some of us indulge in such a hazardous pastime? We rarely succeeded in predicting anything of any real importance. Yet somehow we thought it mattered to try.

By using the past tense, I do not mean to suggest that the movement broadly known as "futurism" or "futures studies" has expired. But its founding generation, the generation that rose to modest prominence and, more rarely, celebrity in the 1960s and 1970s, the generation that included Herman Kahn, Daniel Bell, John McHale, Alvin and Heidi Toffler, Edward Cornish, Donella and Dennis Meadows, Wendell Bell, Bertrand and Hugues de Jouvenel, Robert Jungk, and several dozen others, is now passing from the scene. Although I doubt we shall see their like again, I may be (and usually am) wrong about the future. Fortunately for my family, I never visit racetracks or betting shops.

Still, thinking about the future is one of the inevitable concomitants of being human. My cats — fortunate beasts! — never think about it. Human beings have always done so, which accounts for religion, philosophy, science, governance, architecture, and most of the other trappings of civilization. In the 1960s and 1970s some of us decided that thinking about the future could be systematized, regularized, and transformed into a synthetic new discipline capable of spanning and integrating all the others. This may still happen. So far it has not. *Memoirs of the Future* is my personal contribution to an understanding of the mind-set of the futurist.

But an introduction is now in order. My full name is Walter Warren Wagar. I am the son of an American businessman of the same name who died in 1939 and an American housewife and nurse who died in 1990. My father was of mixed German and English heritage; the first Wagars to arrive in America came from the Duchy of Württemberg in the middle of the 18th Century and settled in upstate New York. In a futile effort to protect the proper pronunciation of their surname, they changed it from "Weger" to "Wager" or "Wagar." After the Revolutionary War, in which they supported the Crown, many of them emigrated to Canada or moved to the Midwest. My mother was of mixed German, Welsh, and Irish heritage, from families that located in southeastern Pennsylvania during the 19th Century. I was raised in the old colonial inland market town of Lancaster, Pennsylvania.

In 1959 I became the first member of my family to earn a doctorate. I have spent all of my postdoctoral years as a professional academic historian, first at Wellesley College, then at the University of New Mexico, and since 1971 at the State University of New York at Binghamton. I have published 16 books, chiefly on ideas of the future, which have been reviewed for the most part favorably and which have sold for the most part poorly. I joined the Washington-based World Future Society a year or two after its founding in 1966 and have been active in its doings ever since; I am also a charter member of the Society for Utopian Studies, founded in 1976. My annual lecture course "History of the Future," inaugurated in 1974 at SUNY Binghamton, has been taken by some 7,000 students, qualifying as a minor campus legend.

In *Encyclopedia of the Future*, the standard reference work in the field from a U.S. perspective, I am ranked 24th among the world's 100 most influential futurists of all time. If this ranking is actually justified, futures research stands in far direr straits than even I would have imagined!

Only one thing remains to be said. Serious study of the future is the most important task in the world. Foolish or wise, dead-accurate or wildly wrong, such study is humanity's best hope for gaining control of its own destiny. The human past occupied some 35,000 years. If we are half as sapient as the name biologists give our species denotes, our future will occupy numberless millions. Into this future we send our sons and daughters; and of this future, if we think well and hard, there will be no end.

CHAPTER 1
EARLY DAYS

The boy is twelve years old, very pale, with fine brown hair, dreaming blue eyes, and arms and legs like pipe cleaners. He has rosy lips that he resents because (so he imagines) they make him look like a girl. Once he went out Hallowe'ening in full costume. Some older boys accosted him, ripped off his mask, and laughed, "Hey, it's a girl!" He has not forgotten.

But now it is the summer of 1944. He has survived seventh grade, the year of passage from childhood, and on his Underwood No. 5 typewriter he is banging out another book, the capstone of his intellectual career, a summa on the history and destiny of humankind entitled *Philosophy of Progress*, culminating in a plan for world peace. Because of his formidable mind, he is obliged to write in formidable prose, a prose so exalted that ordinary folk cannot hope to grasp it. The first chapter, as the Foreword explains, "endeavors the reader to assume the past in a philosophical angle, quite different from the historical or the factual."

Why would a boy of twelve, presumably on the brink of puberty, consecrate his precious summer days to the writing of a book on progress? Why, even in the midst of the greatest war in human history — a war barely cited in *Philosophy of Progress* — would he be thinking of plans for peace? What about baseball with the fellas, Westerns at the Bijou, summer camp, working a newspaper route, building balsa-wood models of heavy bombers?

The summer of 1944 was followed by many others very similar. The boy grew taller, thinner. Puberty finally arrived, far later than normal, but he never lived the life of a teenager. He spent most of his free time at home in his room in the cramped red-brick town house on West Walnut Street, tapping away on his Underwood No. 5 typewriter, creating worlds. Some of his schoolteachers would shake their heads and express sadness for the boy who could not be a boy, for the youth he had foregone.

I might feel a great distance from that boy. How can anyone of mature years recall early adolescence — the freshness of the senses, the discovery of the body, the poorly stocked but inquisitive mind, the vision of an unlimited future, the anxiety and embarrassment, the heedlessness and cruelty, the surges of rebellion? Experience transforms us, in ways both obscure and obvious, so that we are forever separated from our prior selves. We are texts rewritten every day. There is never a final draft.

True. But somehow, and in spite of common sense, I do not feel distant from the pale little boy of the Underwood No. 5. Over the years I have communed with him often, and wondered what he would think of me, and whether he would be disappointed or pleased. This chronicle of my summer 1944 self, and the selves that came before and after, has been torn from me with the greatest reluctance, as if it were a mutilation, even a dismemberment, but not because the past seems out of reach. Perhaps for the opposite reason: because it is here with me now, flesh of my flesh, thought of my thought. How can I take myself apart, how can I peel away the infinite succession of my selves, without pain?

My life began on a Sunday early in June, 1932. The stock market had touched bottom, but the Wagars were flourishing. My father Walter was the manager of the largest Montgomery Ward retail store in the East, in Baltimore, earning something like a hundred dollars a week, in those days a handsome salary. We lived in a house in suburban Catonsville. We owned a car and when I was still a baby, Walter began to build a family library of new books, clothbound treasures of my childhood, from an era — the early to mid-1930s — when book design was bold and muscular. My favorites were those designed by W. A. Dwiggins and published by Alfred A. Knopf: especially *Seven Famous Novels* by H.G. Wells.

But Daddy was a sick man. Our last good year was 1934, when my little sister Winnifred was born. I called her Baby Sister. In photographs she closely resembled my mother Laura, just as I favored my father's side of the family. From the time she could walk, she followed me around wherever I went, always gentle and sweet

CHAPTER 1: EARLY DAYS

and trusting. But although Daddy could never quite bring himself to admit it, he was desperately, perhaps terminally ill with tuberculosis. The time finally came when he had to yield to the disease and take a leave of absence from Ward's. In November, 1935, our little family stowed its bags in our black Pontiac sedan and drove across the country to the small town (as it was then) of Albuquerque, a place frequented by recovering tuberculosis patients, who were thought to benefit from the high and dry desert air.

What Walter needed more than anything was bed rest. No antibiotics were available to treat him, but with prolonged rest, he might recover. His superiors at Ward's did what they could to provide for him, promising to be on the lookout for a store in the Southwest that he could manage after he regained his health.

I have a few vivid memories, which may or may not be accurate, of this cool and dusty place where we came to live. I recall Indians selling blankets to tourists in a hotel lobby, or perhaps just outside. We rented an adobe bungalow on North Fourth Street, where we spent the Christmas of 1935. But it was not a happy time. My father was sick, recovering from a phrenic nerve operation performed in Albuquerque shortly after our arrival, which did him no good. My little sister burned her foot badly on a hot air register, and I came down with scarlet fever. The change of climate had given my mother a brutal cold and our bungalow was quarantined because of my illness. How she coped with all of this she herself could barely remember in later years. Somehow she did.

In January the corporate axe fell. Some higher-ups must have reviewed Walter's situation and decided that Ward's was not a charitable institution. One day Walter received a notice that his paid leave and his employment were terminated. The money stopped coming. Finding suitable work in Albuquerque, with no significant cash reserves and my father's health still wobbly, seemed out of the question. My mother, who had a ninth grade education, could have gone out to work, finding a job as a waitress or a salesclerk, but the the table. In any event my father was sufficiently patriarchal to find such a solution intolerable. He was the man. He had to provide. His wife could not work. Besides, who would take care of the babies? I was only three, my sister not even a year and a half.

The only remedy was to leave the salubrious climate of New Mexico and return to the Wagar family homestead on West Walnut Street in Lancaster, Pennsylvania, until we could get back on our feet. Walter would rest and eventually look for work. Laura would raise her children and help around the house.

Taking us in during the late winter of 1935-1936 was a generous deed to be sure. The home on West Walnut Street was not large and already fully occupied. My grandmother and grandfather slept in the rear bedroom, and two maiden aunts, Winnifred and Louise, had the other two rooms. Grandfather, although now in his late 60s, still worked in a farm machine factory and the aunts were elementary schoolteachers. When the newcomers arrived, the four of us — Walter, Laura, Warren, and Baby Sister — took over the front bedroom, and Winnifred and Louise shared the tiny middle bedroom between them. How all eight people managed to fit around the family table is hard to imagine. I have no personal recollection of this brief era at all, except the celebration of my fourth birthday in the dining room, when the lights were turned out and the be-candled cake arrived from the kitchen.

By the summer of 1936, my father's health had improved and he was able to take a full-time job as the proprietor of the White Swan, a small tavern in the Lancaster county hamlet of Rothsville. Nominally, the White Swan was an inn, a *Gasthaus* in the heart of Pennsylvania "Dutch" land, but we rarely entertained boarders. The point of the White Swan was to provide food and drink, mostly drink, to neighborhood rustics in search of a good time. On weekends it also offered dancing with a live band. The first dollar my father received, a silver dollar, he mounted, framed, and put on display in the tavern. The date on the placard reads July 24, 1936.

Running a country tavern suited Walter in most respects. He was the manager of his own business, he could keep irregular hours, and his able-bodied wife could do much of the work and yet not scar his ego by earning money outside the home. He would not be de-

CHAPTER 1: EARLY DAYS

pendent on a woman's wages. But there was a price to be paid. The hours, if irregular, were also long. To encourage business, my father spent many nights smoking, drinking, and consorting with customers. Often he and Laura did not get to bed until three o'clock in the morning. A few hours later, the children would wake up and need their breakfasts. A tavern is not a tuberculosis sanitarium. Walter, at 35, still had some of his youthful energy and vitality; but he was in the grip of a lethal disease.

Meanwhile, tuberculosis claimed my Baby Sister. She came down in November, 1936, with tubercular meningitis. In the final stages of the illness she was moved to the front bedroom of the house in Lancaster, probably to be nearer medical help, but the doctors could do nothing for her. I remember seeing her lie there, and later a doctor coming down the stairs, as we sat in the living room, to inform us it was all over. My mother later told me that I went out into the alleyway between our house and the next house shouting to the world "Baby Sister is dead! Baby Sister is dead!" I could not have understood death, but I knew something fateful had happened. The little girl, barely two, was buried under a headstone inscribed "Mamma and Daddy's Doll Baby." The loss devastated my father, knowing as he did that she had contracted her disease from him.

1937 and 1938 passed without incident. Somehow my father was able to keep the business going, with much help from my mother and hired hands. It prospered so well that by the end of 1938 the owner of the White Swan decided to become her own proprietor and keep the profits for herself. Walter was, as before, a more than competent businessman, but his tenure at the White Swan had come to an end. In January of the new year we moved to the Warwick House, another *Gasthaus*, this time with actual paying boarders, in the picturesque town of Lititz just a few miles north of Lancaster. By February 1, Walter was able to mount and frame one of the first dollars received at the new establishment. He invested the last of his energies in building up the business.

Then one beautiful spring day he took a short drive in the country, stopped by the side of the road to snatch a quick nap, and in the nippy air of twilight caught a cold that soon turned into pneumonia. On Sunday evening, May 21, 1939, my father's 38th birthday, the Wagars were gathered in the family quarters above the bar of the Warwick House to be with Walter. I heard my grandmother Gertie call to my mother as Aunt Winnifred helped me take a bath. Gertie was not sure that anything was wrong, but best that Laura take a look. Something in the tone of her voice alarmed me. It sticks clearly in memory even now. My mother, who may have been napping, came into the bedroom. Walter died soon afterward — or perhaps he was already dead. The official cause noted by the attending physician was pneumonia, but for lungs ravaged by tuberculosis in those days, pneumonia was routinely fatal. Later that night, my mother asked me to say goodbye to my father. She held me up, and I kissed his cool forehead. I was still only six years old.

Our nuclear family was now down to two. Whether experiencing death at an early age, or being an only surviving child, made me serious and overly concerned with past and future, I cannot say. I seem to have been a serious child all along. "He looks as if he's carrying the weight of the world on his shoulders," a friend of the family once said. I was basically a shy, quiet, brooding sort of little boy, with deep-set eyes and a penetrating, clear voice that began in time to sound ministerial — or professorial.

My father's death left us where we were in 1936, with no place to go but the house on West Walnut Street. One of the maiden aunts, Louise, had married and moved away, so we could fit more easily. In June of 1939 we settled there permanently. Laura shared the front bedroom with her sister-in-law Winnifred, and I took the middle room all by myself. It was here that I wrote *Philosophy of Progress* and many other preposterous masterpieces.

Of course I exaggerate. The years from 1939 to 1944 and beyond were not wholly devoted to literary matters. If my physical development had kept pace with my mental, I might have chosen a radically different path. Through the early 1940s I found a succession of neighborhood friends my own age, with whom I played games, took little jaunts on bicycles, ventured briefly into "gang" wars, smoked a few cigarettes, broke into a warehouse, went to Saturday afternoon movies at the Strand or the Fulton theater. Young Warren even indulged in one or two sexual "experiments" with a wayward lass who lived across the street. The delay of the onset of puberty did not prevent him from developing a few crushes on girls, or from studying with excessive care the representations of female nudity in the art and photography articles in the *Encyclopaedia Britannica*, notably *Bewegung* by Dr. Rudolf Koppitz, a print of which hangs framed above my desk even now.

But all that belonged to a path not taken in adolescence. It was the serious Warren, the Warren of the deathbeds, the Warren of the Underwood No. 5, who prevailed and became the father of the man.

Of my biological father, I have few meaningful memories. I was too young when he died. I know him principally through my mother's reminiscences, almost all adoring. That he was basically a kind and good man, who loved me and treated me well, I cannot doubt. His only flaw was his pride, which combined with ambition to kill him in the prime of his life. Had he stayed in bed for a few years, even in Lancaster, he might well have recovered. But then he would not have been my father. In the 1930s in middle-class America no self-respecting man could allow himself to be kept by his wife. It was a far better thing to die.

ENTR'ACTE: PHILOSOPHY OF PROGRESS

Now let us cut away to explore my first credo, my Ur-text, my *Philosophy of Progress* from the summer of 1944. It was my first credo, but not my first book. The author of *Philosophy of Progress* was also well known on selected parts of West Walnut Street as the writer of such epics of popular science as *The Earth and Its History*, a review of life on earth from the Paleozoic to the Cenozoic Eras in three slender volumes (1941), *The Science of Elementary Chemistry* (1943), and *World Snakes* (1944) in two volumes (one for the poisonous snakes, one for the non-poisonous), with illustrations in color by the author. Only the earliest of these had been pecked out on my typewriter; the others I wrote, laboriously, with a lead pencil. My first aspiration was to become a scientist, but I hardly knew which sort. An extended stay on the east coast of Florida in the winter of 1940 spurred an interest in the shells of molluscs, and so, for a little while, I planned a career in conchology, revived in 1944-45 when I wrote *The Elementary Textbook of Ocean Life*. The dinosaurs of Walt Disney's *Fantasia* may have led to *The Earth and Its History*. I would be a paleontologist. When my mother gave me a chemistry set for Christmas in 1942, I became an ardent chemist. Chemistry took me to a study of the elements and their atomic structure. In *Theoretical Thesis of Atomics* (1944), a wide-ranging fantasy on the subject of nuclear energy and radiation that contained almost no real science, I imagined myself an inventor of incredible high-tech machines. When the summer of 1945 brought news of the atomic bomb, I enjoyed a brief moment of glory among my neighborhood acquaintances, who remembered my "work" of the previous year. Not to mention a short season as a herpetologist in the winter of 1944, when I produced *World Snakes*.

The pattern in each case was the same: a flurry of interest, the devouring of a few volumes from the public library or my father's collection, and then the writing of a book that aspired to outline the whole subject. The point was not so much to "do" science as to englobulate it in a single definitive text.

Philosophy of Progress represented a new departure. Although informed here and there by the natural sciences, and above all by the theory of evolution, this was no digest of scientific knowledge. This was "philosophy."

Do not jump to warrantless conclusions. By "philosophy" I surely did not mean the academic subject taught in universities, of which I knew nothing. The only model available to me in the family library was Will Durant's middle-brow potpourri *The Mansions of Philosophy*. I recall grazing in its pages, but I may not have read it all the way through. In any event, I took "philosophy" to signify meditations on the human condition and prospect: not knowledge as such, not methods of inquiry, not logic and epistemology, but free-ranging commentary and speculation. This was somehow a higher calling than the life of the scientist, setting Warren apart from his fellow scientific toilers. Through philosophy, he would not only enlighten humankind: he would save it.

The new book consisted of twelve brief essays on 49 typewritten pages. Some of the essays were indeed about human progress and destiny; others offered random reflections on lesser matters. The prose is infallibly pretentious and sometimes unintelligible to boot. The young man's vocabulary was far more impressive than his mastery of how such grandiose words actually worked in sentences.

Nevertheless, the main argument comes through more or less, especially in the opening essays, which dealt in sequence with the past, the present, and the future. The human race, I reported, had made enormous strides since prehistoric times. With the help of philosophy and science, it could make many more. Ultimately, it would perish in great wars and be succeeded, perhaps, by a race of intelligent and pacific lizards, but for many generations to come, we could stave off disaster by adopting my "Plan of Peace." Chapter 3, "The Future of the Future" (the only striking phrase in the whole book, later the title of a pioneering study in futures research by John McHale), charts the chief possibilities; and Chapter 4 sets down my peace plan.

The plan consisted of three revolutionary transformations: the elimination of differences among peoples through worldwide interracial marriage and the abolition of independent national states; a scheme for the stabilization of the world economy through direct marketing of goods by producers in domed shopping plazas (no, I had not yet read Edward Bellamy's *Looking Backward*); and the elimination of sexual frustration and competition through the bioengineering of a new hermaphroditic human race. This bizarre third transformation no doubt originated in my sense of sexual inadequacy, as a woefully pre-pubescent lad strongly attracted to girls, who (he was sure) found him too immature to reciprocate his feelings. My long-delayed puberty, together with my general weirdness, kept me from attempting to date anyone until I was a junior in college. Ironically, the science-fiction novelist Ursula Le Guin would later imagine a race of peace-loving hermaphrodites in her classic utopia, *The Left Hand of Darkness*.

But no sooner were the words out of my typewriter than I recanted. I warned readers not to carry out this plan. It would work, if fully implemented, but too many things might go wrong in the attempt. I hinted darkly of "monstrous things," all unspecified, which appeared to leave my plan in ruins. What to do? No answer. Not even the question. Instead, we move abruptly to Chapter 5, "On Astronomy," rich with apocalyptic babble about the creation and eventual destruction of the universe. The rest of the book trails off into musings on the life and achievements of Charles Darwin, a grudging admission that religious feeling is essential to the human psyche, a tirade against physical education, an essay in defense of poetry, a polemic for sex education (with a reprise on the blessings of hermaphroditism), and a last banal chapter on human psychology apparently dredged from an article in the *Encyclopaedia Britannica*.

Clearly, *Philosophy of Progress* lacked the rigor and tautness of my popular science tomes. But comparisons are not difficult to draw. The scale of the book was immense — all time, all space, past and future, humanity, the meaning of life. Once again, I was englobulating, sketching in broad strokes the Big Picture. But I was not without significant mentors, even if they received little credit at the time. My chief inspirations were the *Britannica* — my father had acquired a complete set of the 14th Edition, updated to the early 1930s; H.G. Wells's *Seven Famous Novels*, *The Outline of History*, and *The Science of Life* (the latter in a special four-volume edition autographed by Wells and his two junior co-authors); Will Durant's already cited *The Mansions of Philosophy*; and two books by the Dutch popularizer Hendrik Willem Van Loon, *The Story of Mankind* and *Van Loon's Geography*, all bearing my father's distinctive bookplates. From elementary school days, I also recall two formative experiences — a class touching on prehistoric cultures taken in third

CHAPTER 1: EARLY DAYS

grade, and a class on world history taken in fourth. Nor should I overlook the animated sketch of early life set to the incomparable music of Igor Stravinsky in *Fantasia*, which appealed both to my interest in change over time and to my boyish obsession with global disaster, an obsession I have never been able — never tried or wanted — to outgrow.

Was the Warren of *Philosophy of Progress* a child prodigy, a genius, a *Wunderkind*? He thought so, but I know better. I was a good student with a high but not spectacular I.Q. (whatever such a thing may be worth, 142 in one test, 144 in another). But I was not a prodigy, not even close. In 1944 it would take me at least another dozen years to learn how to write publishable prose. I could play no musical instrument, had no gift for mathematics, learned foreign languages slowly and painfully, and garnered A's in all my school subjects only by relentless, patient, plodding toil.

The single distinction to which I can lay claim is an unusual interest — unusual in a person so young — in matters cosmic, global, and world-historical, in large processes of change through time, from the most remote past to the furthest future. A feeling for what the Germans call *Geschichtlichkeit* — "historicity" is a poor substitute — is ordinarily one of the last faculties to mature in the growing mind. Historians notoriously reach their prime only in middle age, if even then.

I would also argue that a full awareness of *Geschichtlichkeit* did not become possible in the history of human thought itself until the 19th Century, with the emergence of *Historismus*, another concept that can best be savored in German, usually rendered in English as "historicism." To see all human beings — even all living things — as ineluctable products of their unique position in space and time, yet densely intertwined thanks to the seamlessness of both space and time, is to view the world altogether differently from the way the world was perceived prior to the rise of historicism and its close cousin in the natural sciences, the theory of evolution. The place of eternal truths, of divine and natural laws, of all dualities and dichotomies, is usurped by spatio-temporal relativity, but a relativity that also points to the ultimate wholeness and unity of being.

At the age of twelve, I did not see as far as that. But I was clearly on my way.

CHAPTER 2
THE INSTITUTIONAL CIRCLE

In February, 1945, something quite unexpected happened to the boy-philosopher of West Walnut Street. He found a colleague. Or, to be more accurate, a colleague found him. Hudson Cattell, one of my eighth-grade classmates at Reynolds Junior High School, a boy I had barely known the previous fall, became almost over night a close friend. Neither of us recalls how this took place, but I suspect that most of the credit belongs to Hudson, a quiet lad but more outgoing than I, and more inclined to take initiatives. Somehow or other we discovered that we shared a common interest in fantasy and science fiction, as well as science itself. Both of us were bookish, both of us were aspiring writers.

We were also both outsiders. It is a fact of life, to which the American institution of the junior high school pays no heed, that young men mature later than young women and at quite different speeds from one another. So the typical eighth- or ninth-grade classroom flings together, say, five entirely pre-pubescent males and ten who are well along toward manhood. The bulls date the girls, dominate the basketball court, and generally cut impressive figures. The calves are marginalized. Hudson and I were fellow calves. My own situation was particularly sorry because I had skipped a grade in elementary school and was not even the same chronological age as the other calves. The bulls in my eighth-grade homeroom were thirteen, going on sixteen. I was twelve, locked into an unforgiving twelveness for years to come.

The only redeeming feature of marginalization is the company of the rest of the marginalized. Fortunately for our self-esteem, Hudson and I made an appropriate twosome. Strange, unpopular, brainy, and somewhat lonely, we related to one another. By the same token, we aggravated one another's strangeness. If Warren used a typewriter, so would Hudson. If Hudson had no interest (for the time being) in girls, neither did Warren. If Warren was a philosopher, so was Hudson. If Hudson listened to classical music, so would Warren. And so forth. And to hell with the good opinion of our unwashed classmates.

Our first joint decision was to create a so-called Science-Fiction Library, consisting of the handful of books and magazines in our possession, and to "publish" on my typewriter a critical review of the field known as *Science-Fiction News*, which lasted all of one issue. A fractious period ensued, thanks to my ill-considered introduction into our small band of a third eighth-grade calf — let us call him "Modred" in tribute to Arthurian legend. Modred also had an interest in science fiction, but his principal gift was the muddying of waters. By late April he was safely out of the way, and Hudson and I then entered into our golden age, some nine months of multiplying interactions that became central to both our lives, much to the dismay of the young teacher in whose ninth-grade homeroom we were placed in the fall of 1945.

These interactions became known to both of us as "the institutional circle," an interlocking series of joint and individual projects that in various ways replicated the institutions of adult professional life. In May we began a semi-monthly journal entitled *Fantasy & Science-Fiction*, consisting of reviews and stories of our own, with Hudson responsible for the "fantasy" half and I for the "science-fiction." In 1945, almost all new material in both genres appeared in monthly "pulp" magazines of variable quality, with luridly painted covers whose stock in trade was the assault of helpless Aryan maidens by hideous alien monsters. But behind the covers one could often find serious visions of imaginable futures. In all we managed to produce 14 issues of this redoubtable journal.

Meanwhile, in June, we each inaugurated weekly newspapers, *The Wagarian* and *The Cattellian*, designed to chronicle our adventurous lives and comment sagely on current events. We made carbon copies of every typewritten issue for one another's files. We also both adopted the fiction that the newspapers were not our own work, but were reported, written, and published by editorial "staffs"

CHAPTER 2: THE INSTITUTIONAL CIRCLE

consisting of alter egos with names that were variants of our own. These staffs invariably referred to us in the third person: "Mr. Wagar," "Mr. Cattell." As in a real newspaper, each issue usually contained news stories, editorials, and feature stories. Often the "subject" himself — Warren or Hudson — would contribute a column under his own name. On occasion, acting as the voice of conscience, an editor would call one of us to task because of the alleged impropriety of this or that behavior. Editors were particularly upset when either of us deviated from our role as public intellectuals and literati. Attending a party or a school basketball game might result in a severe scolding in the next issue.

None of this prevented us from dabbling in less rational pursuits when it took our respective fancies. Early in April Hudson had become interested in meteorology, and thunderstorms in particular. This led to his "predicting" thunderstorms and holding services, probably starting in May, to make it rain. By June I had decided to sign on as well. We invented a rain god called Tsathaggua, the name borrowed from that of a grisly supernatural creature in a short story by the fantasy writer Clark Ashton Smith. Invoking Tsathaggua's might, we held a number of rain services duly reported in our newspapers. They were almost always a success because Hudson kept close watch on the daily weather bureau forecasts.

At about the same time, discussions of the Bible led me to write my own, *The Book of Wagarism*, in which I cast myself as a divine and immortal being who had come to earth thousands of years ago to rescue humanity from its wickedness. *The Book of Wagarism* was supplemented in due course by various service manuals, prayer books, and other material. At one level, my "scriptures" were merely light-hearted spoofs. But at another level they were proclamations of spiritual independence from the cant and hypocrisy of American religious life. The first sonorous verse of *The Book of Wagarism* read as follows:

> On Earth there was nought good,
> And evil reigned high.
> Hell was upon Earth,

> And its fires consumed men.
> Praise Wagar, O ye desolation!

I should add that to intone this verse properly, one must give "reigned" two syllables and "consumed" three.

We also underscored our profound rejection of the barbarism of contemporary teen culture by reading great works of world literature. In the summer of 1945, we even staged two-man productions in Hudson's yard of selected plays of Shakespeare and Aristophanes. We were perfect, well-behaved, scholarly young men, untempted by vice, pure of heart and body, foes of sloth and idleness, every mother's dream come true — or not?

My own mother was well out of her element, and simply acquiesced in whatever I chose to do, but Hudson's mother Psyche Cattell had earned a doctorate in education from Harvard and was an internationally prominent child psychologist, not to mention a daughter of the founding father of American psychology, James McKeen Cattell. She harbored a number of theories about what constituted an appropriate childhood in mid-century America. Those theories did not find room for exclusive friendships. Warren was acceptable, in moderation, but her son needed other friends, many other friends, to assure his well-rounded development and socialization. He also needed to spend his summers in the bracing atmosphere of a boys' camp. So, much to my chagrin, Hudson was sent off to the Adirondacks for the months of July and August. We lost two precious months of fraternization, only partially compensated by a weekly exchange of letters.

As soon as Hudson returned, the institutional circle came back to life and even expanded. In early September we created the Wagar-Cattell Philosophical Organization, which boasted its own Constitution and its own Philosophical Examination, a battery of questions designed to exclude from membership all but the select few who could share and act responsibly on our cutting-edge views, which included schemes for world order and the engineering of a new unisexed human race. Of special interest are the first three arti-

CHAPTER 2: THE INSTITUTIONAL CIRCLE

cles of the Constitution, already drafted before Hudson's departure for camp. The purpose of the Wagar-Cattell Philosophical Organization, said the first article, was "to convert the world in ways written below."

Convert the world to what? The Constitution did not mince words. We would promote philosophy and science and "exterminate...uncontrolled religion throughout the world." We would end war and educate adolescents "in psychological, scientific, and philosophical manners." We would create "one common moral code of life; one common nationality and one common government." And we would disseminate our ideals among all peoples "regardless of race, present creed or age." Some of the megalomania evident in this document may have been attributable to Hudson, but my fingerprints are all over it. Only the author of *Philosophy of Progress* could have assembled such an agenda. Did we believe that we could actually carry it out? Or was it all an elaborate exercise in Orwellian Doublethink?

Meanwhile, I was hard at work on a second and entirely new edition of *Philosophy of Progress*, begun during the summer months; Hudson was writing a volume of his own philosophy, *The Earth's People Today*. We embarked on mutual study projects in paleontology, herpetology, and various other esoteric matters, while continuing to churn out regular issues of *Fantasy & Science-Fiction*, *The Wagarian*, and *The Cattellian*. Each of us also pursued independent literary careers, in poetry and playwrighting. The institutional circle was wide, encompassing, astonishing. We were, so we imagined, invincible.

Our new homeroom teacher Miss Miles (not her real name) felt otherwise. She assumed that the task of ninth-grade boys was to behave like ninth-grade boys, well-rounded, well-adjusted, not too serious, athletic, vigorous, wholesome, and God-fearing. Hudson and Warren did not fit the pattern. In October Miss Miles asked to see samples of our poetry, which we stupidly provided. As I remember, the stupidity was mine. How could a teacher, of all people, not be happy to find pupils with such extraordinary gifts? So I imagined.

Hudson, the son of a controlling parent in a far less indulgent household, was warier. But he swallowed his reservations and we entrusted some of our most intimate fantasies to this human viper. In my case, it was a long narrative poem entitled "The Master," a story of the gruesome endeavors of Satan in Hell, the worst possible choice to show the pious young Miss Miles.

After school one day Miss Miles returned our work, gave us a fairly harsh review of its merits (no doubt well deserved), and lectured us on the benefits of leading a "normal" childhood. *The Cattellian* shrewdly reported that the session had been "degrading." By contrast (Heaven alone knows why) *The Wagarian* thought it had "gone well."

But a few days later Miss Miles confided to Hudson that plans were afoot to place us in separate homerooms. This would happen for Hudson's good, in view of the bad influence I wielded over him. When he objected, she replied that the decision would be made by the teachers, not by him. As soon as he told me what was in the works, *The Wagarian* ran banner headlines revealing the "scandalous plot." In the end, nothing came of the homeroom teacher's scheme, perhaps because the opinions of the faculty were divided, and I once again relapsed into complacency.

Nevertheless, behind the scenes Miss Miles persevered in her mission to rescue the hapless Hudson. On November 1, 1945, an incident at school furnished her with just the opportunity she needed to stir up trouble. At noon, just before recess for lunch, two boys from the homeroom — including the mischievous Modred who had done his best to break up our budding friendship back in March — tried to pick a fight with Hudson, who refused to fight back. Miss Miles arrived on the scene, feigning horror and outrage, and reported the scuffle to the school principal. The upshot was a three-day suspension for Hudson and one of the other boys. Hudson had become a juvenile delinquent. Clearly, a disturbed child! Miss Miles was left with no choice but to visit Hudson's mother in person and lay bare the details of the whole sordid business. She did so late that afternoon, in a meeting behind closed doors that Hudson was not in-

CHAPTER 2: THE INSTITUTIONAL CIRCLE

vited to join.

As Hudson reconstructs the relevant events of November 1 and the next three and a half months — and I am confident he has worked them out quite accurately — Miss Miles's appearance on Hudson's doorstep was not serendipitous. Rather, it was the first move in what became a well-orchestrated scheme to enlist his mother in her campaign to shatter our friendship, a scheme that neither of us suspected at the time. The "fight" in the school hallway was of no consequence, the sort of roughhousing that occurred routinely among the bulls and was routinely ignored. By blowing it out of all proportion, Miss Miles got her chance to involve Dr. Cattell.

The next day Dr. Cattell went to the school herself and somehow or other convinced the principal to lift Hudson's suspension. The principal also visited Miss Miles's homeroom, no doubt at her instigation, to take a look at the cover of my school notebook, which, as a lark, I had adorned in ink with such inspirational slogans as "Wagar Is Love!," "Wagar Is Power!," "Wagar Is the Creator!," "Exalted Be His Brain!" The principal gravely inspected my notebook and returned it to me without comment. No further attempts were made to curtail my religious freedom. I now wonder if the principal might have been my secret guardian angel, keeping the impetuous Miss Miles in check.

In any case, Hudson immediately began experiencing intensified pressure at home to find friends other than myself. He was not forbidden to see me, but when he failed to cooperate, his mother made arrangements for him to visit, or attend school games with, various members of our homeroom, selected for their wholesomeness by Miss Miles.

Of course none of this came to anything. Parents cannot choose their offspring's friends, especially when the offspring is thirteen years old. Hudson and Warren continued along their deviant paths, with Warren altogether in the dark about the situation in Hudson's home, but wondering to himself why Hudson acted so irritably at times. Entries in a diary I kept for a short while — no hint of this appeared in *The Wagarian* — indicate that Hudson lost his temper with me more than once in the autumn of 1945. The episodes were worrisome, although not serious; they did not keep us from embarking on yet more mutual projects. January, 1946, found us working on two: studies of the anatomy of the human brain and efforts to imagine how the ancient Romans would have used their numerals to solve arithmetic problems. Between January 20 and February 4, no fewer than three issues of *Fantasy & Science-Fiction* appeared. We each completed volumes on Roman numeral arithmetic and began giving "lessons" after school to a sympathetic algebra teacher on the school faculty.

Miss Miles, for her part, found new ways to test our friendship. An English teacher, she gave her students an assignment based on Shakespeare's *A Midsummer Night's Dream*. Hudson produced a parody with mice as the principal characters. I attempted something much more serious, aping Shakespeare's style. Hudson's piece received an A+ and he was asked to read it to the whole class. Mine was dealt a lower grade and dismissed as unoriginal, "too much like Shakespeare." From that point forward, Miss Miles systematically downgraded my work and made a great fuss over Hudson's, hoping, I am sure, that this would lead to jealousy on my part and resentment directed at Hudson. If that was her aim, it did not succeed. All my resentment focused on Miss Miles herself.

There also came a time when the worthy Miss Miles announced to the homeroom that the results of the I.Q. tests we had taken recently were now available. The highest score belonged to an unassuming female member of the class, whose name she then proceeded to reveal. In those days students were never shown the scores they had received on I.Q. tests. It was patently unethical to tell the class anything, but Miss Miles could not resist the temptation to put me in my place. Her news was nicely calculated to subtract some of the wind from my sails, as indeed it did. If anyone in our homeroom needed deflating, it was the insufferable ("Exalted Be His Brain!") Warren; but again, Miss Miles did not play fair.

In February, 1946, the collaboration between Miss Miles and Dr. Cattell reached its grand climax. Miss Miles had been steadily

CHAPTER 2: THE INSTITUTIONAL CIRCLE

feeding Hudson's mother with reports of insubordination by Hudson and Warren in gym and shop classes, classes that both of us viewed with disdain, and in which, on occasion, I am sure our conduct could legitimately have been labeled insubordinate. The campaign to equip Hudson with an alternative set of friends was foundering. The nonsense with Roman numerals and bad poetry and cerebral anatomy and macabre magazines showed no signs of abating. It was time to strike. The first blow fell on February 5, when Hudson's mother announced that he would once again be shipped off to summer camp, the same camp to which he had been sentenced in 1945. Hudson protested vigorously to no avail. On Friday, February 15, in an effort to placate his mother, he told her he would be going to a school basketball game; but when she learned that his companion would be Warren, she refused her permission, on the flimsy pretext that the game would end too late in the evening. Hudson responded angrily. The next day, Dr. Cattell berated Hudson for his "childish" behavior, and a heated argument ensued, in which she offered to buy him some fantasy books he wanted in exchange for seeing me less often. When he indignantly declined the bribe, she delivered an ultimatum: either Hudson spent less time with me and more with other friends, or she would unilaterally decide how much (or how little) time he passed with me in the future.

On Sunday, February 17, the struggle resumed. But this time Hudson capitulated. Assuming that I would not or could not believe the pressure under which he was laboring, pressure exerted not only by his mother but also by his grandmother and by a teacher at Dr. Cattell's private pre-school, he did not take me into his confidence. With his mother in the room he telephoned me to say, frostily and matter-of-factly, that she and Uncle Jaques had decided we would be seeing less of each other, beginning forthwith. He sounded to me like someone reading from a script.

Had Hudson confided in me, I know full well that I would have adopted the same stance I had adopted the previous fall when there was talk of our being assigned to separate homerooms. *The Wagarian* would have run banner headlines and fulminated about dastardly plots. He and I could have tried to continue our friendship underground. But Hudson found himself squeezed between a rock and a hard place, and I lacked the maturity to fathom what was happening. Within days, much to the delight of Miss Miles, our friendship was blown apart. The perfidious Modred, sensing his opportunity, cozied up to Hudson, meanwhile making my life hell for a few weeks.

As she had done earlier for Hudson, Miss Miles turned next to the recruitment of male "friends" from the homeroom to assist in my own rehabilitation. I had my first appointment on February 26, a doubtless repulsive evening at a basketball game with one of the bulls. A few other such occasions presented themselves before the winter came to an end, after which I was mercifully left alone. Early in the spring Hudson began making overtures to regain my ruptured trust. It was no use. *The Wagarian* ranted against him in rage and dismay. He lost the title of "Mr. Cattell" and became known only as the disgraced "H. Cattell." It was a black and evil and unforgiving season. We finally patched things up in January, 1947, but by then it was too late to resuscitate the golden days of the institutional circle.

The break with Hudson matters to the main thread of these *Memoirs* because our friendship had deepened and intensified my interest in "philosophy" and had led to significant additions to the canon: in 1945 a new *Philosophy of Progress*, 151 pages in length; and in 1946 a sequel, *Toward Which We Strive*, 101 pages in length, written after the break but before the afterglow of our friendship had faded. Then full stop. I abandoned philosophy for several years, returning only when a new version of the institutional circle made its appearance in 1950.

ENTR'ACTE: MORE PROGRESS

The main project of my summer vacation in 1945 was to write *Philosophy of Progress* all over again, but not in the sense of revising the 1944 manuscript. I would literally write it again, starting from ground zero. The title would remain, but not a word of the text.

CHAPTER 2: THE INSTITUTIONAL CIRCLE

I was a full year older. I was the member of a flourishing institutional circle. As a founder of the Wagar-Cattell Philosophical Organization, I had a great mission in life. Nothing could equal the importance of articulating my mature thoughts on world salvation.

Dedicated "To my good friend, H.C.", the new *Philosophy of Progress* sported a "Foreward" [sic] dated July 5 and 16 chapters. The writing is not as horrific as in 1944, but still quite grim, with a plethora of misspellings and serious grammatical errors. The earlier chapters reek of the sexism and racism that pervaded most of mid-century American life, including my own household; and this time, surprisingly, there is no explicit "plan of peace," only a bland plea for international "cooperation." I even speculated about the need for a machine that could spot inherited criminal tendencies in the newborn and execute the luckless babes on the spot. So far, so bad.

But as I warmed to my task, my utopian impulses resurged. In the long run, the ideologies and polities of the present-day world would not save us. "There is nothing left," I announced, "but hope in a startling transformation of the world. In other words, the birth of thousands of good-intentioned scientific philosophers." I may have been thinking of the sort of advanced savants who could pass the entrance examination of the Wagar-Cattell Philosophical Organization.

Nor did I retain the lukewarm sympathy for religion expressed in the earlier volume. Religion had once provided a necessary stepping stone, but now it had to be replaced with philosophy, brought to hungry young minds by a whole new system of education. Much of the new book focused on plans for ensuring that schools in the future would rescue humanity from barbarism, ignorance, and unreason. My loathing of gym class led to a proposal for the complete elimination of physical education. I also foresaw churches of philosophy, secular temples where the enlightened millions of the future could attend lectures on morality and hear readings from a new humanistic bible yet to be written. In the purer light of the coming philosophical culture, all human beings would achieve true equality, bridging even the gulf that still divided the white race from the colored races. The barriers between the sexes would fall, too, as a new hermaphroditic race evolved. "One world is essential to peace," I concluded. "Philosophy will make one world which will make peace."

In my third and last juvenile volume of "philosophy," *Toward Which We Strive*, one finds a somewhat different mix of utopian and futurist speculation. In the opening chapter, I anticipated that if all went as all should go, the human race would ultimately shed its simian form and evolve into a single great intelligence, the "Brain," a being whose sole vocation would be philosophy, "pondering the timeless...mysteries of the universe." In a later vision, multiple Brains would evolve still further, leave the earth as immaterial "wisps" and "rise to their final destiny in the Heavens." But if humankind veered from the paths of true philosophy and progressive science, it would destroy civilization in great wars and degenerate into a race of wolf-like savages, "snarling...in the ruins." Or, without any philosophy at all, we might evolve into "dinosimians," brainless apes a hundred feet tall who would perish as the result of their own stupidity during an era of climatic change, like the dinosaurs before them.

But this was 1946, the year after Hiroshima. For now the greatest peril facing humankind was atomic war. Its shadow darkened almost every chapter of *Toward Which We Strive*. In one scenario, I imagined such a war breaking out in four or five years' time and destroying all creatures great and small. Life would eventually come back, bred from "mysterious spores," but millions of years would pass before intelligence re-emerged on our battle-scarred planet.

What hope could I offer? A little. In the short run, the best answer would be to create a world without national boundaries. A mere confederation of nations would not be enough to stop the ravages of war: national sovereignty had to be abolished. Unfortunately I could tender no plan for how to effect such a drastic transformation. Another idea briefly sketched was to create a new form of state, uniting business, science, and government. Monopolies would be established in all industries and the chairman of the board of each monopoly would be elected by popular vote. The chairmen in turn would choose the supreme chief, the Director of the World, who would serve for a term of two or four years. Only one political party would be lawful, "a party that would incorporate Communist, Democratic and Conservative principles." I knew next to nothing about the history of political ideas in 1946, but in effect my scheme brought together in one impossible vision the Comtean utopia of a "positive polity," the Technocracy movement of the 1930s, and Benito Mussolini's conception of the "corporate state." Again, the question of how to get from Here to There was not seriously addressed.

In yet another essay, previewing a theme to which I would return in *A Short History of the Future*, I advocated the transfer of the reins of power to women. Contradicting everything I had written about the female sex the year before in *Philosophy of Progress*, I now speculated that women might be more intelligent than men. True, womankind had produced fewer authentic geniuses. Women also did not apply themselves as single-mindedly to tasks as men. But they were more peace-loving, less emotional, less inclined to commit crimes, and more understanding. Wars would be less likely if they, not men, ruled the earth.

The only individual singled out for special acclaim in *Toward Which We Strive*, however, was a man. H.G. Wells had died in mid-August, 1946, while I was in the middle of my work on *Toward Which We Strive*, and the thirteenth chapter is an obituary notice entitled "Memories of Genius." Although I had read relatively little of Wells at this point in time, I was already an admirer. Word of his death came as a great shock. "Memories of Genius" was a veritable panegyric, hailing Wells as the world's "greatest contemporary author," an accurate prophet, a prolific and powerful novelist, a visionary for all time. My essay included thumbnail sketches of dozens of his books, most of which I had not yet even read. Somehow or other I knew I would like them all, which proved to be, in later years, not far from the truth.

But the chapters on womankind and on Wells were digressions. As *Toward Which We Strive* continued, I turned once more to my main theme, a teleological interpretation of the theory of evolution. Our best and ultimate hope as a species, I insisted, was to learn the "law" of evolution, which decreed the achievement of steadily higher and higher levels of intelligence, until mere bodies could be discarded altogether. In eons to come, if *Homo sapiens* evolved into *Homo superior*, we could transcend the troubles and travails of our physical natures and rise to our "final destiny in the Heavens." I had not yet read Bernard Shaw's *Back to Methuselah*, but I would probably have agreed with every word of that daunting "metabiological" vision of Things to Come.

CHAPTER 3
GROWING UP

The skinny boy with the dreaming blue eyes introduced in the first chapter of these *Memoirs* enrolled in J.P. McCaskey High School in September, 1946. McCaskey was, and remains, the only public high school in the city of Lancaster. My junior high school was within easy walking distance of my home, and even on the same street, but to reach McCaskey, on the other side of town, I had to commute by bicycle and also take my lunches in the school cafeteria.

In the meanwhile, Dr. Cattell had transferred Hudson to an elite private school, the Lancaster Country Day School. Now that we were attending different schools, it would have been easy for us never to see one another again. I certainly had no intention of reviving the friendship. The editorial staff of *The Wagarian* was adamantly opposed to any contact of any kind with "H. Cattell." Fortunately, Hudson felt otherwise. He began telephoning me in October, and by the 23rd of the month we had met to see a movie together. There was also talk of revising our Roman numeral arithmetic books. On October 25 *The Wagarian* ran a lead editorial sternly warning me not to respond to Hudson's overtures. In my personal column, I replied that "common courtesy" required me to do so, although I promised to keep my guard up. Further meetings with Hudson did take place in November and December, although not many, and *The Wagarian* continued to scold me for my weakness and cowardice. In fact the editors did not relent until the issue of January 4, 1947, when they gave their seal of approval to a restoration of the friendship. In June, 1947, they even began referring to Hudson once again as "Mr. Cattell." The last barrier had fallen.

This second round of friendship was on quite a different basis from the first. We now spent most of our time together playing backgammon, bagatelle, cards, and a few commercial board games, including Monopoly and a curiously addictive baseball game based on the lifetime statistics of actual Major League players. Our other chief mutual pastime was to listen to records from one another's classical music albums. Interest in classical music began in 1945 with Hudson, who owned a few albums that he heard on a venerable wind-up phonograph. During the Christmas vacation in 1945, our newspapers report that I was at Hudson's house listening to Rimsky-Korsakov's *Scheherazade*. It took me little time to decide that I, too, should have a record collection. I received a portable electric phonograph for my birthday in 1946, curiously the same model that Hudson had received for his. With birthday money I immediately bought my first album, a recording of Franck's Symphony in D Minor by Pierre Monteux and the San Francisco Symphony. *Toward Which We Strive* contained a learned disquisition on the difference between "good" music and "popular" music, at a time when I knew next to nothing about either one. But I was a fast learner. By the beginning of 1947, each of us had independently acquired a dozen or more cumbersome 78 r.p.m. shellac record albums. It became a fixture of our Saturday afternoon get-togethers to listen to each other's latest acquisitions. I was regaled with Hudson's Mozart and Dvořák; he was regaled with my Berlioz and Tchaikovsky.

At first I may have been drawn to classical music by the same impulse that drew me to Shakespeare and Aristophanes: as a form of pre-pubescent rebellion against teen culture. Teen-agers traditionally rebel against adult culture, so I, as a quintessential anti-teen, would rebel against teen culture. If my peers doted on jazz, swing, and big-band music, obviously I would have to cultivate Beethoven and Brahms. Whatever, it took no time at all for both Hudson and myself to become serious connoisseurs and obsessive collectors. To this day classical music remains a central presence in both our lives, of far greater personal significance than literature or the fine arts. We have immense libraries of LP and CD recordings, attend many concerts together each year, and listen to music almost every day. Our tastes have narrowed from the catholicity of earlier times to a focus on the great European masters of the period from about 1890 to 1960, from Mahler and Debussy to Sibelius and Shostakovich; but there is no longer, if ever there was, anything contrived or rebellious about our passion.

Well and good. But what happened to "philosophy"? What happened to the future of civilization and the salvation of humankind? I have no ready answers. Juvenilia continued to issue from my typewriter, but almost all of it was belletristic — poetry and plays. *The Wagarian* carried on, with editorials that often touched on national and world events, mainly to support the domestic policies of the Truman administration and to oppose the Cold War antics of both the United States and the Soviet Union. My only serious venture into nonfiction was an ill-informed volume on classical music that I threw together in the spring of 1947. Typically, it pretended to cover the whole subject and ventured fatuous opinions on everything. I also continued to bring out monthly issues of *Fantasy & Science-Fiction*, no longer co-edited with Hudson, until January, 1948. But the well of philosophy had, for the moment, run dry.

The dry spell continued throughout our high school years. I graduated from McCaskey at the top of my class in June, 1949. Hudson graduated from the Lancaster Country Day School. In the fall we embarked on our college years, Hudson at Wabash College in Crawfordsville, Indiana; and I on a full-tuition scholarship at Franklin & Marshall College in the west end of Lancaster, almost as close to home as Reynolds Junior High School. I was now 17. So far I had never "gone out" with a member of the opposite sex. I had grown to more than six feet, mostly leg, although I weighed only 140 pounds. My voice had deepened to a pleasant baritone, but I still had no need for a razor.

Because my college campus was less than a mile away, and we could have ill afforded the costs of room and board, I continued to live in the little brick house on West Walnut Street. There were still the five of us, sleeping in the same quarters: Warren in the middle bedroom, my mother Laura and my Aunt Winnifred in the front bedroom, and my grandmother Gertie and my grandfather Willy in the back bedroom. Our circumstances were modest. Laura worked as a receptionist and secretary in a dentist's office, my aunt had become the principal of her small elementary school, and Willy — now past 80 — continued to work in good health at his factory, a job he held until February, 1951, when new owners arrived on the scene and discovered to their consternation that a man nearing his 83rd birthday was on their payroll. I remember the day he brought Gertie his last pay envelope, as he did every Friday afternoon. They sat down together on the sofa in the living room and he wept in her arms. The old gentleman had worked virtually every week of his life for more than 70 years, after leaving school at the age of nine or ten. Retirement was unthinkable.

With Hudson now living in the Midwest, it would have made sense for us to drift apart, but the opposite happened. We kept in close touch by correspondence, exchanging 64 letters during the first college year alone, many of them of formidable length, and we met frequently during our Thanksgiving, Christmas, and Easter breaks, all of which Hudson spent at his home in Lancaster. In June, 1950, we brought out a joint issue of *The Cattellian* and *The Wagarian* to commemorate the five years of our friendship and our respective newspapers. Work also began on *The Memory Book*, a collection of mutual reminiscences. In mid-September, on the eve of Hudson's return to Indiana, we agreed to launch a new monthly journal, to be known as *Archetype*. By the end of 1950, three issues had appeared, containing stories, poems, and, weightiest of all, serialized essays reviving our commitment from the mid-1940s to "philosophy." Hudson's contribution was "A Philosopher's Day," and mine a sprawling, barely coherent three-part opus entitled "Cosmic Progression."

Reviewing "Cosmic Progression" today is a deflating experience. I was now 18, and I had still not learned to write credible prose. But the ideas were as grandiose as ever. I saw human history as a chronicle of progress, life as the handiwork of evolution, the cosmos as a great theater of change and development. Our task was to think holistically, to discard parochialism and pursue "worldmindedness." The prophecy of humanity's teleological advance from body to brain to pure spirit was revisited in Part II. In Part III, I closed with the observation that it might well take a new world war to

CHAPTER 3: GROWING UP

bring the human race to its senses (as I would speculate almost 40 years later in *A Short History of the Future*) and with an appeal for the systematic exploration of outer space, as in the last pages of *The City of Man* (1963) and *The Next Three Futures* (1991).

So it would seem that Warren the futurist, world-betterer, and "philosopher" had survived after all. If he had not yet learned much about writing, he had also not abandoned his juvenile obsession with time and progress. In my sophomore year at Franklin & Marshall College, I took sweeping courses in "Problems of Philosophy" and "Religions of the World" that gave me my first serious exposures to both subjects. I did not take my first college history course, however, until the fall of my junior year. As of 1950 I remained largely a classic example of the autodidact, seldom deeply moved or influenced by anything I learned in the classroom.

Not that I was well read. As of 1950, I had read very little fiction apart from huge batches of science fiction, and very little nonfiction apart from the few dozen titles in my late father's library. The home on West Walnut Street also boasted a complete, leather-bound set of *The Harvard Classics*, but the only volumes I actually read were the 16th and 17th, *The Thousand and One Nights* and *Folk-Lore and Fable*. I no doubt spent more time writing than reading until I reached my early 20s. And after mid-1946 the time available for reading was often filched by the classical music collection. Listening to music was, for me, an experience that could not be combined with any other. I always listened while lying on my bed with eyes shut. Bliss sometimes dissolved into slumber: but until the advent of the LP record, not for long. 78 r.p.m. records needed changing every four minutes or so.

The year 1951 brought unforeseen collisions with reality. In the wake of China's entry into the Korean War, Hudson was classified 1-A by his draft board on February 2. He would be 20 years old in May and a likely candidate for slaughter in Asia. My turn would presumably come a tad later. Two weeks before the outbreak of hostilities in June, 1950, as required by law, I had registered with Selective Service upon reaching my 18th birthday. *The Wagarian* covered the progress of the war in lavish detail from the first, but until China became involved in December, neither of us felt any sense of personal peril. The news of Hudson's classification fell like a hammer blow.

The Wagarian, previously neutral in its commentaries on the Cold War, became almost rabidly patriotic after June, 1950, applauding President Truman's decisive action and supporting American determination to reunify the Korean peninsula and teach the "Reds" a well-deserved lesson for their heinous aggression. But the prospect of Private Wagar dodging bullets in a foxhole, or even surviving basic training, was something else again. Although free of illness and sound of limb, I suffered from a condition for which I still know no medical term. I was weak. My poor scrawny arms and minuscule wrists were largely innocent of muscle. In gym class I could not climb a rope more than half-way to the ceiling. Two or three pushups were all I could manage in a single session. I was the slowest runner in any of my classes. Introduced to wrestling in high school, I was pinned in seconds by every other boy, even, on one humiliating occasion, by a sinewy midget two-thirds my weight. I was also, for good reason, a physical coward constitutionally unable to defend himself in childhood battles. It was my great fortune that even the meanest schoolyard bullies were usually ashamed to take me on.

Hudson had problems of his own, including a long history of severe asthma. Nevertheless, we assumed throughout the first half of 1951 that Selective Service would select us and that we were marked to die nine thousand miles from Pennsylvania. Only the introduction in mid-1951 of an outrageously unfair system of annual deferments for college students in good standing who passed a national standardized examination spared us from further anxiety. Both of us took and passed the examination. We did not complain about the unfairness.

We learned of our passing grades in July, but by then I was on the verge of a second collision with reality. The reality in this instance was young women.

As noted earlier, I had been attracted to females ever since elementary school. My interest doubled during my first year of junior high school, and continued to climb, more slowly, thereafter. Nevertheless, I do not recall ever discussing sexual matters with anyone, not even with Hudson until I first broached the subject in a September, 1951, letter after his return to Wabash. With hindsight, I am sure that many who knew me in the 1940s assumed I was gay. I recall that occasionally a youthful detractor would call me a "fairy," the slang term for homosexuals then in common currency in the United States. The first time it happened, I asked my mother what the word meant, and she explained it to me, all the while assuring me that I was no such thing. She was quite right, although I am not sure how she knew, or even if she knew. It may have been a case of wishful thinking. In any event, my feelings for girls came early in childhood, despite the lateness of my pubescence. One of my chief grievances against the young bulls of junior high school was their attractiveness to girls, whose favors I thought far beyond my reach. I felt the same way throughout my high school years and the first two years of college.

Finally, in the summer and fall of 1951, my hormones demanded an immediate hearing. I was 19. Physically, I bore an astonishing resemblance to a contrivance of matchsticks, but my features were regular, my skin clear, my voice mature. There were certainly more ungainly fish in the ocean. I was also polite, sensitive, even empathetic, except when overcome by arrogance or anger. The time of mating was upon me. But how does a totally inexperienced gangling 19-year-old, terrified of rejection, not confident of his masculinity, shy, awkward, and more than a little nerdish, find a young woman? There were no women in my classes at Franklin & Marshall, which in those days was an exclusively men's college. By mid-September I was plunged into all but paralyzing despair.

My only allies at this time were the editors of *The Wagarian*. Back in February I had "sacked" two of my editors, including the editor-in-chief, for insubordination of long standing. My complaint was that they had orchestrated the campaign against Hudson in the fall of 1946 and had also persuaded me in the spring of 1950 not to accept the offer of a date from a McCaskey senior during my freshman year at F. & M. She was a bright but sallow wallflower who needed someone to take her to her senior prom, and we had met just once, at a teen card party. I had not attended my own prom and of course could not dance a step. Nonetheless, I was tempted. Forever my vigilant conscience, *The Wagarian* vetoed the whole idea as degrading and stupid. The wallflower was turned down. Now, in February, 1951, I had come to regret my cowardice. Bitterly. Regret took the form of a turnover in the editorial staff. The new staff would look with sympathy on Warren's burgeoning sexuality and place no obstacles in his path. By September, 1951, when it became impossible for me to deny my hormones a serious hearing, I had a staff in place that was squarely on my side. The war of Ego and Id had been won, at last, by Id.

    The gravity of my situation was underscored in the September 15 issue of *The Wagarian*, led off by an extraordinary personal statement from Warren himself, confessing his unrequited longing, and by an editorial commiserating with the Subject and calling this "the most terrible and critical period in our existence."

    For the next two years, Id remained firmly in control of Ego, but not of the world of young women. The melodrama of my doleful misadventures would fill several chapters. I never quite succumbed to despondency. Each rejection was followed by the raising of new hopes as I turned from prospect to prospect. After one eventless (and all too typical) date, I asked my inamorata of the evening whether I could see her again. She replied with a simple stab to the heart: "Why?"

    Several of my loves took the wise precaution of not letting me date them even once.

    In 1952, as a last resort, I also began taking dancing lessons (learning in the process that I had anywhere from three to five feet), tanning my chalky face with a sun lamp, lifting barbells, and persuading my bemused general practitioner to give me hormone injections, all in hopes of putting on weight and muscle and accelerating my glacially slow maturation, so as to be more appealing to young women. None of it made the least difference.

    In the winter of 1952-53, I fell most deeply of all for a student at a near-by women's college, who thought me somewhat entertaining but had more serious fish to fry, in the person of a married young sociology professor. Spotted at his home when his wife was in the hospital having his baby, my darling was interrogated by the college authorities, who tricked her into a confession. The caper led to her expulsion — and the professor's summary dismissal. A few months later, I arranged to visit her at her home in Ohio. We had been together only a short time when the doorbell rang. There stood an enormously tall and handsome young man. She introduced him to me as her fiancé. I fled in shame and horror.

Enough of all that! To be continued. Meanwhile, what of the philosopher? Strangely, he managed to co-exist with the would-be lover. One major initiative was taken in 1951, despite everything. In January, 1951, I decided to return to one of my favorite childhood authors, H.G. Wells, and this time to read his entire considerable *oeuvre*, well over a hundred volumes — or at least all of it available in my college library and second-hand book stores. The project absorbed most of my reading time for months to come. Wells introduced me to socialism, deepened my contempt for nationalism and all organized religion, and revived my childhood interest in evolution and world governance. His fluid, rhythmic, muscular breed of English prose helped me hone my own.

In the summer of 1951, as the Wells project continued, I took an intensive summer school course in Russian at the college, hoping to make myself useful (in some capacity other than hand-to-hand combat) to my expected future employers, the armed forces of the United States. Through the summer months I also managed to write twelve essays for *The Wagarian* on "philosophical issues." I addressed a variety of topics from world peace and birth control to physical anthropology and the global history of religion. The essays came to 35,000 words in all, about the same length as *Toward Which We Strive*, and a clear sign that the boy-philosopher had not relinquished his calling, although most of the essays were more like academic papers than flights of speculation. The summer of 1951 was also enhanced by the presence of Hudson, who had managed to talk his mother out of sending him to camp. We were able to hold a few so-called "intellectual cooperation conferences" on comparative world cultures, but a trip to Florida planned for the end of the summer was vetoed by Dr. Cattell.

During the 1951-52 school year, although frequently addled by the sexual problem, I made a fair amount of progress toward shaping my future. The biggest decision was to switch my major from political science to history. A wide-ranging course in English history taken in the Fall 1951 semester proved far more stimulating than any of my political science courses, past or current. I made the switch in November. It was an inspired choice. Not having studied history in college before, I was forced to spend most of my last three semesters repairing the omission, but I found the work easy, enjoyable, and, above all, meaningful. Rapid marches through the centuries exploring a wide range of subjects exactly suited my englobulating intellect. Synthesis, not analysis, was ever my forte.

The Fall 1951 semester was also notable for the launching of two extracurricular academic projects: a paper on the life and work of H.G. Wells for presentation at a meeting of a student literary society, the Calumet Club; and an entry in a college-wide essay competition on the "key" to world peace. The Wells paper was delivered in February of 1952 and later won a prize in English composition; in March I submitted my contest entry, entitled "Education for International Understanding," which finished third but still netted me a check for $200, in those days a prodigious sum of money.

No copy of "Education for International Understanding" survives in my files, and no recollection of its probably insipid contents lingers in my memory, but I still have the Wells paper. It reads reasonably well, perhaps the first piece of writing of mine that I would not be horrified to see in print today. It helped that I went through more than one draft. All the juvenilia so far cited, including every volume of "philosophy" and every issue of *The Wagarian*, were first and only drafts, banged out on my typewriter once and never revised. I had no secretaries, no computers, no photocopiers at my disposal. As soon as the keys hit the paper, I was done. But for the Wells essay,

CHAPTER 3: GROWING UP

I made an exception.

The great task of the 1952-53 academic season was to arrive at a career choice. Finishing my degree in June, 1953, at the age of 21, I could expect to be vacuumed into the U.S. Army with little delay unless I went to graduate school. I considered voluntary enlistment in another branch of service, such as the Navy, but not too seriously. A vocational testing service at the College recommended that I enter graduate or professional school in psychology, divinity, or international relations.

Another possibility was a career in broadcasting. In June, 1952, I was hired as a staff announcer at one of the local Lancaster radio stations, working full-time all that summer and part-time throughout the ensuing school year. I found the work congenial, even though it required me to master the repertoire of current popular music: chiefly big band "numbers" and romantic ballads crooned by the likes of Nat "King" Cole and Patty Page, the "Singing Rage." Mercifully, rock 'n roll had not yet been invented. Late on Sunday evenings, the management let me play a concert of classical music chosen from my own collection, but on other evenings it was "Starlite [*sic*] Serenade" or "Saturday Night Bandstand." Apart from disk jockeying, I read the news, delivered the commercials, and brought in NBC radio network programming, still quite extensive during the pioneering days of television. It was all very much my kind of job, but it would not earn me an academic deferment.

Enter Hudson. He had spent the summer in Chicago working, but the pace of our correspondence did not flag. We exchanged 17 letters during the summer and 72 during our respective senior years in college. We decided to enter graduate school in the summer of 1953. We would choose the same university, with Hudson working on a master's in English or East Asian Studies and I in European history. But which university? And with what financial aid? My college education had been almost free, thanks to my four-year scholarship at F. & M. and living at home, but living at home was no longer an option for either of us. Lancaster had no universities, and in any event we both felt the need to strike out on our own, far from our families and all the old haunts. The likeliest schools were the Midwestern Big Ten or the premiere universities of the West Coast.

By January, 1953, having pored through many a university bulletin, we narrowed the field to four: the University of Michigan in Ann Arbor, Indiana University in Bloomington, Berkeley, and Stanford. In the end the only university that offered me financial aid was Indiana, which therefore became my only choice. Hudson was meanwhile accepted into the prestigious Indiana School of Letters, a summer program featuring some of the nation's leading "New Critics." Destiny smiled on the aspiring friends. It was also noteworthy for me that of all our initial picks, Indiana enrolled the largest percentage of undergraduate women, not a small consideration in days when men outnumbered women two to one on most American campuses. At Indiana the ratio was less than three to two. Better odds for our love-starved hero.

ENTR'ACTE: THE SUMMER REPORTS

Just when it might have appeared that I was over and done with "philosophy" came the twelve "Summer Reports" under my own by-line in consecutive issues of *The Wagarian* between June 16 and September 1, 1951. I am not entirely sure what prompted this unusual series of essays, after four years of almost exclusive devotion to poetry, science fiction, and drama. Engaging the work of H.G. Wells, and especially his non-fiction, must have played a part. The tortuous ups and downs of the Korean War, with all their personal implications for a potential draftee, must have played a part. At any rate, the twelve reports arrived with no prefatory remarks and no rationale. I had submitted them to my editors for their consideration, and, as always happened with submissions from the Subject, they were accepted.

The first of my reports, "Peace in 1951," explored the possibility that the Korean War would degenerate into World War III, either as the result of following the recommendations of the recently sacked General MacArthur to bomb China or as the result of a command decision by Joseph Stalin to crush the West pre-emptively before its post-Korea rearmament was complete. My instincts told me that world war was imminent, and yet perhaps not. "We have been expecting [world] war so long that we no longer expect it." The strategic advantage of the Soviet Union and China was their central position on the Eurasian land mass, enabling them to conquer the rest of Europe and Asia in a matter of months; America would probably refrain from hurling its atomic arsenal at the Soviets for fear of a comparable Soviet attack. Yet Stalin was a notoriously cautious old bird. He might just bide his time. In the end I drew no definitive conclusion about what the near future held in store. Thinking ahead further, I opined that Communism was "the very last bogey" obstructing humanity's ultimate triumph. If world war could be averted, in the long run Communism would fail and the "liberal conscience" could "begin once more the search for a unified and progressive world."

My second "Summer Report" concerned "Populations." Warning that the earth's population could soar to four billion by the year 2000 (the then-current wisdom, a mere two billion short!), I demanded that every effort be made to curtail population growth in the poor nations and among the less fit in the rich nations. College men and women should rear large families, and the hoi polloi everywhere else should be encouraged to limit their fertility. Professors should "drum" into their students "that procreation is more than a pleasant experience. ... You and your spouse have a duty to civilization to make as many children as you can afford to make. ... Every college man and woman should raise four children per couple." (In due course, for whatever reasons, both Hudson and I would heed this call to the letter.)

My only excuse for advocating such racist rubbish was that once again I saw the multiplication of intelligence as the vehicle for human salvation. Although not every college student was superior to every member of the hoi polloi, the run of humanity was manifestly inferior to the cream (read "white"?). Choices were imperative.

"Populations" was followed by a two-part report entitled

"Three Worlds," in many ways the centerpiece of the whole series and the clearest statement in all my juvenilia of the future I expected for humankind. My basic premise was not unlike Auguste Comte's law of the three states: human history, I suggested, had moved through two epochs of immense length and was now struggling to enter a third. The first, which I dubbed the "materialist" epoch, encompassed all of prehistory and early antiquity. Through these many millennia, human beings had lived essentially as glorified animals, "super-chimpanzees," focused on tribal or group survival, beseeching the protection of gods and spirits. They boasted rudimentary sciences and technologies, but no consciousness of a purpose higher than staying alive.

Yet here and there around the ancient world, some societies had advanced to a second level of existence, ushering in a second epoch of world history, the "religious" epoch. Now men found meaning and purpose in a realm beyond the material, through a spiritual relationship with an almighty supernatural being. They learned to deny themselves, to transcend their animality, for the sake of attunement with the divine world order. Not all individuals in a "religious" society reached so high. Many remained at the animal level. But a new modality of existence had become possible.

The third epoch, the "cosmopolitan liberal" epoch, would represent a Hegelian synthesis (I actually referred to "Hegel's dialectic") of the materialist and religious epochs, combining the science, technology, and commonsense survivalism of the one with the self-abnegating higher consciousness of the other, but freed now from all superstitious dogma and fantasy. The cosmopolitan liberal sought "protection against war and 'cut-throat competition' by world coordination. He wants equality of opportunity for the common man, and he wants intellectual stimulus and cooperation [from] the leaders of society." Every individual, following in the spiritual footsteps of the religious man, was obliged to consecrate his life to the progress of the human race as a whole.

Unfortunately, too many of us were the slaves of inertia, unwilling to make the sacrifices necessary to build this third world, this third epoch of human unity. The liberal conscience was still not strong enough. "The only chance remaining is in the wake of a world catastrophe so stimulating and so complete that the remnant of man will be forced to construct a liberal cosmopolitan state; a catastrophe that will destroy all the erroneous and half-true systems that now 'guide' humanity, and leave us free to organize according to the dictates of our new-found world conscience." My chief candidates for the coming catastrophe were "a war, or an economic depression, more severe than anything in recorded history."

Today I would revise some of the language of this 50-year-old manifesto, and add several considerations not addressed in it, but I find my head more often nodding yes than shaking no. And I was nodding yes even then: in the second part of "Three Worlds," in reference to "cosmopolitan liberalism," I claimed that "this has been my own position, more or less, for the past five or six years." Rather "less" than "more," perhaps, but the threads of thought connecting the boy of 12 and the man of 19 are surely not invisible.

The rest of the Summer Reports, except the last, consisted largely of synopses of my sophomore studies of world religions, cultures, and philosophies, but the twelfth, "Evolution in the Modern World Community," revisited the human future. A democratic Utopia, I argued, was within reach, through revolutions in education and government. If the march in 1951 toward wider and wider cooperation among nations continued, we might some day be able to dissolve national boundaries. "The whole course of human history turns toward unity and still greater intellectual achievements." Revolutions and apocalyptic conflicts might still be needed to bring us to the Promised Land; but "Utopia is within the power of man to achieve, and within his power to sustain. Even now it is not too late."

CHAPTER 4
MANIFESTO!

The plan hatched in 1952 for Hudson and Warren to attend graduate school together went awry almost at once. We left for Bloomington in my car on June 15, 1953. The next day we were in Cincinnati, where I had the ill fortune to meet my girlfriend's fiancé, the episode related in the previous chapter. We reached the campus of Indiana University on the afternoon of the 17th and checked into our respective quarters. Mine was a room in a dormitory for single graduate students. Classes began on the 22nd. But on July 3, I introduced myself to Dorothy Bowers, an undergraduate student from Kokomo, Indiana, who had caught my eye earlier. Within a few weeks we were engaged to be married. The engagement was sealed on July 22 when I "pinned" my intended with my Phi Beta Kappa key. July 22 was also her 17th birthday. I saw very little of Hudson throughout July; he found the New Critics of the Indiana School of Letters cliquish, pretentious, and tiresome; on July 30, he packed his bags and returned to Lancaster for good.

It might have seemed, as in the fall of 1949 and as in the spring of 1946, that our friendship was once again destined to disintegrate. Hudson was living in Pennsylvania, I was living in Indiana. He was single, I was deeply in love and soon to be married.

But somehow the friendship survived and even prospered. In mid-August, while Dorothy vacationed with her family, I drove back to Lancaster to visit my own, and Hudson proposed the launching of a new two-man "journal," somewhat like the long defunct *Archetype*, which this time would appear whenever we felt like it, instead of on a fixed schedule. We decided to call it *The Institutional Review*. The first slender issue was dated August 22, 1953, and by the end of 1953, five more issues had seen the light. *The Institutional Review*, a miscellany of essays and stories, survived for three more years. It also gave birth to our grandest project of all, the so-called "integration project," which evolved by degrees into my second real-world book, *The City of Man* (1963).

The integration project originated in meetings between Hudson and myself during my Easter vacation in April, 1954, in Lancaster. I had married Dorothy in Kokomo the previous December. We honeymooned in Florida. I was nearing completion of my master's degree in history at Indiana University. Hudson had been exempted from military service for medical reasons and gone to work for his uncle Jaques Cattell at the family-owned Science Press in Lancaster. Our adult lives were taking shape. But the boy-philosopher, although now a young married man of 21, remained more or less intact. I continued every week to write and "publish" *The Wagarian*, whose staff Dorothy joined as "Domestic Editor" on January 2, 1954. And when Hudson and I met during the 1954 Easter break, I proposed that the next issue of *The Institutional Review* should feature manifestos by each of us, defining our "common objectives," which could then be amalgamated into a single document in June.

Manifestos? Objectives? What we were up to this time? It is one thing, however bizarre, for adolescent boys to daydream about playing philosopher and saving the world, and quite another for grown men to carry on in the same vein, especially if the "publications" involved consist of typewritten manuscripts available in one or two copies with a readership of two or three. Were we hallucinating, or even clinically insane?

Insane we surely were not. At one level, we had simply fallen into the self-mocking habit of referring to ourselves as institutions. So our friendship was not a friendship, it was an "institutional circle." Our manuscripts were "books" and "journals," which we "bound" or "published," not stapled. Most of my "books" bore the imprint of the "Wagar Type-Press Co." Our rooms were "headquarters." When we met, it was not a get-together, but a "conference." So a statement of our goals in life would have to be a "manifesto."

True, but not the whole truth. By 1954 I had begun to think in terms of actually pursuing a quasi-messianic career, as a professional writer of Wellsian books akin to *The Open Conspiracy* (1928)

CHAPTER 4: MANIFESTO!

or *The Shape of Things To Come* (1933), books that would point the way to a new and transformed world far different from our own. So why not draft a manifesto, a real manifesto initiating a movement for global reconstruction? Two Germans almost as young and obscure as we had written a manifesto in 1848 that changed the whole course of world history. Perhaps now it was the turn of Hudson and Warren. With my growing academic connections and Hudson's inside track in the publishing world, in a few more years we might do great things. It was time to begin. The manifesto could clarify and define our objectives, and lead in due course to a real-world book.

We set to work and in the eleventh issue of *The Institutional Review*, which came out on June 11, our respective manifestos duly appeared. We followed this with what *The Cattellian* dubbed "a marathon conference designed to lay the cornerstone for the future," held all day and evening on June 12 at a small cabin in the woods owned by Dr. Cattell. Hudson's essay was entitled "The Future Under Analysis" and mine "A Revolutionary Charter." It should have been apparent from the outset that we occupied almost no common ground, except a generic liberal and rational humanism. Nevertheless, we were to struggle for more than a year to fuse our positions and complete our project jointly, sometimes putting our friendship at risk in the process. Still, one thing is clear: although I was the friend who, in the end, brought the project to fruition, there would have been nothing for me to bring to fruition had we not resolved, in 1954, to try our luck at saving the world. Without Hudson's interest, his counterpoint, and his role as critic and reader, I might well have vanished into the world of routine academic monographs and dog-eared lecture notes — vanished without a trace. (I came pretty close to doing that anyway, even with his help!)

Whatever, our manifestos veered off in different directions. Hudson deplored the low estate of intellectual life in the America of the mid-1950s and appealed for U.S. intellectuals to embark on rational reform of their society. In particular he proposed the establishment of a liberal, enlightened, progressive, pro-capitalist, anti-Communist magazine dedicated to the highest aims. New heroes would be recruited, heroes not of muscle but of intellect.

My "Revolutionary Charter" started out on a similar note, regretting the lack of zeal in the American intelligentsia of the mid-1950s. But from that point onward, we went our separate ways. My response was to call for Revolution, with a capital "r," while acknowledging "the possibility that no revolution can be achieved except in the catastrophe of war, at which time an organization must be ready to guide the survivors to a world state." I also insisted that our home-grown intelligentsia must deal "in larger loyalties," collaborating with colleagues all over the world.

After a Preamble enunciating basic principles, I argued that the only future worth considering was the global future of *Homo sapiens*. "The concept of a national state has long outlived its usefulness in the history of human political organization." The objective of the Revolution was "a confederated world republic, composed of regional federations, national states, and autonomous districts under international mandate, as political conditions may require." The regulation of international trade and communications, the control of space exploration, the command of all armed forces except for local police, the regulation or ownership of all multinational corporations, and the protection of the basic human rights of all world citizens would become the charge of the world republic. A new secular religion of humanity would compete on an equal footing with the traditional positive confessions, and this new humanism would be obligatory for all "members of the Revolution."

The Revolution itself would not, and could not, happen spontaneously. I proceeded, in the next article of my Manifesto, to outline its organization, the structure of its national and international secretariats, the bases of its mass appeal, its tactics and its strategies. I hinted at the possible eventual need for "storm formations" — echoing the demented rhetoric of German National Socialism — to seize power in the shadow or aftermath of global war. But given the rest of the ideological agenda of the Revolution, I think I hewed more closely to the world-view of the Comintern than to the world-view of the NSDAP.

CHAPTER 4: MANIFESTO!

Regardless of its political pedigree, the program I enunciated in *The Institutional Review* in June, 1954, was not congruent with Hudson's, and I cannot, at this remove in time, fathom why we did not scuttle our joint project forthwith and move on with our lives. The notes I jotted down on the day of our June 12 "marathon conference" survive, but offer no explanation. I surmise that we were just too close, personally, to let a rift occur. It did not suit us to confront and acknowledge the obvious.

In the event no serious effort was made to consolidate the two manifestos into one, but we did agree to produce a full-length book that we would somehow or other contrive to publish. Certain chapters were assigned to Hudson, the rest to Warren. I set to work almost immediately, but Hudson, except for one more essay in *The Institutional Review*, was unable to follow through. His responsibilities at The Science Press doubled and redoubled through the rest of 1954 and well into 1955, by which time he was working at the Press 12 to 14 hours a day. Worse yet, I had reached the decision as early as September that our book could not attract funding or a publisher or even readers unless it synchronized our own thinking with the ideas of a substantial array of leading contemporary minds. To achieve this objective, we needed to read widely and deeply. A letter dispatched to Hudson from Bloomington on September 27, 1954, called for a crash research program to "pile up evidence" confirming the relevance of our ideas. From that point forward, I all but bombarded Hudson with lists of books and authors that he should consult without delay.

But my letter of September 27 and its many sequels, however well intentioned, doomed our collaboration to failure. Hudson did not begin to have the kind of time available to me, as a graduate student, for research and writing. Nor did he enjoy access, as I did, to a large university research library. In the summer of 1955 Hudson withdrew from the project altogether, except as a reader and critic, and I took over his chapters as well as my own. A further complication beginning in June, 1955, was his courtship of Maria Gleaton, a senior at Swarthmore College. Hudson and Maria were married on

December 24 of that year.

Nevertheless, I think I was quite right about the need to lard our book with the ideas of other thinkers. As nobodies in our early 20s, we could hardly expect anyone to take our schemes seriously unless we supplied evidence that many other and more senior minds were thinking along parallel lines. I spent much of the 1954-55 academic year reading widely in the work of contemporary prophets of a new world order, from Arnold J. Toynbee and Pitirim A. Sorokin to Lewis Mumford and F.S.C. Northrop. Then, in the summer of 1955, after Dorothy's graduation from Indiana University, I transferred to Yale University to complete my doctorate, hoping to work under the tutelage of Professor Franklin Le Van Baumer. My academic focus had wandered from an initial interest in Balkan history in 1953 to English history in 1954 and, finally, in early 1955, to European intellectual history, especially as defined by Baumer in his magisterial anthology, *Main Currents of Western Thought* (1952). Baumer took me on, and we worked together well and closely for several years. He was for me the ideal *Doktorvater*.

But when I moved to Yale, the book growing out of my project with Hudson was still not finished. By this point in time, it had virtually become a study in the recent history of ideas, especially ideas of world cultural, economic, and political integration. Still, it was not "school work." At Yale I enrolled in four year-long seminars, all of them assigning extensive research papers, and I held a readership with the late Professor Leonard Krieger that required me to grade all the examinations in his large undergraduate course on the making of modern Europe. How would I find the time to finish my *magnum opus*? And why even try?

All I can remember is my urgent sense that the project had to be finished, and finished quickly. Humankind was in dire crisis. For most of my 23 years on earth, it had been fighting gigantic wars. Another was perhaps just around the bend. At any moment we might succeed in blowing ourselves up. If my book could help mobilize the world's intelligentsia to respond effectively to this vast crisis, and respond in a timely fashion, it was essential that I waste no time finish-

CHAPTER 4: MANIFESTO!

ing it. How much of my concern was naked ambition to make a "name" for myself, to join the ranks of the Great Thinkers, I cannot say. Certainly ambition, spiced with more than a pinch of megalomania, played its part. But I had also persuaded myself that the Day of Judgment might well be at hand. Nor was I alone in thinking apocalyptic thoughts in those early years of the Cold War, the nuclear arms race, the collapse of the great European empires, and the surging appeal of Soviet-orchestrated Communism. The 1950s have been written off by American cultural historians as the "placid decade." There was nothing placid about my 1950s.

So I worked at a furious, haunted pace to complete my book and type up a final draft. A letter to Hudson dated February 17, 1956, announced that I stayed up all night to finish the typing. The final product bore the title *Integration: Formulas of Response to the World Crisis* and ran to 263 triple-spaced pages. I had prepared three copies, the top copy and two carbons, one earmarked for Hudson. At some point during the spring term I lent a copy to Professor Baumer, soliciting his opinion and advice, and intended, after further revisions, to show it to F.S.C. Northrop, also a professor at Yale, and one of the thinkers most often cited in my text. Baumer returned his copy to me in April, with a few guarded but favorable comments, and advised me to set the manuscript aside until I had completed my dissertation.

After all the urgency and haste, could I accept such wise, prudent, unexciting counsel? You might think not. You would be wrong. Somehow or other, his words soothed and settled me. *Integration* was transferred to a back burner. I relented. No further revisions took place. Northrop never saw the manuscript. The world would have to stumble along for at least another year or two without its wake-up call from W. Warren Wagar.

ENTR'ACTE: INTEGRATION

One significant point has not yet been addressed. If Hudson

and I usually referred to our joint project as the "integration project," what the devil did we mean by "integration"? I am not sure we ever really succeeded in pinning it down. At first we may both have meant an attempt to compress the sciences and humanities into a unified super-discipline, and also to bring the nation's — or the world's — intellectuals together under some sort of common front.

But as I pursued our project in 1954-56, the term came to mean, for me, much more than that. It denoted a synthesis not only of science and scholarship, but a synthesis of all the cultures and tribes of humankind: in short, the emergence of a coherent unified world civilization. This was not what is meant today by "globalization." It was also not "modernization" or, in particular, "Westernization." Globalizing forces, such as advanced technology and the capitalist world marketplace, were clearly propelling all of us into ever more intimate contact with one another, but none of that would necessarily make for peace or understanding or metamorphosis. The task before us, I argued, was to subsume all the extant cultures of humankind in a higher, organic, transformed world culture. Such a culture would preserve the most valid and viable ingredients in all parochial cultures. It would not be European, or Asian, or American, or African. It would be Terran.

Let us now explore this last and longest sample of my juvenilia, the strange text of *Integration: Formulas of Response to the World Crisis*, as it issued, hot and intemperate, from my typewriter in the winter of 1955-56.

The final draft consisted of an Introduction, eight chapters, an Epilogue, and a brief bibliography. Endnotes were planned, but never compiled. The Introduction called attention to the rise of a new consciousness in the years since the Second World War. Thinkers of many persuasions had reached the sober conclusion that the modern world, with its lethal plurality of states and cultures, stood on the brink of collapse. The time was at hand to forge an integrated global civilization.

In the first chapter, I sketched "The Mid-Century Challenge," an inventory of all the woes of the world in the 1950s. In the second

CHAPTER 4: MANIFESTO!

chapter, "The Mid-Century Response." I furnished an overview of the new "integrative" thought now aborning, which closed with six fundamental propositions that "thinking men" everywhere were obliged to endorse: humanity's responsibility to take charge of its own evolution, the "free surrender of the ego to the demands of humane love," the integration of all knowledge, the central role of "the creative individual," the need for a global movement of the "most able men," and the replacement of sovereign nations by "a common world law" and "world councils competent to govern their intercourse and arbitrate their disputes."

These six propositions were further developed in the next four chapters, the first and second in a chapter entitled "The Ethical Dimension," the third in a chapter entitled "Synthesis," the fourth and fifth in "Liberalism and Leadership," and the sixth in "World Government." I generously sprinkled each chapter with learned references to the chief architects of integrative thought. "The Ethical Dimension" drew on the work of Erich Fromm, Julian Huxley, M.F. Ashley Montagu, Lewis Mumford, Edmund Ware Sinnott, Pitirim A. Sorokin, and Arnold J. Toynbee. For the chapter on cognitive and cultural synthesis, I cited, among others, Bhagavan Das, Carl Gustav Jung, F.S.C. Northrop, Sir Sarvepalli Radhakrishnan, Oliver L. Reiser, H.G. Wells, and Lancelot Law Whyte. The chapter on the leadership role of the intelligentsia collected ideas from C.E.M. Joad, Joseph Wood Krutch, Walter Lippmann, Karl Mannheim, and José Ortega y Gasset. In "World Government" I referred to many of these same thinkers, such as Northrop, Toynbee, and Wells, together with Stringfellow Barr, G.A. Borgese, Norman Cousins, Robert Maynard Hutchins, Frederick L. Schuman, and Clarence Streit. The "Select Book List" at the end consisted of 87 titles by 53 authors or editors. Not quite a cornucopia; but it was the first bibliography ever to appear in any of my juvenilia.

Chapter Seven, "The Disintegrative Pattern in Modern Culture," charted the rise and fall of modernism between 1890 and 1955. I used Alfred Kroeber's theory of the "culture burst" to track this powerful efflorescence in art, literature, music, science, and philosophy; and then showed how, in the past quarter-century, modernism had exhausted its premises, creating space for the emergence of a new, post-modernist, integrative culture that would express the values of the coming world civilization. As modernism had been raw, negative, splintering, and centrifugal, so the new integralism would be a culture of synthesis and healing. As the Renaissance of the 15th Century had led to the Reformation of the 16th, so the new integralism would "contribute in many ways to World Reformation." But I could provide no examples of what I had in view: the new culture was not yet here.

To charges that I was dealing in delusive utopian fantasy, I replied in Chapter Eight, "On Prophecy," that myopic self-styled "realists" were the deluded ones. The "realist," clinging unimaginatively to the status quo, failed to grasp that status quo's are always in process of subversion by the great tidal forces of world history. Better to wear the mantle of the prophet and anticipate and help to shape the future than to play "the 'realist,' stuck fast to the flypaper of the two-dimensional present." I gave several examples from recent history of how "realists" had time and again failed to foresee what was coming by mindlessly assuming that the future would simply continue present-day trends, along present-day tracks. Accurate prediction was never easy, but the true prophet usually outperformed the realist, if only because the prophet understood that man has the power to create himself anew, "to spin the future from the cravings...of his soul." The prophet understood the "godlike power of ideas," how they could, with ample nurturance, become "warheads of revolution or epochal change."

The last few pages of the text of *Integration* consisted of an Epilogue, subtitled "The Deep End." The future, I wrote, would not end with the achievement of an integrated world civilization. In fact, it would never end. On the far horizon were prospects we could only feebly glimpse. I cited William H. McNeill's speculation in *Past and Future* (1954) that a world civilization might eventually become stagnant and uncreative. But I doubted this would happen, because of all the frontiers still before us: the exploration of space, as outlined in a recent book by Arthur C. Clarke; the possibility of extra-sensory perception; and much more. To that distant future "we send our sons" and from that future, " — in man's unimaginable flight through time — they will never return."

In the summer of 1956, I prepared a 44-page synopsis of *Integration*, entitled "The Twentieth-Century Search for Synthesis," which I asked my mentor, Professor Baumer, to help me place in a suitable journal. This article became my first serious submission of any work for actual publication, but it was rejected, even with Baumer's recommendations, by *The Journal of the History of Ideas* and *The Journal of Modern History*, after which we agreed to desist. By then I was deep into work on my doctoral dissertation, which soon took full precedence over any other project.

It may be misleading to lump *Integration* with my juvenilia. The manuscript was by no means publishable, yet it was also more professional than anything else I had written, except for various graduate school seminar papers produced during the same time frame. It did not bear the imprint of the Wagar Type-Press Co. Unlike earlier books, it had been intended all along for publication in the real world. It was also not reviewed in *The Wagarian*, because that mighty house organ had fallen silent at the end of January, 1955, never to be revived. The last issue, for January 22, 1955, contained an editorial forecasting the eventual collapse of Soviet Communism as the result of decay from within, a vision I would have done well to revisit before writing *A Short History of the Future* in 1987! But in any case *The Wagarian* was no more. With its demise, and with the filing away of my unpublished *Integration*, I had finally left the *Wunderkind* of West Walnut Street in the dust.

Do not believe it.

CHAPTER 5
ALL'S WELLS

In the late 1950s, it would have been difficult to think of a writer recently famous who commanded less respect or attention from the nabobs of literary criticism than Herbert George Wells. His body of work was the antithesis of everything that counted. Meticulous craftsmanship, dissection of the psyche, non-linear narration, linguistic invention, multiple levels of metaphor and paradox, erotic candor: all were lamentably missing in Wells. In the eyes of the keepers of the canon, he had turned out a few passable fantasies in his youth, degenerated into a practitioner of middlebrow social-realist fiction in mid-life, and misspent his dotage huckstering windy ideas. He was, in short, the anti-Joyce.

Fortunately I was not a member of the fraternity of literary critics. With my newly acquired credentials as an intellectual historian, I found Wells an ideal topic for a doctoral dissertation. Professor Baumer concurred. It was Baumer, for that matter, who gave me the courage to proceed. Wells was just the sort of writer, he said, that our discipline was uniquely qualified to study, not a towering genius whose immortal work would fall mainly into the province of specialists in science or philosophy or literature, but a public intellectual with a gift for disseminating and popularizing ideas. Who else would find him an appealing subject? He might not have been "great," but he had been a potent force in the lives and minds of millions of people all over the world for half a century. He belonged to history, and therefore to historians.

Of course I harbored an ulterior motive for studying Wells. To me, he was not just a writer or a popularizer or an influence. He was a prophet of world integration, the foremost prophet of his generation, and in this sense an authentic Great Man, an original and creative thinker, his drooping reputation among the literati notwithstanding. Through him I could gain an audience for some of my own ideas. Besides, I had already digested most of his work in college. I was half-way to the finish line before I even began. Best of all, I hugely admired and warmly connected to his way of writing. A book about Wells would virtually write itself, unlike the majority of doctoral dissertations, which are pried loose from their authors as if by instruments of Gothic torture.

A few hurdles remained. I had completed my course requirements in May, 1956, but during the Fall semester I served once again as a graduate assistant, this time in Baumer's undergraduate survey of European intellectual history. I also audited a seminar taught by F.S.C. Northrop, one of my prime "integrators," and undertook a crash program of reading for my comprehensive oral examinations, scheduled for mid-December. Baumer's lectures turned out to be the best organized and most provocative I had ever heard, furnishing me with a model of excellence I have tried to follow in my own undergraduate teaching ever since.

By the end of 1956 the coast was clear for my attack on Wells. Work proceeded much as I had expected. In the first eight months of 1957, I read or re-read all of Wells's books and many of his unreprinted articles and skimmed the writings of his most prominent contemporaries, including everything I could track down by way of criticism and commentary, in 1957 a task far less formidable than it would be today. I filled two file boxes with typewritten note slips.

In March I had also become the first outside scholar authorized to explore the just-catalogued Wells Archive at the University of Illinois. My week in the Wells Archive, which held most of the books, manuscripts, and letters in Wells's possession at the time of his death in 1946, was a heady adventure for the young scholar, my first and — as it turned out — my only taste of serious archival research. Since Wells rushed everything he thought into print, and wrote few letters that contradicted or significantly amplified his published writings, I gleaned only a few sidebars and footnotes for my dissertation.

But the experience of holding in my own hands original letters to Wells from the likes of Beatrice Webb, Bertrand Russell, and Bernard Shaw, as well as carbon copies of his responses, and exam-

CHAPTER 5: ALL'S WELLS

ining the handwritten drafts of many of Wells's books, was worth far more to me than anything I managed to tuck into my dissertation. I remember with greatest pleasure combing through the exchanges between Wells and Shaw — the letters of Shaw long, eloquent, and inimitably Shavian, those of Wells brisk and less imposing. Today, this whole correspondence is easily available in a scholarly edition prepared by J. Percy Smith, replete with illuminating footnotes, but in 1957 I was one of a privileged few.

In September Dorothy and I embarked on the S.S. *United States* for a year of study in London on a Fulbright Scholarship. To be truthful, there was not all that much left to "study." I made occasional use of London's major research libraries, including the Reading Room of the British Museum, but I had more than broken the back of my project at Yale and Illinois. Most of my work time was invested in writing drafts of chapters and having them read by Baumer and a professor of English literature at the University of London assigned to me by the Fulbright office.

I also took the chance to visit some of Wells's former homes, including his last residence at 13 Hanover Terrace, opposite Regent's Park; and in April, 1958, I interviewed Wells's oldest son Gip (G.P. Wells, a co-author of *The Science of Life*), a marine biologist at the University of London, as well as Gip's ex-wife Marjorie, Wells's last personal secretary. From letters in the Wells Archive, I had gathered that Wells was usually put off by earnest young (male) admirers, which Marjorie confirmed. "I'm sure he would have found me a dull lad," I said. "Oh yes, but Mrs. Wagar," she continued, smiling and looking pointedly at my lovely 21-year old wife, "now that would have been a different matter altogether!" In 1958 much less was publicly known about H.G.'s inveterate womanizing than we have all learned since. The Estate had taken care to withhold his love letters from the Archive. But I knew enough even then to appreciate the joke. I also knew that, given half a chance, and as much as I loved Dorothy, I would have gladly walked in my hero's iniquitous footsteps.

Meanwhile, the late 1950s were a troublous season for aspiring academics. The early postwar explosion in enrollments made possible by the "G.I. Bill" in aid of returning veterans had ended, and the stampede into colleges by the "baby boomers" of the 1940s was still in the future. But I was in luck. Wellesley College needed a junior intellectual historian. The chair of the History Department at Wellesley, Henry Schwarz, a scion of the F.A.O. Schwarz family of toy retailing fame, behaved as chairs in those incorrect days usually did. He wrote to the leading Ivy League schools, including Yale, to inquire about promising rising stars. Yale sent him Baumer's endorsement of me, and without further fuss, he wrote in December, 1957, to solicit my interest in an entry-level job at Wellesley. He was under no mandate to scour the market for women and minorities. No affirmative action guidelines constrained his search. All he had to do was to invite the likeliest Ivy League candidate, assuming that he (almost always he) would fit the bill, even if he (almost always he) had to be hired sight unseen.

In December, 1957, Schwarz wrote to ask if I was interested. I said yes. In January he wrote again to tender me an instructorship at a salary of $4,500. I accepted the next day. It was the only offer I received that winter. Many of my fellow equally qualified Yalies received no plausible offers at all.

And so it happened that in September, 1958, after a summer of touring and camping throughout Europe, from Scotland to Turkey and back, Dorothy and I relocated to the Commonwealth of Massachusetts, where I inaugurated my long career as a history professor, on the "Campus Beautiful" of Wellesley College, just outside Boston. Now 26, I no longer needed deferments from my draft board. Selective Service policy at the time was not to draft men over the age of 25.

In the 1950s Wellesley was not yet a feminist college. It was a college for privileged young women in the thrall of the Feminine Mystique. Uniformly bright, my students dreamed chiefly of marrying young bucks from the Harvard Business School and settling down in a leafy suburb of Cleveland (or wherever) to raise a large family and live what passed at that time for the good female life. Only a fifth of Wellesley's alumnae even attempted graduate or professional school. Their low self-esteem may be illustrated by a remark I overheard one day on my way to the Library, as two fair Wellesleyans discussed a somewhat effeminate male professor — "Well, what other kind of man would teach at a girls' school?" Although they were not talking about me, my cheeks burned for hours.

But in 1958 and 1959, I did not allow myself to be overly distracted by the pros and cons of teaching at a women's college. The great mission was to complete my dissertation and earn my doctorate. It was a brutally busy year, preparing scores of brand-new lectures and working even longer hours on the dissertation, still only two-thirds finished as of September. Nor was I a born teacher. Writing to Hudson on December 2, 1958, I confessed that I had "long since ceased to look on my students as tempting morsels. They are my task-masters, my pitiless critics, my Furies." My classes were "sometimes miserable failures, on which I brood." During that first year, I sat at a desk reading my lectures from a typewritten script punctuated now and then by a question pitched at the class, for which only one answer, also typed in, would do. My experience at Yale as a graduate assistant had consisted only of grading papers. Like most beginning college teachers in the 1950s, I had never taught a day in my green life before stepping into my first classroom as a credentialed and salaried professor. Shy, unsure, more intimidated than enticed by the "tempting morsels" under my faltering tutelage, I must have cut a forlorn figure.

Somehow or other, I was able to complete my dissertation. I had the last of the draft chapters ready by early December. Revisions occupied me for the next few months, and the final draft was shipped to Yale in April, 1959. I entitled it *The Open Conspirator: H.G. Wells as a Prophet of World Order*. My dissertation committee gave it the necessary stamp of approval. I received my doctorate on June 8, 1959, three days after my 27th birthday.

The next five years were surely the best of my life, a succession of triumphs that would have delighted the editors of *The Wagarian*. Frank Baumer (academic protocol allowed — almost required — proteges to call former Ph.D. supervisors by their first names after receiving their degrees, but not one day sooner) recommended my dissertation to his publisher, Alfred A. Knopf. In August, 1959, Frank forwarded me a letter from Knopf himself asking to see the manuscript. Knopf soon rejected it, on the grounds that it was more appropriate for a university press. Professor John Morton Blum, another member of my dissertation committee at Yale, then recommended it to his own publisher, Houghton Mifflin of Boston. In late October two Houghton Mifflin editors took me to lunch in Boston. They liked the manuscript, but liked its voice even more. Although they did not find *The Open Conspirator* suitable for commercial publication, they urged me to consider writing another book that might appeal to a wider reading public. Within a week I had dashed off the prospectus for a new book with the tentative title of "The Organic World Society," based on the work I had done for *Integration*. Just before Christmas, 1959, Houghton Mifflin bought an option on "The Organic World Society." Visions of sugar plums danced in my head. The boy-philosopher was on his way!

Meanwhile, I had received assurances from Frank that Yale University Press would offer me a contract for *The Open Conspirator*; and Dorothy presented me on November 25 with our first child, John Alden Wagar, named after her own most famous ancestor. I wrote to Hudson on December 29 that 1959 had turned out to be an "*annus mirabilis*, from start to finish." Looking back, I see no reason to alter that judgment. Despite my modest background as a member of the *petite bourgeoisie*, I had managed to hook into one of the principal old boy networks of my era, a network of power and privilege, male, white, chiefly Protestant, Ivy League, and inbred, a network that took good care of its own but did admit a limited number of outsiders as long as they possessed certain gifts and played by the rules. My single most important move had been to transfer to Yale in 1955. After that, all the right doors began to open in just the right sequence.

"The Organic World Society" evolved into my second book, *The City of Man*, the centerpiece of the next chapter. But for now, I prefer to concentrate on my intellectual love affair with H.G. Wells. As Frank had promised, Yale University Press did indeed accept *The

CHAPTER 5: ALL'S WELLS

Open Conspirator: H.G. Wells as a Prophet of World Order. The letter of intent arrived in January, 1960. By late April I had finished revising and typing up the manuscript, and sent it off to New Haven. The revisions required were not substantial. I do not remember any superhuman toil, certainly nothing like the labors of the previous year. The production process went smoothly, and in March of 1961 my first book was in print. I had changed the title for some reason (not at the insistence of the Press) to *H.G. Wells and the World State*. Perhaps I should have adhered to the original title. Wells did often use the phrase "world state," but what he had in mind was not so much a "state" as an apolitical system of interlocking world controls, a global technocracy. Either title, however, pointed to the focus of the book. It was not a life of Wells, not a literary appreciation, not even an intellectual biography, but a study of Wells as a futurist, and one kind of futurist in particular: a visionary with a formula for the salvaging of modern civilization.

For a university press monograph on a largely forgotten writer, *H.G. Wells and the World State* received a surprising number of reviews in prominent places. I probably expected none at all, except in one or two professional history journals. The major coup was "One Planet Indivisible," a piece in *Saturday Review* by the British M.P. and world federalist Arthur Henderson, which began with an eminently quotable sentence: "Warren Wagar has written a brilliant, scholarly, and incisive analysis of one of the great writers and thinkers of the past century." The review went on for more than a page, turning on its second page to an assessment of an anthology of writings on world peace by Albert Einstein. I was delighted that Wells, not Einstein, had received top billing in Henderson's essay.

In the British journal *Time & Tide,* Martin Green published a double review of *H.G. Wells and the World State* and another dissertation on Wells, *The Early H.G. Wells: A Study of the Scientific Romances,* by Bernard Bergonzi, which appeared at about the same time as my Yale book under the imprint of Manchester University Press. Green felt that I had done the better job, although Bergonzi's book was soon to garner far more attention in literary circles. Having heard that Bergonzi was writing a dissertation on Wells, but not knowing what his angle might be, I had looked him up at his Oxford digs during my year in England. The first thing I noticed as I entered his room was a crucifix hanging on the wall. I was relieved at once of all anxiety that he and I might be writing the same dissertation.

As it happened, we were writing opposite dissertations. Bergonzi hailed Wells as a youthful genius persuaded of the secular equivalent of the Augustinian doctrine of Original Sin, whose later "acceptance of a collectivist ideology and the Fabian ideal of 'social service' destroyed the autonomy of his imagination, and radically reduced his stature as a literary artist." Indeed, Wells all but ceased to be an artist after 1901, allowing his creativity to be "dragooned into the didactic service of his sociological ideas." Wells soon became little more than a propagandist for a hollow adolescent dream of utopia, a soap-bubble dream burst by the rampage of world events during the balance of his life. I no longer remember my conversation with Bergonzi, but it was brief, and we may have agreed to disagree. Perhaps he had me in mind when he wrote, on the last page of *The Early H.G. Wells*, that for anyone interested primarily in literature, all that really mattered about Wells were his first scientific romances, "however absorbing the historians of society or ideas may find the rest of his work."

My passion for "the rest of his work" led me, in August, 1962, to propose to Craig Wylie, my editor at Houghton Mifflin, the production of an anthology of Wells's journalism and prophetic writings. Wells, I suggested, was one of the greatest journalists and futurists of the century. In addition to the prophetic element in his scientific romances and other books, he had published more than 20 volumes of collected newspaper and magazine articles combining astute commentary on world events with insightful visions of things to come. Most of these volumes were now entirely forgotten, dense with dust on the shelves of used-book stores, but if Wylie were to nose around in them, he would see their potential. I offered to prepare a volume of carefully selected excerpts from Wells that would trace the history of the world in the first half of the 20th Century and limn possible

CHAPTER 5: ALL'S WELLS

futures; I also sent Wylie a list of books and chapters that he might find especially appealing.

Wylie shelved my suggestions until a phone call from me the following spring prodded his memory. He did now read a bit of Wells and on April 29, 1963, he wrote me a letter expressing serious interest in my idea of an anthology. The selections he had scanned were "truly fascinating stuff." In May and June I assembled a liberal assortment of appropriate items, received a contract from Houghton Mifflin in July, revisited the Wells Archive at the University of Illinois in early August to hunt down some additional materials, and delivered the finished manuscript to Houghton Mifflin before departing, on August 17, for another full year of research and writing in London jointly financed by an "Early Leave" from Wellesley College and a fellowship from the American Council of Learned Societies. As before, we sailed on the S.S. *United States*, but this time with a Ford station wagon in the hold and three little boys sharing our stateroom. In addition to John Alden Wagar, Bruce Alan Wagar had been born in December, 1960; and Steven Lawrence Wagar in February, 1962.

The Wells anthology, entitled *H.G. Wells: Journalism and Prophecy, 1893-1946*, and 447 pages in length, duly made its appearance in the autumn of 1964, by which time I had already arranged for a British edition to be published in London by The Bodley Head. The British version would contain 16 fewer excerpts, at the request of the publishers. On the whole it may have been not only a leaner but a better book.

Both editions received abundant, and chiefly charitable, notices. The reviews of the American edition included essays in *The Nation* and *The New Republic*, a semi-sour piece by Bergonzi in *The New York Review of Books*, and a sweet piece in *The Humanist* by Isaac Asimov. "Reading this book," wrote Asimov, "is an exciting experience, all the more so because of Wagar's illuminating editorial notes." Many newspapers across the land chimed in as well. Even the *Book-of-the-Month Club News*, in its issue for January, 1965, printed a favorable review, although only in its feature "Other New Books to Know About," captioned "Book Dividend Certificates Not

Given with These Books."

The British edition, published in January, 1966, was awarded reviews in most of the leading papers, from the *Daily Telegraph*, *The Sunday Times*, and *The Guardian*, to *The Daily Worker*. Kingsley Martin reviewed it in *New Statesman*, A.J.P. Taylor in *The Observer*, Anthony Burgess in *The Spectator*, Michael Foot in *Evening Standard*. The pattern in each review was much the same: perfunctory comments on my success in pulling together Wells's thoughts, followed by criticism or defenses of the thoughts themselves, depending on the politics of the reviewer. But I could not complain of having been ignored. Both publishers did a respectable job of promoting and advertising the book, and it could have been a winner.

It was not. Sales were flat both in the United States and the United Kingdom. Houghton Mifflin ruthlessly remaindered the American edition after only six months. They notified me of this development in a form letter addressed to "Dr. Wagar W. Warren," with the salutation, "Dear Dr. Warren." No more lunches with Craig Wylie at oak-paneled Boston eateries. My Wells boomlet was over.

ENTR'ACTE: H.G. WELLS AND THE WORLD STATE

H.G. Wells and the World State is a lightly touched-up doctoral dissertation, peppered with hundreds of footnotes and all the usual paraphernalia of academic research. The first printing of 1,000 copies was soon exhausted, and a second of 500 followed. The conversion in the 1960s of many American four-year colleges to research institutions with graduate schools created an additional market for university press books; in 1971, a third printing was needed.

But *H.G. Wells and the World State* was never intended by its author primarily to help fill the shelves of research libraries. Of course it would do that, and also keep food on the table, by entitling me to tenure somewhere. Nevertheless, I had an agenda quite different from most young scholars. *H.G. Wells and the World State* would

CHAPTER 5: ALL'S WELLS

enable me to pick up where Wells himself had left off. It would supply me with some of the credentials I needed to become a prophet of world order in my own right. If you suspect I had now begun to lose my mind, you have not read the preceding chapters of these *Memoirs*. The boy-philosopher of West Walnut Street knew all along that he had a unique mission in life. He did not choose the "topic" of his dissertation lightly. If he was demented in 1961, which may well have been the case, it was not for the first time.

Anyone glancing casually at the text of my first book might have decided that the boy-philosopher had produced a work of real philosophy. Instead of presenting Wells's ideas in some sort of chronological sequence, I organized my material thematically: after a biographical introduction ("The Prophetic Office"), my next four chapters were entitled, in order, "Fundamental Assumptions," "Education," "The Open Conspiracy," and "Cosmopolis." In the last chapter, "H.G. Wells and the Twentieth Century," I inventoried the failures and the successes of Wells's career as a prophet. *The New York Times*, in its "Other Books of the Week" for April 2, 1961, listed *H.G. Wells and the World State* under the heading of "Philosophy."

Perhaps, in a way, the *Times* had got it right. Organizing my text thematically was a device to foreground the logic and priorities of Wells's thought. In "Fundamental Assumptions," I expounded Wells's view of nature (derived chiefly from Charles Darwin and T. H. Huxley), his conception of humankind as "Prometheus," his faith in the powers of science to enlighten and order human affairs, and his quasi-religious conception of "the Mind of the Race," an evolving, collective consciousness that gained ground steadily in its struggle with superstition and tribalism. "Education" explored Wells's ideas on schooling; his role as a popularizer of world history, biology, and the social sciences; and his schemes for what I called "intellectual integration," the synthesis of all the cognitive disciplines, especially as argued in one of his later books, *World Brain* (1938).

But for Wells intellectual integration was not an end in itself. The last sentence of the chapter on "Education" set the stage for the rest of my book:

> Wells assumed that the movement for educational reform and reorientation would grow by degrees into a much broader movement with tentacles reaching into business and government, an Open Conspiracy of men of wealth and power and learning, to seize, sabotage, or bypass the political institutions of the old order and organize a world state.

"The Open Conspiracy," my fourth chapter, discussed Wells's antidemocratic concept of leadership and his strategy for world revolution; and "Cosmopolis," my fifth, his vision of a global and postcapitalist technocratic utopia. Throughout, I drew as heavily for my evidence on Wells's novels as on his non-fiction, seeing them as a seamless body of work aimed at world reconstruction, from start to finish.

Finally, in my summary assessment of Wells's effectiveness, I described him as the builder of a bridge, a bridge of ideas, between the fragmented, warring humanity of his own time and "the coming world civilization." Wells had helped to make all of us more "world-minded." The "sheer logic of survival will force men of every faith and culture to commit themselves to more and more far-reaching experiments in world integration in the years ahead." In that inevitable one-world commonwealth of the future, whether it chose to remember him or not, and whether it would be organized along Marxian, Wellsian, or liberal democratic lines, "there will always remain indelible traces of H.G. Wells."

From my current vantage point, early in the 21st Century, the one great inexcusable moral flaw in all of this was my tacit endorsement of Wells's chronic elitism. In one of the subsections of the fourth chapter, "The Salt of the Earth," I traced his elitism from the vision of scientifically trained "functional men" seizing the reins of global power in *Anticipations* (1902) all the way down to some of his last novels, including *The Holy Terror* (1939), whose hero Rud Whitlow, clearly modeled on Adolf Hitler, was represented as a necessary evil, needed to ignite the world revolution.

CHAPTER 5: ALL'S WELLS

Not that Wells ever became in any meaningful sense a fascist. But he lodged no faith in the "common man." His hopes were always pinned on the emergence of a movement of volunteer aristocrats, selfless and wise, hardened by the unsparing discipline of science, determined to rescue the rabble from themselves. Once in charge, Wells's Open Conspiracy of natural noblemen would build a world state untrammeled by politics of any kind. In place of pointless struggles for power would come the administration of human affairs by qualified experts. Liberated from capitalism, nationalism, and all sectarian faiths by the illuminating power of science, Wells's global utopia would resemble a Platonic Republic of Guardians, not a democracy of equals. In one of his mid-life fictions, *The World of William Clissold* (1926), he had even looked to the moguls of multinational industry for leadership in toppling the despised regime of national states.

But the Warren of 1961, as anyone can tell from reading his juvenilia, was just as unimpressed by the circuses of popular democracy as H.G. Wells. Nor had he learned (or even read) much of anything from thinkers on the political Left. The United States in the late 1940s and 1950s was a poor place to bump into Leftist literature. I doubt that I ever knew or met a person of the Left in high school, college, or graduate school. There were few if any Left books on my father's, the businessman's, shelves. All that I knew about socialism, in particular, was what I had learned from U.S. Cold War propaganda or from Wells, a nominal socialist who detested Marxism.

There were also, I am sure, deeper reasons for my elitist posture. Throughout my school years, to the very end, it was always a question of Warren ("Exalted Be His Brain!") versus the coarse, ill-bred, violent, ignorant, and conformist riffraff. In order to carve out a zone of self-defense and self-respect, I had to assume that a great gulf yawned between "my" kind of human being, naturally superior creatures such as Hudson or myself, and the lumpish throng. Clearly, "the salt of the earth" had to prevail. It may well be that "H.G." himself was a similarly scarred victim of a difficult and delayed adolescence. Photographs of Wells as a child and as a college student show us a slight, skeletal, underdeveloped youth. Both of us were also tortured, no other verb will do, by cravings for the ardent companionship of the opposite sex, a companionship not easily achieved in our earlier years. And both of us rose from exactly the same social class, the breeding ground as well of the German *Führer*: the petty bourgeoisie.

I offer this moment of pop psychoanalysis for whatever it may be worth. At any rate, although I have significantly overhauled my *Weltanschauung* since 1961, I still dote on H.G. Wells.

CHAPTER 6
COSMOPOLIS REVISITED

Earlier, I described the years from 1959 and 1964 as the "best" of my life. The culminating event was the publication not of my two Wells books but of *The City of Man: Prophecies of a World Civilization in Twentieth-Century Thought* by Houghton Mifflin in March, 1963. The prophet was now unleashed. He freely addressed the world in his own voice. All that remained was its astonishment and its capitulation to his irrefutable rhetoric.

First entitled "The Organic World Society," the manuscript I signed to write in 1961 with Houghton Mifflin attracted early favor, but the staff of three editors who read it recommended cuts. At a luncheon with Craig Wylie in February, 1962, I agreed to comply. I wrote to my mother in March that I had bled 55 pages from the original draft and prayed it would be enough. It was. Houghton Mifflin offered me a contract in May. The title had changed, at my suggestion, to "World Integration."

Given my sense of world-historical mission, I am reasonably sure that in early 1962 I entertained few doubts about my personal future, not to mention the hoped-for future of *Homo sapiens*. The long labors of a misunderstood youth were now reaping their just rewards. The boy-philosopher stood on the threshold, not just of global glory, but of compensation for all the imagined neglect and contumely of past decades.

To promote the new masterpiece, I wrote an article summarizing its message that Houghton Mifflin offered to place in a likely national journal. The article was written in the summer of 1962, and Houghton Mifflin referred it confidently to *Harper's*. No sale. Then to *Saturday Review*. In January, 1963, Norman Cousins himself made his apologies to me; *Saturday Review* had lately suffered from a surfeit of war-peace essays and needed to give the theme a rest. On to *Foreign Affairs*. Still no sale. Houghton Mifflin kept trying, and finally my essay, "Beyond the Peace Movement: The Idea of a World Civilization," became the lead article in the Summer 1963 issue of *The Virginia Quarterly Review*.

There was still the question of the title. In my files I have preserved the dust cover, colorful and striking, of "World Integration," sent to me for my approval a few months before our book was due to be published. We had come that far. But at the last minute, Houghton Mifflin sales representatives from the states of the former Confederacy weighed in with negative impressions. In the early 1960s, the word "integration" meant only one thing to most Southerners: the opposite of racial segregation. If Southern whites by and large detested the idea of integrating the races in Alabama or North Carolina, would their hackles not rise still further if they saw a book proclaiming *world* integration, the end of *Apartheid* worldwide? Might not a visit to a bookstore by an unwary racist in Jackson or Selma even carry the risk of death by apoplexy?

Of course "World Integration" was not about racial matters at all. The issue never arose in its pages. Nevertheless, I was obliged to re-think my title. What about "Cosmopolis"? Too arcane. In the end I opted for *The City of Man*, which I thought not very original or clever, a rough translation of cosmopolis, but uncomfortably close to the title of Frederick L. Schuman's important study of world government, *The Commonwealth of Man* (1952). There was also the possibility of confusing my phrase with St. Augustine's *civitas terrena*, "the earthly city," the city of the damned, sometimes (wrongly) rendered as "the city of man." Of course in 1963 I had no inkling that ten or fifteen years down the road the generic usage of "man" or "mankind" would fall under fierce, warranted, and ultimately lethal assault from feminists. To avoid the appearance of anti-racism, I had tricked myself into the appearance of sexism. But not yet, not in 1963. So *The City of Man* it was. I dedicated the book to Hudson.

The City of Man got off to a rousing start when *The New York Times* chose to review it as its book of the day for Friday, April 5, 1963, under the byline of Kalman Seigel. "Dr. Wagar pleads his case brilliantly and with intensity," in a style both "vigorous and sure." It was "a provocative book, and a deeply serious book but not an easy one to read." Seigel failed to explain why *The City of Man* was not easy to read. The implication, from his previous remarks, was that it addressed so many disturbing issues and called for such sweeping transformations on so many levels that it might be hard to take in all at once. It would certainly not be fun. Whatever he may have meant, I did not take offense.

April was a good month for *The City of Man*. Walter Robinson, writing in the *Chicago Sunday Tribune* on April 14, called it "an inspiring light for a darkening world." "Only a man of serene scholarship, high moral lucidity, unblanching spiritual qualities, and perhaps, most importantly, youth, could have managed this remarkable accomplishment." Stringfellow Barr commended *The City of Man* in *Saturday Review* for April 13. I was "philosophically competent in high degree." My book supplied "a road map for those who have kept their heads and want to know what ideas are in circulation."

There were dozens of other reviews throughout the spring of 1963 and beyond, most of them equally complimentary. The historian Ralph H. Gabriel, in his review for *The Washington Post & Times Herald*, called *The City of Man* "a sane, sophisticated, imaginative, and eloquent book." But another historian, Loren Baritz, writing in *The Chicago News*, complained that I was heedless of hard realities. My "well-intentioned day dream" of a new world civilization would not prevent Armageddon. "If we are as close to annihilation as Wagar thinks, it is offensively luxurious to dream of Elysium." And in *The Annals of the American Academy of Political and Social Science*, the Yale political scientist H. Bradford Westerfield, after dubbing *The City of Man* "a literary work of inspirational idealism...distinguished in quality far beyond the average of this genre," feared that it would "repel most of the skeptics whom Professor Wagar might have hoped to convert" because of its "deliberately uncritical approach. ... Wagar is simply unwilling to dissect." If the cost of world peace included the suppression of critical inquiry, "many intellectuals would find such a rerouting of the quest for truth too high a price to pay."

But the problem with *The City of Man* was not its reviews. The problem was its failure to sell. In a letter to Hudson dated July 10, 1964, I reported that only 1,560 copies, from a printing of 5,000, had been purchased. The rest would have to be remaindered. "The book is finished," I sighed, "and must be set down as a failure, at least commercially." *H.G. Wells and the World State* had done no better, but expectations for university press books and for trade books, then as now, were quite different. *H.G. Wells and the World State* had sold out its first printing. *The City of Man* had wasted a goodly stand of timber.

Of course college administrations care much less about how many copies of a book are sold than about how many books and articles their professors manage to publish at all. In the fall of 1962, I was an assistant professor at Wellesley on a term appointment that expired in the spring of 1964. I would not be eligible for tenure until 1967. With one book in print and another under contract, how could I miss receiving it? Very simple. In the fall of 1962, so far as I knew, I had no chance whatever of tenure at Wellesley. Because of the college's inflexible policy of keeping no more than 50% of the members of any department on tenure at any one time, and taking into account the ages of the senior members of my department, my fate was sealed, no matter how many books I published. Frank Baumer urged me to begin looking for another job. He apparently put in a word for me at Princeton, where a junior opening in 19th-Century European history was expected, and early in December, 1962, a letter of invitation to journey to Princeton for an interview appeared in my mail.

At about the same time I received news from Wellesley's president, Margaret Clapp, that I was one of three junior faculty to be awarded an "Early Leave" — in effect a sabbatical — for the academic year 1963-64. Wellesley had hired quite a few productive young faculty in the late 1950s (among those in my "class" were the now world-famous philosopher Richard Rorty, the economist Marshall Goldman, and the critic Patricia Spacks, all destined for eminent Ivy League careers). The idea of the Early Leave was to try to hold on to these future stars, although in my case, it seemed an empty ges-

CHAPTER 6: COSMOPOLIS REVISITED

ture, given the lack of room at the top in the History Department. A few days later, simultaneously, came a letter from Frank urging me to take the job at Princeton, if it was offered, and news that I had also been awarded a research fellowship by the American Council of Learned Societies, which would make up the difference between my Early Leave stipend and my regular salary.

What to do? Turn down a guaranteed full year of research and writing or turn down Princeton? It is difficult to reconstruct my state of mind during that long-ago December. At the time there were three things I did not know: first, I did not know this would be almost my last chance to ascend the academic ladder; second, I did not know that schools in Princeton's league routinely discarded most of their junior hires after a few years; and third, I did not know that I would soon be promised tenure at Wellesley because of a sudden death in the ranks of my senior colleagues. With the limited information at my disposal, the obvious strategy would have been to accept the grants, interview at Princeton anyway, and, if offered a job, take it, and return the grants. But that would have been duplicitous. Was I above duplicity? The poorly informed *Chicago Sunday Tribune* review hailing my "high moral lucidity" and "unblanching spiritual qualities" was still several months away, so it could not have shamed me into living up to my alleged saintliness. But, yes, I would have been uncomfortable telling Wellesley College one thing and Princeton University another.

In the end, I wrote to Princeton expressing my regret that I was not available for 1963-64 and would be unable to come down for my interview. I suspect that my "high moral lucidity" played less of a part than my arrogance as a young man apparently on the way up for whom many more such interviews surely loomed. Today, I have to wonder if I was good enough — good enough as an academician — to earn tenure at Princeton. Whatever my strengths, they were probably not the sort required to astound the search committees of premier universities. I was a makeshift scholar, a plausible scholar with a hard-earned facility for writing well and thinking widely, but not a denizen of the proverbial cutting edge — any more than my mentor,

Frank Baumer. I had no talent for sniffing out the way the breeze was blowing. In short order, and thanks in part to my loyalty to Baumer's persuasive (but doomed) species of intellectual history, I would be stranded for 20 or 30 years behind the prevailing winds.

I could not have imagined this, in 1962 or 1963 or even 1964. What mattered to me then, in addition to personal vindication, was the conversion of humankind to a program of world synthesis, to a crusade for the metamorphosis of the dissolving local civilizations into a pan-human planetary civilization, living under one law, one faith, and one commonwealth.

In the academic year 1963-64, as reported in the previous chapter, my growing family and I lived once again in London. The project for which I had won an ACLS Fellowship and a Wellesley College Early Leave was a study suggested by a new upper-division seminar that I had taught in the Fall 1962 semester on the idea of general and universal human progress from the mid-19th to the mid-20th Centuries. It appeared to me that here was the master-idea of the past one hundred years: championed in the period from 1850 to 1914, powerfully challenged in the agonizing decades of the World Wars, but still alive and — perhaps — even well. A modest literature on the history of the belief in progress already existed, devoted mainly to the thinkers of the 17th, 18th, and early 19th Centuries, from Fontenelle to Comte, but what about the last one hundred years? I would carry the story, warts and all, forward and down to the present.

Since most theories of human progress claimed predictive power, enabling the theorist to imagine future felicities, once again my research would involve visions of human destiny. But this time on a much broader scale: not just ideas about a coming world civilization, but all conceptions of human betterment, from all points of view. If *H.G. Wells and the World State* was the square root of *The City of Man*, so *The City of Man* would be the square root of the new book. I would englobulate not just Wells, not just a whole generation of post-Wellsian prophets of cosmopolis, but all the visionaries of the past one hundred years.

So back once again in England, I embarked on a systematic

CHAPTER 6: COSMOPOLIS REVISITED

program of study at the major London research libraries, collecting thousands of pages of notes and writing the first several chapters of what would eventually become *Good Tidings: The Belief in Progress from Darwin to Marcuse*. Dorothy and I also partook liberally of the rich cultural life of London, at that time absurdly inexpensive, attending dozens of concerts, operas, ballets, and plays. Laurence Olivier and Michael Redgrave in *Uncle Vanya*. Joan Greenwood in *Hedda Gabler*. Patrick Magee in *Endgame*. Mahler symphonies with Horenstein, Klemperer, Solti; even the world premiere of the Deryck Cooke performing version of Mahler's Tenth Symphony at the Royal Albert Hall. Vishnevskaya in *Aida*, Sutherland in *I Puritani*, Collier in *Tosca*. Monteux conducting the Sibelius Violin Concerto with Isaac Stern. Dorati conducting the Bartók Violin Concerto with Yehudi Menuhin. Kenneth MacMillan's *Rite of Spring*. Fresh from Broadway, Uta Hagen and Arthur Hill in *Who's Afraid of Virginia Woolf?*.

With three toddlers in tow, we were unable to travel as much during this second year in England as during the first. But we managed a number of day trips and, boarding the boys at a "children's hotel" in Bexhill-on-Sea, a week in Paris and two weeks of touring in France and Catalonia. Especially memorable was a late spring snowstorm in the Pyrenees as we were attempting to return to France through Andorra. Our station wagon slipped this way and that on a steep mountain road without guardrails, and all I could think of was who would take care of our children after we plunged into the abyss below. Somehow I managed to turn us around and retreat to safety.

The 1964-65 academic year began with the death of the chairman of the history department at Wellesley. His demise brought the tenured ranks below 50% and opened the way for me to stay on. But by now I aspired to greater things: a position at a major university where I could emulate Frank Baumer and train graduate students. My third book, the Wells anthology, came out in October and I did begin to receive expressions of interest from various institutions. Princeton still needed a specialist in 19th-Century Europe and requested my dossier from the placement office at Yale. Inquiries arrived from the University of Colorado and from Indiana University, as well as a few four-year colleges. On December 21, President Clapp notified me that I would soon receive a remarkable offer from Wellesley: early promotion in 1965 to Associate Professor. The appointment would not include tenure, but "we all agree that an action like this commits us as of now to favorable action on tenure unless you manage to turn into a two-headed monster before the formal vote is taken."

At the end of December, nevertheless, I went to the annual meetings of the American Historical Association in Washington, where I was interviewed by Indiana University for its opening in European history. Princeton scheduled no interview for me and when I spoke to its chairman at the Princeton "smoker," an informal reception for Princeton faculty and alumni, I detected no glimmer of interest. The reason may have been quite simple: Princeton wanted a 19th-Century specialist and after reviewing my credentials, any fool could see that I had clearly become a 20th-Century specialist. But Indiana was serious. On January 13, the chairman at Indiana, Professor Robert Byrnes, wrote to inform me that I stood "at the head of the list for the new appointment in Recent European History." He expected to invite me to an on-campus interview "within a couple of weeks."

Then began a classic academic squeeze play. On January 18, Miss Clapp formally offered me a three-year appointment as an associate professor without tenure. At the end of January Indiana put its search on hold because Byrnes had gone off to Russia for several weeks. On February 12, Miss Clapp gave me one more week to make up my mind. On February 13, I visited the campus of the University of Massachusetts at Amherst, where a senior opening had become available. The chairman at Massachusetts expressed strong interest in my candidacy. On February 19, the last day before my deadline expired, and hearing no further word from the competition, I signed the Wellesley contract. Hours later, Byrnes called to invite me to come to Bloomington for an interview and I received a firm offer of an associate professorship with tenure from Massachusetts. Good grief.

Another splendid opportunity for duplicity — or triplicity? Whatever, I said no to both Indiana and Massachusetts. The ink was not yet dry, but I had given my word to Miss Clapp. I was weary of the whole business. I would stay at Wellesley, a far from disgraceful choice, and try not "to turn into a two-headed monster."

ENTR'ACTE: THE CITY OF MAN

The publication of *The City of Man* in March, 1963, and its remaindering in the summer of 1964 after a dismal sales record did not quite end the story. In 1967, it returned to life for a few years, with minor revisions and a new Preface, as a Penguin paperback (in the United States only) priced at $1.65. This time sales were much more brisk, eventually passing the 10,000 mark.

But *The City of Man* still did not accomplish what I had fatuously imagined it would accomplish. Both from my recollections and from my letters at the time to Hudson, it is clear that I expected the book, all by itself, to launch a new planet-wide movement for "world integration." In the process I might well be called upon to don the mantle of a messiah. The prophets of integration celebrated in *The City of Man* concurred in envisioning an organic global civilization beyond the parochial good and evil of previous cultures. I would enlist their light in illuminating the path to Cosmopolis, the City of Man, the World State. My time, and by extension the time of all humankind, had come.

If this sounds exaggerated, consider my letter to Hudson of December 29, 1959, shortly after Houghton Mifflin had purchased an option on the project that eventually became *The City of Man*. I marveled at my good fortune. I pledged to write this book, but I added that it must be published, that it must become "a kind of best-seller," and that it must "launch a genuine movement...a great intellectual movement." Here was "my chance...to make some permanent contribution to the relief of human distress in our century." I might become the "Aristotle of integralism," and Hudson (who had written a futuristic manuscript of his own, *The New World*) "its Plato." When Houghton Mifflin actually accepted my book, I wrote to Hudson on

May 11, 1962, that the forthcoming volume was the "first substantial milestone on the road to a self-conscious movement for world integration." The mental climate might not yet be propitious for such a vast transformation, but sooner or later, "we will integrate. Of that I have not the slightest doubt."

It was all moonshine. No "great intellectual movement" emerged in response to my pleas, no movement at all. In retrospect the thinkers I viewed as the avant-garde of a world revolution turned out to offer only fading echoes of early postwar liberal internationalism. Had my book appeared in 1948 or 1949, or even as late as the mid-1950s, it might have drawn more serious attention. But in 1963, the intelligentsia had moved on to other concerns — nuclear disarmament, civil rights, and by the time of the paperback reprint, the New Left, protests against the Vietnam war, women's and gay liberation, and the chemically mediated ecstasies of the Flower Children. To young activists of the late 1960s, *The City of Man* must have seemed like stale beer indeed.

But it was not a bad little book, in and of itself. It began as an overview of world history since ancient times, arguing that the vision of an organic world civilization was thousands of years old, and not just the vision, but sometimes the reality as well. Humanity's golden ages were the eras of its greatest spiritually healthy empires, when local cultures fused and authority consolidated in the later examples of Toynbeean "Universal States." In my first chapter, "The Biography of a Vision," I pointed to the neo-Confucian China of the Han Dynasty, the Buddhist *raj* of Asoka, the Stoic Pax Romana of Marcus Aurelius, the Carolingian ideal of a Christian New Rome, and the medieval Arab caliphates with their theology of the *dar al-Islam*, all aspiring world orders that attempted, in their time and place, to unify humankind.

Since the 17th Century, the dream of world integration had been reduced once again to just a dream, but its dreamers were men and women of extraordinary vitality: my heroes included Comenius, Leibniz, Saint-Pierre, Kant, Comte, and the neo-Confucian philosopher K'ang Yu-wei. And in the 20th Century, the "world crisis" had called forth a host of prophetic integrators, from H.G. Wells to Toynbee, Sorokin, Teilhard de Chardin, Northrop, and Radhakrishnan, whose thought provided most of the grist for my mill in subsequent chapters. In this latest generation of prophets I descried the possible successors of all the master-teachers of world history, who would achieve for the coming world civilization what Confucius, Buddha, Christ, and Muhammad had achieved for the ecumenical cultures and polities of antiquity.

My second chapter, "History as Prophecy," turned to contemporary theories of world history and biological evolution with cosmopolitically futurist implications. The last six volumes of Toynbee's *A Study of History* furnished the fullest case in point. His belief, articulated in Volume XII (1961), that the cyclical history of civilizations might be ending at last, to be succeeded by an ascent of the "next ledge" to Cosmopolis, the "sacred union" of all nations, received extensive treatment. So too did the work of his fellow cyclicalist, the Russian-American sociologist Pitirim A. Sorokin. Of believers in linear or spiraliform progress to world integration, I cited Karl Jaspers, Lewis Mumford, and Erich Kahler. Biologically-grounded thinkers who had reached comparable conclusions about human destiny were Sir Julian Huxley and Pierre Teilhard de Chardin.

I turned also, in a final sub-section, "The Doctrinaires," to the exponents of visions of world unity who represented some of the great dogmatic faiths in modern culture, party-liners such as Muslim futurists, Roman Catholic philosophers, the prophets of the Baha'i World Faith, and Marxist-Leninists. Their beliefs were in many ways congruent with those of my independent prophets, but with a vast difference: each belief-system was rooted in a basically unquestioned and unquestionable revelation. Devout Muslims, Catholics, Baha'is, and Marxists all wanted to see the present-day divisions among humankind closed and healed, but only on their own terms. I avoided drawing the obvious conclusion that these heated partisans were blinded by their own fanaticism, but I recognized that all of them were also, in their own ways, would-be builders of the City of Man.

Chapter Three, "The Concert of Cultures," came to the heart

of my thesis. Before there could be an integration of nations, before we could found a viable global polity, the cultures contending for hegemony in the modern world needed to reconceive their founding premises and fuse at a higher level of collective consciousness. No system of global governance could work or survive until it could flourish in a pan-human cultural matrix, an organic planetary civilization capable of making all of us one universal people, committed to many of the same objectives and values.

I studied the prospects for a concert of cultures under four headings: synthesis in philosophy, the emergence of a global religion or confederacy of religions, the integration of the sciences and the humanities, and the rise of a planetary art. Here my chief sources were Northrop in *The Meeting of East and West* (1946), studies of the possible fusion of liberalism and socialism, the ecumenical theology of William Ernest Hocking, the speculations on a syncretic world faith of Toynbee, Erich Kahler, and others, studies of the prospects for a unified language of science, and Sorokin and Ernest Mundt (*Art, Form, and Civilization*, 1952) on a new "organic" art. How long would it take before this ecumenical cultural matrix would be ready to nurture an embryonic world state? I did not guess. The idea that no baby can grow without a womb made sense, but the timetable was something else again.

What, finally, did *The City of Man* have to say about matters economic and political? Since my primary concern was to present my prophets' visions of a world culture and civilization, it was necessary to defer consideration of such issues until near the end of the volume, but consider them I did in my fourth chapter, "The World Commonwealth," with abundant reference to the relevant thoughts of Toynbee, Northrop, Mumford, Schuman, and many others.

Here I argued the case for an integrated world economy, in which the developed countries would generously help fund the industrialization of the rest; the emergence of a "sane compromise" between capitalism and communism, as in Sweden or Tito's Yugoslavia; and a federal world government, once the cultural and psychospiritual groundwork had been laid. At the very end of the chapter, I touched briefly on the question of democracy, arguing that the "form of government [of the world state] will obviously be democratic," although "democratically recruited 'elite' groups, with high standards of professional and humane responsibility" might also be needed to prevent the world commonwealth from degenerating into "a mobocracy pandering to the tastes of the mass-man." At this distance in time, I cannot say for sure why my previous concerns about the failings of democracy and the tyranny of the common man had shrunk, in *The City of Man*, to just a sentence or two, barely an afterthought. The likeliest explanation is that since my principal prophets did not share Wells's aversion to democracy, I felt compelled to swallow my own doubts. Or perhaps, by the early 1960s, I had actually warmed a bit to the democratic ethos.

Two more chapters remained: Chapter Five, "Who Will Integrate the Integrators?," and an Epilogue, as in *Integration*, "The Deep End." In the fifth chapter, I introduced what I thought was a novel proposal, and possibly still is. William James had written at length of "The Will To Believe." I altered this to "The Will To Agree." Through most of late modern history, the hallmark of the free-floating intelligentsia in Western civilization was its resolute rejection of all orthodoxies and its insistence on every thinking man and woman's right to dissent from every received idea in the name of untrammeled critical inquiry. The inevitable result was a cult of conflict and rebellion which almost ensured that any thinker not prepared to debunk all of his or her colleagues was poised for well-deserved oblivion. Knee-jerk dissent had replaced humble compliance as the mark of the true mage.

This understandable new fashion had produced many important breakthroughs in human thought, but it was now obsolescent. The imperative of the future was consensus, the reconciliation of differences in a higher synthesis capable of undergirding the emergent world civilization. Otherwise our maniac quarrels and our parochial allegiances would tear humankind apart. Let the watchword of the future be the will to agree, the determination to "bang heads together" in the pursuit of a higher ecumenical truth.

Truth by whose criteria? To what ends? And what is truth? By the soon-to-flare lights of poststructuralist criticism, all of this was ludicrously naive. To be sure. But I still know what I was driving at. In some ways deconstruction is a cheap shot, a fusillade aimed at sitting ducks. In my old age I have become the ultimate relativist. But what if the scalpels of deconstruction dismember us and leave us without cells, muscles, or neural synapses? What if we commit racial suicide by our infinite cleverness?

And then the Epilogue. It was much as before, in *Integration*. The perils of technology, and above all the technology of global Armageddon. The possibility of world ennui and cultural heat-death. The challenges of outer space. "Into this future we send our sons, and from it, in man's relentless flight through time, they will never return." The same words as in *Integration*. This time, I had three wonderful sons to send. A beloved daughter had not yet arrived.

CHAPTER 7
REVOLUTION!

As soon as I had made the decision to stay on at Wellesley, presumably for good, I changed my mind again. The academic year 1965-1966 turned out to be my last in the Commonwealth of Massachusetts. A restlessness overpowered me that I still cannot entirely explain. Various considerations entered into my thinking, which in an earlier draft of these *Memoirs* I recounted in shrill detail. Reading the story over again, I find it too tangled and self-serving to be worth wearying anyone else, so I will simply draw the curtain and say that Dorothy and I resolved to quit the Commonwealth.

With Wellesley College I had no quarrel, and my last year on the Campus Beautiful went well. (It was also Hillary Rodham Clinton's freshman year at Wellesley, although she did not take any of my courses.) I even fulfilled an old ambition, deferred through the high school and college years because of my contempt for my eternally adolescent body. Finally grown up and in my early thirties, I appeared in a play. With help from assorted males on the faculty and at other colleges in the Boston area, Wellesley students staged remarkably professional productions of major plays. The theater director, Paul Barstow, was superb. On February 25-26 I appeared in the role of the cuckolded schoolmaster Kulygin in his production of Chekhov's *Three Sisters*. Long suppressed histrionic impulses came to the fore. I felt entirely at ease and at home on the stage.

A month later I gave an all-college lecture on the apparent failure of feminism. Another new departure for me? Yes, but by now I had been teaching at Wellesley for eight years. I had watched class after class of intelligent and privileged young women disappear into suburbia on the arms of Harvard Business School graduates, or the like, with no thought of making anything more out of their lives. They were excellent students, but by their senior years, the eyes of most of them had glazed over, and they looked forward only to matronhood.

The triggering event for me was reading a free-verse poem inked on the side of a carrel in the college library, which I quote verbatim:

> Study hard
> Get good grades
> Get your degree
> Get married
> Have three horrid kids
> Die, and be buried.

I do not know who wrote that poem, but whoever it was, it had to have been a young woman, peering, with revulsion, into her probable future as a graduate of Wellesley College. When I published it years later in a chapter of my book *Building the City of Man*, an outside reader for my publisher, a young law professor by the name of Ruth Bader Ginsburg, not yet Justice Ginsburg of the U.S. Supreme Court, was sufficiently moved to quote it in a footnote of one of her law articles. I have lost track of the citation, but her reader's report on my book is still in my files.

My well-attended public lecture was entitled, "Whatever Happened to the New Woman? The Struggle of Women To Become People in Historical Perspective — with a Long Glance at the Future." Of course I had read a great deal about the "New Woman" of Edwardian times in England because of my interest in Wells, who had written some of the signature novels of what passed for feminism in his generation, most notably *Ann Veronica* (1909). His own lovers had included such formidable New Women as Rebecca West and Margaret Sanger. As my former student Cliona Murphy has shown, he was not so much of a feminist as he thought. Nevertheless, the struggle for women's suffrage and women's rights had figured importantly in the history of the late 19th and early 20th Centuries. Yet in the 1950s and early 1960s the women's movement appeared moribund, if not simply dead. Women everywhere, including Wellesley College, were under the seductive spell of Betty Friedan's "Feminine Mystique." My wife Dorothy and Hudson's wife Maria fell for most of it,

CHAPTER 7: REVOLUTION!

too, at the time. Each gave birth to four children and kept themselves enormously busy with cooking, housekeeping, child-rearing, and cherishing Hubby. Later, they would return to school, earn doctorates, and become professionals in their own right, but that was later. Not in 1966.

I no longer recall much of what I said to my female audience in March, 1966, but I am reasonably sure of the gist of it. Women had lost their way, dragooned into domesticity by the postwar *Zeitgeist* so eloquently described by Friedan. The heroic times of the past were no more. The hour had come for women to wake up and resume their struggle to become full-fledged human beings, with lives and work of their own. I hoped this would happen, although I beheld few signs on the horizon. No signs at all were evident in the reactions of the students in the open discussion that ensued. They had been remarkably attentive throughout my talk, but virtually everyone who made comments or asked questions said, in effect, Professor Wagar, you've made some interesting points, but what would become of our children in your scenario? What about the integrity of the family? For all I know, one of my interrogators was Hillary Rodham. She could certainly have been in the room, since this was a public lecture.

Of course the irony of all this is that a new women's liberation movement had already begun to form in the heart of our culture. By the end of the 1960s, so I am told, Wellesley was to become a nursery of feminist and even Lesbian activism, in part because it was, and remains, one of the few women's colleges in the country not to open its doors to male students. Yet when I submitted the text of my lecture to *The Virginia Quarterly Review*, a female editor turned it down, with a comment to the effect that although I had obviously enjoyed writing the piece, its topic lacked the gravitas appropriate to essays deserving of publication in *VQR*.

But by March my days at Wellesley were almost over. On March 12 I received an attractive offer from the University of New Mexico in Albuquerque. The day before I asked the Wellesleyans "Whatever Happened to the New Woman?," I had already written to President Margaret Clapp asking to be released from my contract. On

June 22, the Wagars — two adults, three children, and a beagle — set foot in Albuquerque to begin house-hunting. We rented a suitable place a week later, and before we had gotten entirely settled in, early in the morning of July 4, I rushed Dorothy to the hospital where she gave birth to our fourth and last child, Jennifer Lynne. Jenny came a month ahead of her predicted arrival time, but she was a healthy, lusty child. Our family was complete.

The years in the Land of Enchantment passed quickly and happily. Before I met my first classes in September, I returned to the stage, starring in a Broadway comedy, Ira Wallach's *Absence of a Cello*, at the Albuquerque Little Theatre. This was a more arduous affair than *Three Sisters*. I had a far bigger part and we offered something like a dozen performances. I came to appreciate that an actor's life is mostly hard work, especially on Saturday evenings, when we put on two shows, one at 6:00 and one at 9:00. Much as I enjoyed the challenge, *Absence of a Cello* was my last turn on the stage.

Classes at U.N.M. began September 19. My first courses were "Modern Europe, 1815-1914" and "European Social and Intellectual History, 1762-1870," both new to me. I must have been no more than a week or two ahead of my class throughout the semester, since my summer travels and acting had left almost no time for course preparation. I worked whenever I could on my book on the belief in progress. Over the next three years I published three anthologies designed for the college text market in intellectual history, two with Harper and Row, one with John Wiley.

There was also the reissue, with minor revisions, of *The City of Man* by Penguin Books in 1967. This led to an invitation to give a paper based on the book and take part in three days of colloquia on its thesis at Robert M. Hutchins's Center for the Study of Democratic Institutions in Santa Barbara. Serious talk ensued about my joining the Center as a resident fellow, although the offer never came. *The City of Man* brought me a small flurry of other speaking engagements in various parts of country, as well as the keynote address at a meeting of the International Fellowship of Reconciliation just outside Oslo. I also took a seat on the Board of Directors of the Council for the Study of Mankind, an assortment of distinguished humanist scholars headquartered at the University of Chicago. I was easily the youngest and least eminent of the members.

Dorothy and I somehow found time to participate in the life of the community. We had both been raised as middle-of-the-road Presbyterians, although neither of us harbored a smidgeon of Christian belief. Now joining the First Unitarian Church of Albuquerque, we soon became active in its doings, with Dorothy organizing vast church dinners and I serving as a lay minister, in charge of several Sunday morning services a year. As in most Unitarian churches, theology was never an issue. No one had to be a Christian. The centerpiece of the church building was a great curved standing art-work emblazoned with the symbols of all the world's faiths. *The City of Man* had advocated a synthesis of all religions. From such a pulpit I could preach in good conscience.

But these were the late 1960s. As I lived the good life in Albuquerque, hundreds of thousands of younger Americans had been shipped across the Pacific to help slaughter millions of Vietnamese, in order to prevent — ? No one was sure. At first, while still at Wellesley, I had thought that perhaps the United States was rightfully there to assist the legitimate government of South Vietnam in putting down an insurrection inspired by malign foreign powers. By 1967 the legitimacy of that government was in grave doubt, and its lack of support by the majority of the South Vietnamese people was patent. I also began to read the writings of spokesmen of the New Left, notably Herbert Marcuse; and, when teaching European intellectual history, to take more seriously the texts of some of my primary sources, from Marx, Engels, Lenin, Trotsky, and Kautsky to Erich Fromm and Ernst Bloch. The boy-philosopher had spoken of global transformation, of revolution in the service of all humankind. Toward which we strive! Could I seriously believe that the Cold Warriors in Washington were striving toward anything I ever wanted to behold?

The turning point came in 1969. Richard Hudson, editor of the journal *War/Peace Report*, invited me to submit an article, which became its cover story in mid-year, "The Bankruptcy of the Peace

Movement." Here, for the first time, I urged the formation of a multinational political party, a World Party, that would take as its goal the mobilization of people all over the world to supplant the nation-states with a global republic, the only feasible alternative to continuing anarchy and eventual major war. A reader of my article, Ian Baldwin, Jr., of the New York-based World Law Fund, visited me in Albuquerque late that year to solicit a volume for its new "World Order Series." I received a contract in December. We would call the new book "World Integration: Building the City of Man." It would bear the imprint of Richard Grossman Publishers, a subsidiary of Viking Press.

The City of Man had given me considerable latitude to speak in my own voice, as well as in the voices of many others, but the World Law Fund volume was to be a true and unadulterated personal manifesto, harking back to the ancient essay in *The Institutional Review*. Early in 1970, I finished work on my book on the belief in progress, at 705 manuscript pages my longest ever, which I placed in the hands of a literary agent. The way was now clear to begin writing "World Integration." I wrote most of it in a blaze of inspiration in the summer of 1970, adding the final touches during the winter break of 1970-71.

By then, although I did not know it, I would soon be leaving New Mexico. As a home owner and the paterfamilias of a family of six, I could barely squeak by on my salary at the University, one of the lowest in the nation for academics at that time. I commuted to campus by bicycle. Our only car was ten years old and beginning to limp. In 1969 Dorothy had enrolled in the U.N.M. School of Law, aspiring to become a lawyer. Meanwhile I was the only breadwinner, and the bread I won was just barely enough. My chairman was sympathetic, but unable to help. The only way I could hope for a significant raise in salary, he told me, would be to snare a firm offer from another institution.

So at the American Historical Association meetings in December, 1970, I met with a delegation from the History Department of the University of Illinois, which had a senior opening in European history. I was a candidate. But Illinois could make no promises. The

CHAPTER 7: REVOLUTION!

Department had not even firmly decided whether the opening would occur in a "traditional" field, such as intellectual history, or something more trendy. I was a bit chilled to hear that intellectual history, so daring in the mid-1950s, now already figured as "traditional." Since then I have heard the same tale about virtually every fashion in academic life. Cutting edges nowadays lose their sharpness in three to five years. No matter. In the end I received no offer. It would have been comforting somehow to work on the same campus that housed the H.G. Wells Archive.

But on the morning of February 6, 1971, I was flying a kite with my boys near our house when Dorothy answered the telephone. It was the chairman of the history department at the State University of New York at Binghamton (SUNY), Professor Norman F. Cantor. Dorothy called me to the house. A senior opening existed at Binghamton for a modern European intellectual historian. Binghamton, the former Harpur College, had been transformed almost overnight into a state university and research center with a large and vibrant graduate program. It was young, it was growing, it was bound for the stars. Give us a look!

My interest in moving to upstate New York at that point in time was less than nil, least of all to a university I had probably never heard of. The name "Binghamton" still elicits many blank stares. On my flight into the town for the interview, the stewardess indicated that our next stop was "Birmingham." (Actually, because of a strike, we were diverted to Syracuse.) In any case, I did agree to an interview because I remembered the fateful words of my chairman at U.N.M. You must secure a firm offer from another institution before we can consider a raise in salary.

In short order I did get a firm offer from SUNY with a 40% raise in salary and fringe benefits far greater than anything in my package at U.N.M. The authorities in Albuquerque were flustered. The state had imposed a freeze on salaries at just that time. Nothing could be done. Later, I learned that the jealousy of several senior department members whose salaries would have been lower than mine if "something" had been done, and not the state-imposed freeze, prevented my chairman and dean from making a plausible counter-offer. Even without a counter-offer, I decided to stay, but Dorothy — shrewdly — talked me out of it. Cantor had even arranged for her to interview at Cornell and Syracuse Law Schools, so that she could finish her degree in the vicinity, and their acceptance of her as a third-year transfer student overcame the last hurdle.

In the summer of 1971 we moved to Ithaca and bought a house. Dorothy would complete her studies at Cornell University Law School and I would commute to Binghamton, 50 miles away. In November Richard Grossman Publishers brought out my manifesto. Grossman had personally talked me out of the title "World Integration," on the grounds that it was not sexy enough. We settled on the original subtitle, *Building the City of Man*, with a new subtitle, *Outlines of a World Civilization*.

If *The City of Man* merited an inquiry into my loyalty from the Federal Bureau of Investigation, *Building the City of Man* probably merited immediate arrest. But although it became a reasonably successful book, it apparently lacked the key words and its author lacked the criminal credentials to attract federal attention. It was just another of those many New Left tracts that could be allowed to fester and bubble and spew its venom, and spend its harmless life, and pass away.

ENTR'ACTE: BUILDING THE CITY OF MAN

The ostensible starting point of *Building the City of Man* was that in 1963 I had drafted the blueprints for a new organic world civilization, and now, at last, I would advise the world how it might set construction crews to work to actually build this remarkable conurbation.

Fair enough. But first, we need to revisit the times in which *Building the City of Man* was written.

When commentators and historians speak of the "Sixties," they are seldom thinking of the first several years of the decade. The

CHAPTER 7: REVOLUTION!

era of short-haired young men in suits and skinny ties, of glamorous breathy damsels in tight sheath dresses, of Eisenhower and Jack Kennedy, of Adenauer and Macmillan, of Khrushchev and Nehru, was not the "Sixties" of memory and legend. For the most part the statesmen who presided over those first years of the new decade were the same people who had presided over the last years of the old decade. Eisenhower's reign lasted from 1953 to 1961, Kennedy's from 1961 to 1963, Adenauer's from 1949 to 1963, Macmillan's from 1957 to 1963, Khrushchev's from 1957 to 1964, and Nehru's from 1947 to 1964. The political tenor of the times was much the same in 1963 as it had been ten years before. The Cold War continued, economies were still booming, university students behaved themselves, and such rebels as we had were rebels "without a cause," typified by the apolitical Beat novelists Jack Kerouac and William Burroughs.

But in the mid-1960s, a sea-change swept over the United States and the world. The "real" Sixties arrived, a period of about eight years that began with the assassination of Kennedy on November 22, 1963, and ended with Richard Nixon's visit to China in February, 1972. Older readers will need no reminders of the turbulence of this era. In the United States, it was the era of political assassination, race warfare, women's liberation, Vietnam, the Hippies and Yippies, and the New Left. In Europe, it was the era of Maoist-inspired urban terrorism, the "Prague Spring," and a major uprising of students and workers in France that briefly threatened to destroy the Fifth Republic. In China, it was the era of the disastrous Cultural Revolution. Everywhere university students were on the march, protesting the policies of governments and/or issuing calls for revolutionary transformation. As a university professor meeting and interacting with young people every day, I found myself in the front lines.

How would I respond to the challenges of this post-Camelot world? Various scenarios present themselves. One can imagine a profoundly radicalized Warren, bearded and beaded, in jeans and work shirt, haranguing his students with New Left mantras, leading them into battle against the Establishment, hoisted again and again into paddy wagons by sneering blue-uniformed "pigs." One can imagine a cynical burned-out Warren, reduced to wry smiles and shrugs of indifference, suffering stoically in his provincial hell. One can imagine a hectic Warren, falling for some dangerous and irresponsible temptress, his career and marriage in ruins, and, finally, a bullet in his brain. One can imagine a reactionary Warren, rebelling against his youthful indiscretions and utopian pipedreams, becoming a curmudgeonly pillar of political conservatism, a born-again fascist.

None of these hypothetical Warrens materialized, and I think for two reasons. The first was the steely persistence of my sense of continuity with all the Warrens who had ever been. At no point in the troublous period between 1965 and 1970 did I ever think of repudiating my earlier self, as I remembered and understood him. My earlier self still lived in and through me. I was he, and he was I. The call to utopian prophecy rang just as loudly in my ears in 1970 as it had in 1945. My past was all I had. It would have been psychologically impossible for me to set aside my past and start afresh. My ideas might change, my priorities might change, but never my loyalty to myself. Therefore, my task in the late 1960s was not to invent a new self, but to find new ways of restoring the old self to vigorous life.

The second reason that I did not become a firebrand, a cynic, a wastrel, or a fascist was the kind of political vibrations I was picking up from the mental climate of the late 1960s. In the 1950s, I had hoped that an enlightened elite of cosmopolitan integrators would be able, with a little prodding from Hudson and myself, to transform the world by the sheer force of their leadership, intellect, and charisma. The existing religions, states, and multinational institutions would pool their energies and, voilà! — the City of Man would spring forth, all grand and gleaming.

But in the bitterly disillusioning late 1960s, who could believe such a dénouement? Young radicals everywhere were re-examining the premises of their societies, re-examining issues of class, race, and gender, of nationhood, of democracy, of corporate capitalism and Soviet-style state capitalism. The liberal assumption that fundamental change could be effected from within the established order, peacefully and legally, came under massive assault, and

CHAPTER 7: REVOLUTION!

above all in the groves of academe, where men and women had the time and resources to read, think, and converse in depth about the state of the world. In due course, what they were saying began to seep into my reluctant consciousness and re-direct much of my own thinking. I remained the utopianizing world-saviour of yore, but with a significantly altered political agenda. At the same time, I was far too buttoned-down to spring for marijuana and love beads. Nor could the partisan of H.G. Wells and Gustav Mahler readily switch his allegiance to Allen Ginsberg and Bob Dylan. As for head-on collisions with uniformed pigs, I had neither the physical courage nor the faith in the transformative power of sidewalk scuffles to collide with anyone.

It did not take long for me to experience the "real" Sixties after we moved to Albuquerque in the summer of 1966. Within a year or two, the campus of the University of New Mexico had become a playground for bead-bedecked Hippies and a public forum for the national movement to end the Vietnam war. The first documented indication of a turn in my political orientation can be found in my letter to Hudson of April 27, 1968. The last two paragraphs are worth quoting:

> I have had the oddest feeling this spring of things breaking up, of vast changes at work, of ice jams melting and rushing out to sea. Some of it originates in my personal life, some of it in the outside world, and I don't know where it is leading, but I think it's for the good.
>
> At any rate, I refuse to be mired. Never have I been so far from that youthful *Weltschmerz* which was so often paraded in the pages of these letters. I feel younger than I did five or ten years ago. I also find that each year adds to my anger and my feeling of alienation from established structures of power. When I think that fifteen years ago I was taking an examination to enter the C.I.A., when I think that even four years ago I imagined that it would make a difference which "major" party occupied the White House.

I offered no illuminating detail, but reading between the lines and drawing on memory, I can readily decipher what I was trying to say: my growing exposure to New Left doctrine on issues of class, race, and political economy had eroded my allegiance to the bromides of New Deal liberalism. The old tacit acceptance of capitalism, as long as it was reined in by a caring and watchful government, had disappeared. The old technocratic elitism had crumpled, as I peered more and more skeptically into the doings of "the best and the brightest" in Washington and Saigon. Irritation over the blunders of U.S. foreign policy had hardened into a wholesale repudiation of the Cold War and the pathological "better dead than Red" philosophy of U.S. strategists. It no longer made any difference whether Democrats or Republicans prevailed, Tories or Labourites, Christian Democrats or Social Democrats, Gaullists or Socialists. Indeed, it had never made any difference, since they all belonged to the same Establishment. They all played on the same team.

As the war in Vietnam intensified, as casualties rose steeply on both sides, I lost all patience with U.S. policy. Before, I had described U.S. involvement as lawful but misguided, because the South Vietnamese government had lost popular support. Now I joined with the radicals who diagnosed the U.S. role in Vietnam as a simple case of racist imperialist aggression. I stood in picket lines on campus in silent protest. As described in the Prolegomenon above, I was the faculty member chosen to introduce Jane Fonda when she addressed a public meeting called to denounce the U.S. attack on Cambodia in May, 1970. When the New Mexico National Guard invaded the campus by helicopter to storm the student-occupied union building after Fonda's visit, I took my place in the front line of the demonstrators taunting the armed guardsmen and daring them to fire on us. Earlier, these same guardsmen had hacked their way through the campus with fixed bayonets, injuring almost a dozen people.

But this is not the whole story. Let me repeat. Moving to the Left did not mean feeling any affinity with the emergent counterculture of drugs, rock music, anarchism, or aberrant religiosity. I re-

CHAPTER 7: REVOLUTION!

mained the professor in jacket and tie, who refused to turn his classroom into a launching pad for revolution or share the ecstasies of the Flower Children. I had lost all faith in the Establishment, perhaps, but I was equally dismayed by the mindlessness of most of those who sought to bring it down. The typical ranting activist left me quite cold. I was attracted to the discourses of Erich Fromm and Herbert Marcuse, men of intellectual substance, but not to Abbie Hoffman or the Black Panthers. All this comes out quite clearly in my letter to Hudson of March 10, 1969, a stinging tirade against both student radicals and black nationalists. Their brainless strategy of premature anarchist violence would lead, I foresaw, to massive backlash on the part of "white bourgeois conservative reaction." The radical lambs would be slaughtered and "we liberals" would go down with them. Notice that I was still clinging to the "liberal" label, perhaps because New Left spokesmen used it scornfully to apply to anyone left of center who had not embraced their militance and countercultural zeal. To call myself a "radical" at that point in time would have been to cast my lot in with the Abbie Hoffmans and Jerry Rubins and Bobby Seales, and this I resolutely refused to do.

Nevertheless, I had become a radical of another sort, probably by 1969, and certainly by 1970, when I wrote *Building the City of Man*. Despite the title, *Building the City of Man* was not a revisiting or reworking of *The City of Man*. In 1963 I had argued the case for a movement of ideas that would help speed the transition from the separate nations and civilizations of today to an integrated world civilization incorporating the best of each — the best of capitalism, the best of socialism, the best of Christianity, the best of Islam, and so forth. I had identified a miscellaneous assortment of prophets who were producing the intellectual raw material for such a grand synthesis. I had called for an end to partisan bickering and knee-jerk dissidence: the new world civilization would be a community of consent, mediated by the "will to agree."

Building the City of Man was an entirely different book, a call not for the integration of existing cultures but for a world revolution to construct a new culture. The existing cultures, since I wrote

The City of Man in the early 1960s, had given us the Cuba missile crisis, a wave of political assassinations, race war in America, the Vietnam War with all its attendant horrors, the Israeli seizure of the West Bank, the Soviet invasion of Czechoslovakia, government-sponsored terror in China, the Kent State massacre, the bayonetting of the innocent at the University of New Mexico, and deep disenchantment with established orders everywhere, especially among the young. The existing cultures had failed. It was time to move on, and move forward.

The new book stayed in print until 1979, a run of eight years, selling reasonably well all that time. Its strongest review came from one of the most respected wise men of the New Left, Richard J. Barnet, co-director of the Institute for Policy Studies, in *Saturday Review* for November 6, 1971. I used *Building the City of Man* as a textbook in my new course at SUNY-Binghamton, "History of the Future," from the spring of 1974 until the fall of 1979. I would surely change a lot of it if I had the book to write over again, but the prose (and the poetry at the end) holds up remarkably well.

The most unacceptable chapter, from my current perspective, is the first, "The Great Explosion," which could have given the reader no clue of what was coming next. In diagnosing "the crisis in civilization," I pointed not to imperialism or capitalism or even nationalism as the real enemy of modern man, but rather to a Great Explosion of change taking place in all aspects of human life. Too much change of all kinds coming too fast had left us dizzy and confused. We could not keep up with it, and yet we had no choice but to try. From an article by Alvin Toffler, I picked up the phrase "future shock" (I had not yet seen his book of the same title) as an appropriate descriptor of the late 20th-century state of mind. The Great Explosion of social, political, economic, cultural, and technological change had traumatized us. Adapting to the headlong pace of the transforming forces in our civilization was like trying to paddle a rowboat out of a maelstrom; however much we flailed at the black swirling water, in our numbed state the currents might be too terrible to resist.

In a further section of the first chapter, I also introduced my

CHAPTER 7: REVOLUTION!

first version of the theme to which I returned in the early 1990s, the spectacle of the world simultaneously coming together and falling apart. Here I called this phenomenon "Fission and Fusion," and cited various examples of how integrative and disintegrative forces were contending for mastery in our time. Benjamin R. Barber was later to popularize this idea in his excellent book *Jihad vs. McWorld* (1995), but I was 25 years ahead of him.

The problem is that the Great Explosion of Change and the ding-dong battle between Fission and Fusion, although they certainly tell us a great deal about life in the second half of the 20th century, are almost ideology-free concepts. So, too, are the five specific dangers that I saw arising out of the Great Explosion and the battle of Fission and Fusion: international war, underdevelopment in the Third World, environmental degradation, enslavement to the logic of the machine, and the death of religious and ethical belief-systems. With the partial exception of the second (underdevelopment in the Third World), these are not ideologically charged issues, at least not in the sense of the classical ideological warfare waged in the 20th Century among socialists, liberals, conservatives, and fascists. I was fingering processes that were really the consequences, rather than the underlying causes, of our predicament.

So one finds scant evidence of a sharp leftward turn in Chapter One. The only hint of a swerve came at the very end, where, to illustrate the contemporary clash of cultures, I supplied thumbnail sketches of an imaginary father and son, one a ruthless capitalist driving a gas-devouring Chrysler, the other a gay hippie helping a friend procure an abortion. My sympathies lay clearly with the hippie, not with his dad.

But in the next chapter, "Half Measures and Red Herrings," I waded bravely into the ideological fray. The title referred both to political initiatives that did not go far enough and to initiatives that were, in my judgment, beside the point and likely to lead us astray. The world lay in the clutches of a totalizing crisis, and only a totalizing response could rescue us. I assailed pacifists, partisans of the United Nations, world federalists, and cultural pluralists (my term for what today we call "multiculturalists") as good-hearted dreamers offering little more than pabulum when what we needed was red meat. Then came the scientists and behavioral engineers who imagined that humankind could be rescued by teams of experts. These learned folk were more intelligent than the dreamers, but they fatally ignored the essentially political nature of civilization, the strategic role of will and motive and judgment. "Knowledge...is in itself entirely neutral and can be turned to any purpose whatsoever." Finally, I addressed the agendas of the late 1960s New Left, lauding its willingness to scuttle the old order, but severe in my criticism of its insistence on working only on behalf of shrinking proletariats, or oppressed nationalities, or alienated youth. The human predicament was a planet-wide predicament, afflicting all races, all classes, all nations, all sexes. We were all in the same sinking boat, and only by moving to a new one could we hope to survive.

Well and good, but from my present-day angle of vision I still have to wonder why I was satisfied to enumerate the salient consequences of the world crisis and the shortcomings of the most frequently proposed solutions without attending to the likeliest undermost causes. In any event, I did not, not in the first two chapters, although I must have thought I had. Chapter Three, "World Revolution," put forward my own alternative to the half-measures and red herrings of Chapter Two, and here I came much closer to ferreting out causes. The old fragmentary and disintegrating world order, I wrote, had to make way. Its fate was to yield inexorably to a new global civilization with its own distinctive overarching ideology and religious faith, facilitated by a great new World Party waging world revolution in its service. With formations in every country operating above or below ground as local circumstances dictated, the World Party would recruit most of its followers from the political left. However — and this was the heart of the matter — it would disavow "the official Left."

> By traducing the hopes for change of Leftists everywhere, the official Left has in any case forfeited all claims upon

CHAPTER 7: REVOLUTION!

our loyalties. It has sold out to the nation-state system and made its peace with capitalism. It deserves no sympathy, and no further support.

An interesting choice of words. My report of the sellout of the organized Left to the "nation-state system" and to "capitalism" suggests that I had identified the real causes of the world crisis in spite of myself — not tumultuous change or the conflict between centripetal and centrifugal forces, as analyzed in Chapter One, but the roots of such change and such conflict in a world system comprised of sovereign armed polities co-existing in a predatory global economy dominated by the insatiable profit-hunger of multinational corporations. I was not fully aware of what I was saying. Chapter One had not been a Trojan horse concealing what I really thought. But why this choice of words in Chapter Three? Why bemoan the sellout to the nation-state system and capitalism, if "the official Left" was, in fact, guilty of selling out to the Great Explosion and the clash of Fission and Fusion? Was I unwittingly shifting my ground in Chapter Three? I think so.

The shifting became still more obvious in the last part of *Building the City of Man*, where I ventured beyond analysis and prescription to sketch the outlines of a world civilization in being. Even then political matters occupied only a single chapter. Elsewhere, my focus fell chiefly on the coming world culture, the relations of men and women, education, and the search for extraterrestrial life. But Chapter Seven, "Commonwealth," discussed in some depth the political and economic shape of things to come. Building the City of Man, I argued, would require the creation of a world state, and the world state would be simultaneously unitary, democratic, socialist, and liberal — unitary rather than federal, democratic rather than technocratic, socialist rather than capitalist, and liberal rather than authoritarian.

I have no quarrel with those priorities even now. I favored a unitary world republic over a federal world government because I could not bring myself to believe in divided sovereignty or in the willingness of any state on the globe to surrender its sovereignty to a higher authority. The people of earth, through revolution, had to appropriate sovereignty from national states and invest that sovereignty in a unitary world state. By "the people," of course, I meant all the people — choosing suitable leaders, acting in concert, expressing the Rousseauian general will of humankind. Hence the world state would be democratic. It would also legislate a socialist system of relations of production "because private capital is monopolistic by nature and tends to usurp the authority and wealth of the people." And it would be a liberal state "because the end of all government is to set men free to become what they choose to become in conformity with the unique conditions of their own being." In short, my political credo was not "Liberté, Egalité, Fraternité," although it came close, but rather "World Unity, the General Will, Social Justice, and Personal Freedom."

The rest of Chapter Seven filled in the details. There was an elaborate plan for the government of the global commonwealth, to consist of four equal branches — the World Assembly [legislature], the World Council with its seven ministries [executive], the World Court [judiciary], and the World Chamber of Tribunes [ombudsmen]. Another section described the "law of citizenship," a statement of the fundamental rights and responsibilities of citizens, which included the "right to live," the "right to education," the "right to work," and a broad array of civil liberties, from freedom of speech to freedom of "consensual erotic life," together with such responsibilities as care for one's children, public service, and custodianship of the environment. Under the "right to live," I specified the right of all citizens to enjoy from society "an income sufficient for their fundamental needs" regardless of how much or how little work they performed.

But the longest section of the chapter, entitled "Welfare," provided a blueprint for world socialism. This was surely the most radical element in my reformulated political philosophy, which takes us almost light-years beyond the Warren of the 1950s and early 1960s. Part of the "Welfare" section suggested strategies for ending

CHAPTER 7: REVOLUTION!

gross economic inequality among the nations and eliminating toil, waste, and pollution. In the rest, I made a clear choice of economic systems. "Will the world economy be capitalist or socialist? We have already answered this question in the most direct way: it will be socialist." I proceeded to explain, in classical Marxian terms, how successful private corporations in their inevitable contest with less successful private corporations acted to strangle competition, acquire vast power over public life, and redistribute wealth undemocratically. The world commonwealth would do better, avoiding also the mistakes of the command economies of the Soviet Union and Communist China. Its economy would "combine the best features of both capitalism and socialism, in a predominantly socialist framework." The big corporations would be expropriated by the world government and turned over to its "ministry of welfare," but the right of free enterprise would be enjoyed by individuals and cooperatives, subject to limitations of size and capital. As much as one-quarter of the world's adult population would find gainful employment in small-scale private enterprise.

Of course my nod to the "right of enterprise" could not have fooled any follower of Adam Smith or Milton Friedman. In a market economy, there are no limitations on the accumulations of plutocrats. Whatever John D. Rockefeller or Bill Gates "earns" is rightfully his. If A.T. & T., Shell, and General Motors call the tunes in their respective industries, so be it. The Warren of *Building the City of Man* would have none of that. The only legitimate private enterprise was small business. Very small.

So I conclude that by 1971 a significant change had occurred in my political allegiance. I remained stoutly committed to world integration, but the erstwhile moderate liberal, the erstwhile elitist, the erstwhile technocrat, had become a democratic socialist. I only regret that my friendship with Hudson had reached its nadir at just this time, so that no confirming or for that matter disconfirming epistolary evidence is available of my leftward swerve. I tend to trust this correspondence more confidently than anything I say in print. But I sent no letters at all to Hudson in 1970, the year I was writing

Building the City of Man, and only one in 1971 and one in 1972, both of a personal nature with no reference to matters political. Now that we were living at almost opposite ends of the continent, we had all but lost touch. Letters to my mother of this period are frequent, but they are almost entirely centered on family news.

Nevertheless, *Building the City of Man* witnesses to a major and enduring reorientation. Nothing was ever quite the same again.

CHAPTER 8
BELIEVING IN PROGRESS

Why, upon reaching mature years, did the author of two youthful "books" entitled *Philosophy of Progress* abandon the idea of progress? I am baffled. The closest I came to a belief in progress in my work published through 1971 was the cyclical (or spiraliform?) premise of *The City of Man*, the premise (based on Toynbee's *A Study of History*) that in the past a number of civilizations had achieved unity and equilibrium through the sharing of a common ecumenical culture and imperial legal order, and therefore the next stage of human history should be the building of an authentically planetary culture and legal order. But this was not quite an idea of progress, certainly not a rectilinear idea. The City of Man would represent an advance over the Pax Sinica or the Pax Romana, but more in size and scope than in form and substance.

In short the boy-philosopher with all his grandiose ideas had been unable, as a young man, to link his vision of the future with a progressivist reading of the past. And yet he was now a professional historian! Also a convert to the New Left, with all its Left — both New and Old — philosophies of history. Somehow, the connections were not made. One clue perhaps is the barmy dedication page of *Building the City of Man*. In an excess of eclecticism, I dedicated the book to 27 "prophet-fathers of the coming world civilization." My fathers included such stalwarts of progressivist thought as Condorcet, Kant, and Comte, as well as Marx, Wells, and Marcuse. But the list did not stop there. I also cited Baha'u'llah (Persian founder of the Baha'i World Faith), the Indian mystic Sri Aurobindo, Nietzsche, Sorokin, Teilhard de Chardin, Mumford, and Toynbee, and, by a process of ***reductio ad absurdum***, the French astrologer Dane Rudhyar, who had written a book that I fleetingly admired, *The Planetarization of Consciousness* (1970). Anyone who could have actually coordinated and reconciled the writings of this jumbled lot would have been a savant indeed! Or an *idiot savant*?

At least I cannot be accused of toeing anybody's party line. I was trying to reach out to as many traditions as possible, in the search for "synthesis." But the very act of reaching out in so many directions at once precluded the adoption of a coherent philosophy of history, progressivist or otherwise.

The history of the idea of progress that I wrote between 1963 and 1970 did nothing to untangle me, mostly because it was intended from the first primarily as a contribution to academic intellectual history, not as a sequel or underpinning to *The City of Man*, although in some respects it may have been both. My goal was to look at the rich *mélange* of faiths in general human progress that had flourished since about 1880, as well as the almost equally rich profusion of assaults on such faiths. Loyal to the Diltheyan hermeneutic I had learned at Yale in the 1950s, I resolved to suspend my own beliefs as much as humanly possible, inhabit (by *Einfühlung*, "empathy") the consciousness of my prophets, and faithfully re-think their thoughts. By showing how many diverse paths the belief in progress had followed since the late 19th Century, I would overthrow the reigning notion that progressivist thought had died with the 19th Century itself. At the same time, it would not be amiss to disclose that one of the chief visions of human progress in our own time was the prophecy of a coming world civilization fulfilling the highest aspirations of all its parochial predecessors.

But the prophecy of a coming world civilization did not hold center stage in the new book. I felt a need to strengthen my credentials as an academic intellectual historian, not to reiterate *The City of Man*, which in any case was doing pretty well on its own at this time. I knew enough about academe to appreciate that scholars type-cast as shallow popularizers or cantankerous prophets seldom earned the respect of their peers. Toynbee, for example, was probably more revered among academicians for his lengthy learned footnotes than for his grandiloquence about the future. To secure the pulpit I sought, I would have to prove myself in the trenches of primary source research.

CHAPTER 8: BELIEVING IN PROGRESS

In retrospect it is clear that I had boarded the wrong bus. Diltheyan *Einfühlung* would soon be "out." Poststructuralist relativism would soon be "in." No one could inhabit the mind of another. The most we toilers in the vineyards of ideas could do was conduct imaginary "dialogues" with the texts of dead thinkers. My exploits in the 1970s at Binghamton contrast pitifully with the meteoric ascent of my fellow intellectual historian Dominick LaCapra just 50 miles away at Cornell. Also in retrospect, I think LaCapra was epistemologically right — the only problem with his being right is the pragmatics of his correctness. Can we really speak with the dead, and if not, what is the point of our speaking at all?

But this is surely another issue, and another debate, altogether. I strove, with the training and equipment at my disposal, to make a difference. As an intellectual historian, I sank out of sight with few traces.

Of course I knew nothing of my imminent submersion in the academic year 1971-1972. This was an ambitious year, marked by major federal grant proposals that I helped to write, one on behalf of the whole History Department to establish a center at Binghamton for the study of the teaching and learning of history by college students, the other to create a graduate program in world futures studies, to which we shall return in the next chapter. Both proposals did well in the review process, but not well enough. We lost. I also worked on new courses and became the chief mentor of several doctoral students. But despite all my doings, despite the encouragement I received from my new chairman Norman Cantor, despite warm welcomes from faculty and students alike, I remember the 1971-1972 academic year with little fondness.

The problem was that I had never really wanted to leave Albuquerque. I also formed an almost instant dislike for our old, sprawling, once-elegant, but somewhat decrepit house in Ithaca, and for Ithaca itself, with its arrogant "Heights" and its half-impoverished old town below. To boot, our neighborhood was devoid of young children, and we had four, with no one but each other for company. Shortly after I whined about my lot in a letter to a faculty friend in

Albuquerque, my former chair at U.N.M. called to ask if I was interested in returning to New Mexico, this time as chair of the department myself. My recollection is that I expressed strong interest. His recollection was that I did not. Whatever, I received no further overtures.

In mid-April, 1972, my long gestating book on the recent history of the idea of progress finally made its appearance. The literary agent — himself a distinguished Pulitzer-Prize-winning historian — who tried to place it with some of the top publishing houses in New York had had no luck. In the end I persuaded the press of one of my own *almae matres*, Indiana University, to do the honors. I.U. Press performed creditably, and the result was *Good Tidings: The Belief in Progress Since Darwin and Marcuse*, a tome of 398 pages, my longest original book.

Meanwhile, the University of New Mexico Press had, in 1971, brought out my symposium volume for the Council for the Study of Mankind, *History and the Idea of Mankind*, to which I contributed two chapters of my own; and in 1973 Indiana University Press would publish my *Books in World History*, a bibliographical guide for teachers and students. So the academic round went on, but without the *éclat* of my earlier work. No more world crises, no more formulas of response, no more stentorian appeals for integration. The globe once again — so much the worse! — was on its own.

In the summer of 1972 Dorothy passed her New York State Bar examinations in Albany, after graduating in the top 10% of her class at Cornell. I was immensely proud. We took the inevitable step of selling our house in Ithaca and moving to Vestal, New York, five miles from the campus of SUNY Binghamton, so that she could set up a practice in this much larger community and I could be close to my workplace.

ENTR'ACTE: GOOD TIDINGS

Good Tidings was not *The City of Man* revisited, but it was

CHAPTER 8: BELIEVING IN PROGRESS

yet another book about the destiny of humankind, as contemplated by a great swarm of thinkers. I chose each word of the subtitle carefully: *The Belief in Progress from Darwin to Marcuse*. Almost every previous and subsequent study of the subject called it the "idea" of progress, or occasionally the "theory" of progress, but I favored "belief" in hopes of covering a broader terrain. The believer might or might not have a well worked-through, systematic, and methodical concept of history as progress; the essential desideratum was belief, however arrived at, and however defended.

As for "progress" itself, it meant "general improvement, by whatever idea of the good and by whatever agency, in the temporal life of mankind, extending from the past into the predictable or at least possible future." I further defined "general" improvement as "net gain," rather than what the poet Whittier once called "the steady gain of man." Progress did not have to be continuous; it was simply a question of accounting; if, after all the credits and debits through all the centuries of history had been totaled, humanity was found to be in the black, humanity had progressed. And by whose idea of the good? Clearly, by the idea of the good of the thinker or thinkers under investigation. The intellectual historian, *qua* historian, had no business meddling in values. He or she had to remain on the sidelines, and rest content just to watch and keep score.

Why "from Darwin to Marcuse"? It was another way of saying "since about 1880," from the deaths of the 19th Century's most paradigmatic thinkers, Charles Darwin (d. 1882) and Karl Marx (d. 1883), to one of the latest in a long series of contemporary prophets, Herbert Marcuse, by the early 1970s at the peak of his influence and celebrity. J.B. Bury and dozens of others had detailed the history of the belief in progress down to the thinkers of the Darwin-Marx generation. It would be my task to trace what had transpired since then.

Two brief opening chapters took care of my definitions and offered a short synopsis of the idea of progress in earlier centuries. I disputed the widespread notion that progress was merely a secularized version of Augustinian "providence," or that any idea of general human progress had existed anywhere prior to the 18th Century. Despite inevitable debts to the Judeo-Christian and Hellenic heritage, the belief in progress was a specifically modern faith, a modern reading of history with organic ties to the "religion" that had in effect displaced Christianity: a rationalist and liberal humanism, which "has always been, at its roots, a religion of man, a faith in man and human possibility, which ultimately evolved into a faith in history, or, what amounts to the same thing, a faith in progress." Its spiritual forefathers were not Jewish prophets, Greek philosophers, or Christian apostles, but Bacon and Hobbes, Galileo and Newton, Descartes and Locke. Its first exponents were not St. Augustine or Joachim of Floris but the *philosophes* of the Enlightenment, such as St.-Pierre and Turgot. Had there never been such phenomena as Christianity and Hellenism, modern thinkers would have reached a belief in progress all the same.

Just so! Imagine an ancient Western world in which Carthage had won the Punic Wars or a medieval world in which Islam had conquered all of Europe (and not just Iberia and the Balkans). I cannot doubt that in due time there would still have been a Renaissance, a Scientific Revolution, and an Age of Enlightenment in Western Europe, a Western Europe with a quite different "heritage" to outgrow and dismiss, but with the same geographical features that frustrated empire-building, spurred the maritime rivalry of the early modern kingdoms and city states, and inspired the rise of agricultural and commercial capitalism. The timing, the cast of characters, many of the details would have been dissimilar, but not, I think, the main lines of advance. And from such keen rivalries and from such rapacious capitalism came the intellectual space for the growth of modern science, philosophy, and the religion of liberal humanism. On these points the Warren of 1972 and the Warren of today concur.

The remainder of *Good Tidings* was divided into three large parts: "Sons and Heirs," an exploration of the varieties of belief in progress that emerged between the 1880s and 1914; "Progress on Trial," a survey of the repudiation of progressivism by thinkers both before and after 1914; and "The Survival of Hope," six chapters examining the many writers and texts in the Western world that had

CHAPTER 8: BELIEVING IN PROGRESS

reaffirmed a belief in progress between 1914 and 1970. In an Epilogue, I gave myself the opportunity to chip in with my own thoughts on these great issues.

"Sons and Heirs" reconnoitered turn-of-the-century prophets of progress under four major headings. In the first, "The Cult of Science," I reminded readers that the hypothesis of a *fin-de-siècle* "revolt against positivism," first documented in eloquent breadth by the Harvard intellectual historian H. Stuart Hughes in his *Consciousness and Society* (1956), was not in all respects faithful to its times. If what we could, now and advisedly, recognize as the avant-garde had revolted against positivism, nevertheless the rank and file of intellectuals and their literate public in Europe and America between 1880 and 1914 had not revolted at all. The cachet of science, both natural and social, had never been more powerful. It continued to generate visions of progress, past and future. I began with the second generation of Positivists, the disciples of the late "High Priest of Humanity," Auguste Comte, who included Pierre Laffitte and Frederic Harrison. Germany produced Darwin's champion Ernst Haeckel and Wilhelm Ostwald. Alfred Russel Wallace was a firm believer in progress, although he rejected the atheism of his German contemporaries. In the social sciences, the belief in progress enlisted Emile Durkheim, Guillaume De Greef, Sir James Frazer, Franz Müller-Lyer, Lester Ward, L.T. Hobhouse, and that remarkable amateur sociologist H.G. Wells.

The merit of "Sons and Heirs," as I see it now, was to infuse fresh energy into thinkers and tides of thought flagrantly neglected by almost all intellectual historians of the second half of the 20th Century. The great game of historians has always been to cheer on the "winners," the writers and texts and ideas that have the most to say to our own era, while turning away with barely concealed yawns from anyone who now strikes us as musty, exploded, or sterile. But this powerfully distorts the past.

My most vivid graphic image of this distortion comes from an hour I spent in Highgate Cemetery in London in 1964. As I was trudging down the pathways, I came upon the overgrown, weedy patch surrounding the singularly modest gravestone of Herbert Spencer, one of the two founders of sociology, a devout believer in progress, arguably the most influential thinker in Great Britain and the rest of at least the Anglophone world in the last four decades of the 19th Century. Any Anglophone intellectual in the year 1880 or 1890 asked to identify Herbert Spencer would have had no difficulty. A few yards further on, I came to a much more splendid grave site, piled high with fresh flowers and topped with an immense bust of the deceased: the burial place of Karl Marx. I have no problem recognizing the significance of Marx, but who in 1880, in 1890, could have foreseen the glum obscurity of Spencer and the ongoing glamour of Marx?

Of course a revolt against positivism did occur in the quarter-century or more before the First World War. In my next chapter, "The Will to Power," I investigated another facet of it, the appearance of anti-positivist philosophers who all the same did not reject the idea of progress and in many instances gave it their fervent blessing. I argued that in the higher circles of philosophy "most of the leading schools — vitalist, spiritualist, neo-idealist, neo-Kantian, pantheist, pragmatist — proclaimed the good tidings of the faith in progress with enthusiasm."

First taking on the most problematic of philosophers of the era, I built what I still think is a credible case for regarding even Friedrich Nietzsche as a believer in progress, in some respects although clearly not in many others, and especially as he was understood by the generation that made a hero of him, the young people of 1890 to 1914. (In a later chapter I also explored him as a hostile critic of the belief in progress in its most typical late 19th-Century manifestations.) But my other exhibits in evidence are more straightforward, some of them nowadays ignored, if not entirely forgotten: from Germany, Wilhelm Wundt, Rudolf Eucken, Hermann Cohen; from France, Alfred Fouillée, Emile Boutroux, Jean-Marie Guyau, Henri Bergson; from Britain, Samuel Alexander, Bernard Shaw; from the United States, C.S. Peirce, William James, John Dewey.

Another whole category of thinkers, the theologians of the

age, were also in many instances converts to the idea of progress, guided more by secular thought than by Jewish or Christian tradition. In "The Theology of Progress," I examined the followers in Germany of Albrecht Ritschl, especially Adolf von Harnack, the modernist wing of Roman Catholicism as represented by Alfred Loisy, and the liberal camp of Anglophone theologians, including Henry Drummond, Lyman Abbott, and Walter Rauschenbusch, all exponents of the belief in progress. Finally came "Progress and Politics," a study of the leading political thinkers who put forward ideas of progress from Lord Acton and Friedrich Naumann through J.A. Hobson and Herbert Croly to the first post-Marxian generation of socialist prophets, notably Karl Kautsky, Eduard Bernstein, Jean Jaurès, the Fabians, Henry George, and G.V. Plekhanov. The last pages of "Progress and Politics" wrestled with the question of what to do with Vladimir Ilyich Lenin. Did he — or for that matter did Marx himself — "believe" in progress?

I contended, and still contend, if perhaps less confidently, that Marxian metahistory is a doctrine of net progress extending from the Paleolithic Era to the future victory of socialism and the transition to pure communism. The apparent fly in the ointment, Marx and Engels's quasi-idyllic description of the life of humankind in a state of primitive communism, and even their favorable contrast between the lives of medieval serfs and the still more degraded and commodified lives of 19th-Century wage-slaves, must be understood in the light of their dialectic. The higher humankind advanced in its conquest of nature and its creation of wealth, the deeper its descent to injustice in the realm of the social relations of production; but all stages were inevitable, necessary, and liberating, liberating at first for the few, but in the long run, in days to come, for all. So Marx, Engels, and Lenin were not latter-day disciples of J.-J. Rousseau. Much that ailed civilization was deplorable, but civilization for Marx and for Marxists is, in a metahistorical sense, good. Without it, no conquest of nature, and no material preconditions for a future world of abundance, equality, and security. Translated into theological terms, Marxism-Leninism holds that God and Satan are working together, not at cross purposes, to prepare humankind for a new Garden of Paradise.

We have now arrived at page 143 of *Good Tidings*, with more than 250 still to go. Let us pick up the pace. The middle chapters put "Progress on Trial." Belief in progress fell under heavy attack long before 1914 from many azimuths, from romantics, from positivists, from the infamous "Decadents," from Anatole France and Thomas Hardy, even from my beloved Wells in some of his earliest scientific romances. Progress was also a well targeted victim of the rise of the academic "relativisms" — historical, psychological, anthropological. After 1914, it was bitterly assailed by Oswald Spengler, by neo-orthodox theologians, by the existentialists, by the writers of dystopian fiction, and a thousand others.

All this was easy to pull together, but in the six last chapters, I discovered that hopefulness, the utopian imagination, and the belief in progress, although badly bloodied, had survived after all in the years since 1914. A chapter on "Holy Worldliness" explored revivals of progressivism in contemporary Catholic thought and in the new "secular theology" or "theology of hope" expounded by Harvey Cox, Dietrich Bonhoeffer, and Jürgen Moltmann. There were "Philosophies of Hope," as well, from Bertrand Russell to Karl Jaspers to Pierre Teilhard de Chardin to Arnold J. Toynbee to Ernst Bloch. Scientific thinkers joined the chorus, such as Julian Huxley and J.D. Bernal. The social sciences? Think only of V. Gordon Childe, Margaret Mead, Robert Redfield, Karl Mannheim, Morris Ginsberg. And in the last chapter, "The Meta-Psychology of Progress," I spoke of "the fertile meliorism of Freud's thought," as carried further by Erich Fromm and Herbert Marcuse.

In an Epilogue, only seven pages long, I ventured my own tentative thoughts. I entitled it "The Great Explosion," the same title chosen for the opening chapter of *Building the City of Man*. It began in quite a different vein. Instead of a litany of all the tumultuous changes plunging humanity into future shock, I opened with a brief, sobering sermon on the impossibility of finding objective criteria for discriminating between what is "progressive" and what is not. Even if such criteria could be found, I posited the impossibility of measuring "net gain." Even if we could measure it, I argued the impossibility of

CHAPTER 8: BELIEVING IN PROGRESS

discerning what would come next. "Mankind perpetually wishes to know...but prophets invariably fail." Even what is possible cannot be known, "as a matter of cognition."

My thinking here may seem to anticipate poststructuralism, but I cannot make such a claim. Although the text of *Good Tidings* offers no clues, I am quite sure that my epistemological wits derived almost entirely from bracing draughts of logical positivism imbibed in college and graduate school, laced with a jigger of French existentialist skepticism. Who can know *l'en-soi* (J.-P. Sartre)? What is ethics, in a cognitive sense, but "meaningless noise" (A.J. Ayer)? "Killing is bad" has the same cognitive force as "I like my steak medium-rare." To revert to my plea in *The City of Man*, all that remained was "the will to agree," a phrase that deliberately blended William James's "the will to believe" and Nietzsche's "the will to power." But then I asked the ultimate question: "If I cannot pretend to know, why should I dare to believe?"

I resolved the issue by sundering my self as "scholar" from my self as "human being." The scholar could not know, but the human being could dare to believe. Indeed, it was commanded by common humanity that each of us try our best to gauge the meaning of human history and weigh the good against the bad. Tossing aside my cap and gown, I stated unequivocally: "I must...affirm my belief in the progress of mankind since the first appearance on earth of the genus *Homo*." It was even "a kind of moral infantilism" not to believe, a mindless and childish deference to past eras that none of them deserved.

What followed was a paean to the intelligence and good will of humankind, increasing almost imperceptibly from millennium to millennium. In every respect, I maintained, not just in this or that, humankind had progressed: in knowledge, technological mastery, material wealth, personal comfort, security of life and limb, longevity, freedom from pain, individuation, self-awareness, scope and sensitivity of aesthetic and intellectual culture, fellowship among cultures and races, equality of status and opportunity, in everything that mattered most. The trend, with many setbacks and failures and regressions along the way, was always upward. "The longer the spans of time considered, the easier it is to see progress." Should we ignore the horrors of the 20th Century? Not at all. "The very fact that modern man so vigorously lashes himself for his shortcomings is in itself evidence of the progress of moral sensibility."

Then finally I got to the "Great Explosion." What had happened in the 20th Century was not a halt to progress but a geometrical increase in the technological and organizational powers of humankind, arming evil as well as good, magnifying malice as well as benevolence. Nonetheless, the good — up till now — had generally prevailed. I closed with a scorching rebuke of "the contemptible *Schadenfreude* of the neo-Augustinian theologians, the obscurantists, and all the pious and mystical refugees from progress who detect a fatal moral insufficiency in the heart of man." For thousands of years we had listened to thousands of excuses from the hallucinating faithful, explaining why Almighty God had fashioned "His" creatures to be so frail. Why not turn "the tables on these tiresome apologists"? Why not contrive "anthropodicies that explain why a fallible and predatory race of recently evolved apes has not yet succeeded in building its own paradise"? Indeed: "Why should we not acknowledge that we have even done rather well, we who are not gods?"

I can add nothing to that final question. My contempt for the *Schadenfreude* of the neo-Augustinian orthodox is limitless, even today. Damn them to the Hell they themselves, and their mad saints and fathers, long ago invented! Who disbelieves in the higher destiny of humanity disbelieves in all that can ever be.

CHAPTER 9
HIGH CHURCH

Having done, for the time being, with the history of the belief in progress, I turned in 1972 to two more projects, both with futurist implications: a study of what I called "comparative world views" and a survey of visions of the world's end in imaginative literature, which I dubbed "secular eschatology." The first would culminate in a forecast of "the next world view," the second would follow the formula of *Good Tidings* in exploring ideas of the future, save that now the ideas in question were apocalyptic, "the literature of last things."

Writing two books simultaneously was nothing I had planned. I had already signed with Holt, Rinehart and Winston in February, 1971, to write a volume for their ambitious new series of college textbooks, *Dimensions in Comparative History*. I received a large advance for signing. A further inducement was that all volumes in the series would be published simultaneously in Britain by Jonathan Cape. When I started teaching at SUNY Binghamton, I also succumbed to the temptation to apply for a SUNY-wide summer research grant that Norman Cantor virtually guaranteed I would win. I did apply and did win, both for Summer 1972 and for Summer 1973. The catch, of course, was that I needed a project, and it could hardly be the same as the one for Holt. So I came up with the not uninspired idea of a study of visions of the world's end.

The idea was not uninspired, perhaps, but writing two books at the same time ran against my personal grain. Ever since childhood I had always finished one book before starting another. I had a mania about finishing. I would start a new book with great reluctance and trepidation, but once well into it, I could not let go. It has been much the same with everything else in my driven life: I never want to start a vacation, meet a new class, come to dinner, go to bed, or wake up in the morning. Yet having finally put out to sea, I never want to return to port. There is probably a psychiatric term for my condition. But it does have one merit: it leaves me with very few aborted manuscripts.

The summer of 1972 was further complicated by the need to wrap up a third project, still not quite complete, my annotated bibliography for Indiana University Press, *Books in World History*. It was already six months overdue when the summer began, partly because of unforeseen surgery Indiana had asked me to perform on the manuscript of *Good Tidings* in 1970, as well as the fuss of moving house twice and working up new lectures for my courses at SUNY Binghamton. My summer grant was only for June and July, so I reserved August for finishing *Books in World History*. What I managed to accomplish in June and July for the other two books eludes memory. Both were still just embryos. Presumably all my available time went into research.

The publication of *Building the City of Man* the previous fall led to a number of invitations to give talks on the future and these, too, absorbed a fair amount of energy, further delaying work on the new books. In September, 1972, I spent several days in Los Angeles teaching a seminar at the headquarters of the International Cooperation Council, a seminar entitled "Modelling the Future World Civilization." One of my students was the veteran actor Lew Ayres, who later that month sent me a four-page letter assessing my book. He liked the earlier chapters, but when I veered off into my version of secular humanism, he could not follow me. Only by tapping into "divine wisdom" could humankind be rescued. Later in 1972 and on into 1973, I spoke to the Graduate History Society of SUNY Binghamton on "History as Futurology," guest-lectured on world futures at Colgate University and New York University, gave the keynote address at a conference of philosophers at SUNY Geneseo ("Cognitive Synthesis and World Civilization"), and returned to my role as a lay preacher at the Unitarian Universalist Church of Binghamton with a sermon billed in the Church bulletin as "a short introduction to the history of the future."

By then I was probably well into the planning stages of a new undergraduate course that Cantor encouraged me to teach. His original idea had been for me to develop something in the area of world or comparative history, but when I hit on the idea of teaching a course on world futures, he was immediately receptive. Cantor had a good nose for what might be marketable in the classroom. His instincts in this case did not fail him. I taught the first edition of "History of the Future" in the Spring 1974 semester, and I have offered it almost every year since. Even on its first try it enrolled 121 students, far more than I usually attracted. Except for Western Civilization survey courses, it was the largest class I had ever taught.

As older futurists will recall, futures studies got off to a brisk start in the late 1960s and early 1970s. Major books by Buckminster Fuller, Herman Kahn, Daniel Bell, Alvin Toffler, John McHale, Donella and Dennis Meadows, and others, were selling steadily. Edward Cornish founded the World Future Society in Washington in 1966; I joined soon thereafter and by the time I introduced my course its worldwide membership had climbed to well over 20,000. Inspired by the work of Bertrand de Jouvenel, the *Association International Futuribles* was founded in Paris in 1967. The Club of Rome opened shop in 1968. Lester R. Brown launched his Worldwatch Institute in 1974. Writing in the same year, a Dartmouth sociologist counted some 475 futures-related courses on North American campuses. Graduate programs were initiated at the Amherst campus of the University of Massachusetts (1970) and the Clear Lake City campus of the University of Houston (1974).

Whether I viewed myself specifically as a "futurist" before teaching "History of the Future" is doubtful, but I was surely ripe for the arrival of the futures studies movement. In the academic year 1971-72, my first year at SUNY Binghamton, I had already submitted a two-year grant proposal to the Office of Education in Washington for a "Program for the Study of World Integration," a program that would have featured as its co-director the noted futurist John McHale, then the head of a futures research center at Binghamton and best known for his splendid book, *The Future of the Future* (1969). I wrote virtually all the language of the proposal myself and recruited, besides McHale, a number of likely Binghamton faculty members from several departments to act as associates.

This happened five years before the world-systems scholar Immanuel Wallerstein moved from Columbia University to Binghamton to inaugurate his Fernand Braudel Center for the Study of Economies, Historical Systems, and Civilizations. Had my grant come through, Wallerstein and I might have wound up as rivals; or I might have joined forces with him, who can say? With hindsight it is difficult to imagine the cloistered Warren as the Grand Panjandrum of a Center or Institute or whatever. Nor would I have been likely to recruit the impresssive army of graduate students from around the world who descended on Binghamton after Wallerstein's arrival in 1976. In any event, Washington rejected our proposal, and McHale himself was soon thereafter retrenched during a year of disastrous budgets for the SUNY system, one of several retrenchments authorized, ironically, by Cantor, who had since become the University Provost.

But "The History of the Future" evolved into an institution in its own right, enrolling (so far) more than 7,000 students and enlisting the services (so far) of at least a hundred graduate teaching assistants. My debt to Cantor and to all my colleagues at Binghamton who have welcomed or at least tolerated the presence of this behemoth in our departmental life is warmly acknowledged. With 6,000 years of recorded time on six continents to manage, not many history departments would have troubled to house an annual course that chose perversely to invent (or at least to explore in imagination) the next few hundred. But this is a trademark of the SUNY Binghamton history program: its encouragement of difference.

The course as first given in 1974 diverged in several ways from the one I give today. In other ways it was almost identical. The four course objectives, as printed at the top of the syllabus, were virtually the same in 1974 as they are now, although worded a bit differently:

> 1. To identify main trends in the history of humankind from the Stone Age to the Stoned Age, singling out those which may have the heaviest bearing on our future evolution.

2. To analyze recent research by social and natural scientists on the shape of the human future.

3. To explore visions of the future in literature, utopography, and films.

4. To clarify our personal expectations of what may happen to humankind, and define the world we would prefer to see emerge during the next hundred years.

The droll (or not so droll?) phrase "from the Stone Age to the Stoned Age" was of my own coinage, although I have seen it in print elsewhere in recent years, and it may well have been used by others long before 1974.

The lectures of the course were divided into five sections. I can still think of no better way to divide the turf. An introductory section examined futures studies (then styled "futurology") as a discipline, and the second explored "Patterns of the Past." I marched my students through all 6,000 years of the history of civilization, with special attention to the transition in the early modern period from "traditional" to "industrial" society. The last three lectures in the set explored three principal concomitants of the Industrial Revolution: secularization, the globalization of trade and warfare, and the democratization of politics, all of which, I suggested, might well continue or even accelerate through the next hundred years. For this part of the course, I required students to read the then-current edition of William H. McNeill's text, *A World History*, which they despised. They had not signed on to take a course in world history!

Nevertheless, I insisted, and still insist, on attention to the past, even though our forced march nowadays takes only three lectures instead of six. All informed guesswork about the future of civilization derives all of its information and most of its guesswork from studies of past events, whether directly by historians, or indirectly through the historically-situated research of other disciplinarians, such as health scientists collating the results of trials of new drugs or economists investigating the vicissitudes of the business cycle. Information about present events is impossible to gather, since by the time anyone can take note of them, they have already occurred and belong by definition to the past. Information about future events is impossible to gather because they have not yet happened, and have therefore left no witnesses and no traces.

In this sense all "knowledge" of the future is knowledge of the past, and the more we know about the past, the better we can speak with some authority and credibility about the future. Not with more accuracy: accuracy has nothing to do with it. But with more authority and credibility than otherwise. Anyone can say that next year all cows will turn bright blue, sprout wings, and develop the ability to recite the sonnets of Shakespeare. But anyone who so speaks will have some serious explaining to do to the worldwide community of biologists.

Of course the future of civilization as a whole does not consist only of drug trials, business cycles, or the color of cows. Those who argue that accurate prediction of "the" future is possible usually mean that certain individual events are always or usually predictable. The rising of the sun in the east tomorrow morning is the best example, but there are others. Demographers can predict to within, say, one hundred thousand the size of next year's global population. Statisticians of crime can come close to forecasting the number of homicides in France between the year 2001 and the year 2010. Market researchers can give us a canny estimate of how many bottles of Fizz-O will be sold in supermarkets in London over the next twelve months. The probability of a presidential election in the United States in November, 2004, is very high, close to 100%.

Still, this is not really what we mean by predicting "the" future. "The" future is what will become of all humankind in the 21st Century (and beyond). To forecast what will become of all humankind in the 21st Century (and beyond) requires knowledge of how all people everywhere, with all their cultures and institutions, and with all the environmental support supplied or withheld by Mother Earth, will act and react and interact during the next one billion hours (and beyond). Can any scholar or conceivable consortium of scholars hope to procure such knowledge? Of course not. The question is frivolous.

But it is possible to construct credible alternative scenarios of coming times that take full advantage of what we do know about human interactions and the carrying capacity of the earth. And I would argue that the kind of scholar most fit to make a credible stab at telling us what might happen is the student of world history. World historians are in the hazardous business of considering all relevant inputs and limits on a terrestrial scale through the course of hundreds, even thousands of years. They are synthesists. They can be hilariously wrong, as can anyone, but at least they are trained to fill large canvasses.

So I tell my students that our job is to study and write the "history" of the future, not in the sense that history supplies cabalistic answers, but in the sense that the future will continue along the same time-stream as the past. Looking up river, in fading light, we see the past. Looking down river, we glimpse (through dense morning fog) the future.

The third segment of "History of the Future," then as now, was devoted to environmental prospects. From the beginning of serious futures inquiry, exploring the synergy between the environment and civilization has been a major stock in trade of the enterprise. Consider only the outstanding success of Lester R. Brown's Worldwatch Institute, which tends to sidestep political, economic, and cultural conundrums in order to focus on "commonsense" ecological imperatives. How many natural resources are left, how many people will there be, what impact will they exert on the biosphere? How can we build a sustainable relationship between *Homo sapiens* and Mother Earth?

So in successive hours the class dutifully inspected six fundamental ecological concerns: the systemic nature of the relationship between nature and civilization, global population increase and control, reserves of non-renewable resources, pollution, the "limits to growth" proclaimed by the Club of Rome, and the prospects for advances in technology ("Deus ex Machina") to extend those limits. In later years I added segments on energy futures and global warming.

However, we could not stop there. The Worldwatch Institute might be able to dodge political questions, but "History of the Future" could not. Beyond the issue of how many people needed how many resources lay the issue of which people got which resources and why and how. In the fourth segment of the course we turned to the future of institutions, from "The Warfare State" and the world economy to the future of families, education, and behavioral engineering ("The Biocrats" and "The Psychocrats"). Much of our attention, too much, centered on war prevention through the achievement of a world state. I devoted three lectures to issues of global security and war prevention, but only one to the fundamentals of economics and class conflict. (Nowadays it is one lecture to issues of global security and three to the fundamentals of economics and class conflict.)

In the final segment, we inquired into cultural futures, including "The Idea of a World Civilization" and "Strategies for World Renewal," focusing on assigned readings from my *Building the City of Man* and Richard A. Falk's *This Endangered Planet* (1971). With ideas filched from *The City of Man*, I also found time for a lecture on the search for a world religion and two lectures on selected futurists, chiefly Wells and Teilhard de Chardin. (By 1976, the lectures on religion and selected futurists had disappeared from the syllabus.)

The problem with this first edition of the course, as I see it now, was too much propaganda and too many pre-cooked lectures about "the coming world civilization." As a teacher, one does not enlist proteges — or should not — by loudly beating the drums for a single point of view. Students of the future deserve exposure to many scenarios reflecting a broad variety of ideological perspectives. One of those perspectives may be the teacher's own, but only if the teacher makes clear that it is indeed his or her own, and only if the teacher fully respects the academic freedom of students to dissociate themselves from it. Even in the first edition of "History of the Future,"

CHAPTER 9: HIGH CHURCH

I think I managed to protect the academic freedom of my students, but I did not give them enough exposure to perspectives other than my own. Of course the alternative pedagogical strategy is for the teacher to wear a mask of value-neutrality, but this is a mask I have long since discarded. The self-styled *wertfrei* professor abstracted from the real world of contending values is only a figment of his or her own imagination. No such animal has ever existed.

Another feature of the course was the weekly film night, the so-called "Future Film Festival." In the 1970s we showed real films on real reels, rented for the evening from distributors at considerable cost. Attendance was voluntary, but most students came anyway. I would soon add novels to the course, as well, but the first edition in 1974 included only films, primarily films about more or less plausible near futures connecting in some way with the lecture material for that week. The selections for 1974 began with Fritz Lang's *Metropolis* and continued with the 1956 version of *Nineteen Eighty-Four*, François Truffaut's *Fahrenheit 451*, Stanley Kubrick's *2001* and *Dr. Strangelove*, Stanley Kramer's *On the Beach*, Jean-Luc Godard's *Alphaville*, Elio Petri's *The Tenth Victim*, and George Pal's 1960 adaptation of H.G. Wells's *The Time Machine*. Most of these films would be hooted off the screen by today's typical student audience, with its craving for state-of-the-art special effects, but I think the 1974 "Festival" set appropriately high aesthetic standards.

I also distributed to students a check-list of "Selected Books for Further Reading and Research." The handout, on two sides of a single sheet of paper, comprised 51 non-fiction titles, 21 novels, and two journals. Today my check-list has swollen to thousands of titles on 60 or 70 pages, and students have to buy it in the campus bookstore, but it all began with this strange little acorn, recommending what are now the venerable classics of futurism, from Daniel Bell's *The Coming of Post-Industrial Society* (1973) to Alvin Toffler's *Future Shock* (1970) and the Club of Rome's *The Limits to Growth* (1972).

Winning a National Endowment for the Humanities Senior Fellowship plucked me out of the classroom during the 1974-75 academic year, but returning to teach in Fall 1975, the first course I offered was "History of the Future," this time with an enrollment of 125; and in Fall 1976, the size of the class almost doubled, to 230. It kept growing for many years to come, peaking at an absurd 462 in 1986, when nine graduate teaching assistants were required to staff the weekly discussion section meetings. Of which more later.

In 1974-75, while on leave, I completed the manuscript of my study of comparative world views and waded more deeply into my book on secular eschatology. The former should have been ready at least a year earlier, but I had received no complaints about the delay. When my agent wrote to acknowledge receipt of the manuscript in August, 1975, everything appeared to be in order and on track. Meanwhile, now that I was back in the Northeast, I renewed my friendship with Hudson Cattell, who had undergone sea-changes of his own, and we now resumed our old intellectual intimacy.

But the principal event of the 1974-75 academic year was not the recovery of Hudson or the writing of books. The principal event was my conversion to what my wry former colleague in the History Department, Tom Africa (blessings be upon him!), was wont to call "high church" Marxism. Nothing happened on the road to Damascus, no single epiphany, no compelling revelation. I simply reached the conclusion, over a period of months during the winter of 1974-75, that the austere stand-alone revolutionary liberal socialism of *Building the City of Man* was a dead end. A revolutionary and cosmopolitical movement already flourished in our world, some ingredients of which I found distastefully doctrinaire. But why not extract my head from the clouds and join this movement, which claimed at least the nominal allegiance of one-third of the earth's population? Why not, in short, become a Marxist? Marxists repudiated all national chauvinisms. Marxists spoke for and acted to achieve social and economic justice the world over. Marxists sought to build a secular world civilization.

More than a quarter-century later, I remain persuaded that my conversion was well advised and long overdue. At the time I probably did not realize that much of the leadership of the planet's

CHAPTER 9: HIGH CHURCH

so-called socialist "camp" had already lost its faith, but that is another issue. Trying to build socialism in largely agrarian societies in the teeth of the armed hostility of the entire capitalist world was an enterprise no doubt doomed from the get-go. And doomed not only to fail: doomed to resort to paranoia and terror in the process of failing. But Marxism, as such, did not create the Gulag or topple the U.S.S.R., any more than Christianity, as such, massacred native Americans or caused the collapse of Tsarism in Russia.

One further point: when I speak of "conversion" to Marxism, I mean precisely that. It was an act of faith, not an acceptance of Marxism as a science. Engels's famous contention that with the discoveries of Karl Marx "socialism became a science" struck me as almost ludicrous. I did not believe in such a thing as social science. Some theories explained social phenomena in at least certain places in at least certain times better than other theories, and Marx had made important contributions to social theory. But the heart of Marxism, for me, was simply a complex of ethical assertions about the best rationally conceivable future for humankind. In Karl Mannheim's use of the term, it was a "utopia," arguing that human beings are fundamentally productive, sociable creatures who can learn to live together harmoniously once they have risen above their historic dependency on property systems to create wealth. Those systems (culminating in capitalism) were necessary evils, but the time of their supersession might be drawing near. Unlike Marx and Engels, however, I did not (and still do not) see this supersession as inevitable or required by the "laws" of a "science."

Once converted, I sought an appropriate forum to make my *confessio fidei*. This turned out to be the Second General Assembly of the World Future Society, meeting in Washington in early June, 1975. Before an audience of 250, I delivered a paper with the title "The Next World-View." It was at all odds a turning-point.

I began my talk with an apology. "What I wish to say here today is in the nature of a confession. A confession of past sins, and a public declaration of my resolve to go and sin no more." I went on to explain that in my previous work, including *Building the City of*

Man, I had fellow-travelled with a host of "utopian, liberal, eclectic" world-betterers, calling for a "new" ideology and a "new" global party pledged to save humanity from its otherwise imminent doom. This was all well and good, but hopelessly Olympian and pitiably irrelevant to the harsh realities of the rapidly disintegrating world order of here and now. "The thirty years of gentle agitation for world peace, world government, and world order conducted by the American liberal establishment since the end of World War Two have achieved precisely nothing." With time fast running out, the hour had arrived to rally around the one solid movement of thought and action already in being and already pledged to build a new world civilization, a movement with roots in every country on earth: Marxism-Leninism and the international brotherhood of Marxist-Leninist parties.

Notice that I was referring here not just to Marx, but also to Lenin. The distinction is crucial, going far beyond my initial decision to brand myself a Marxist. In effect I had now aligned myself with the CPSU and every other Communist party in the world loyal to Moscow or Beijing. I now supported the revolutionary overthrow of capitalism under the leadership of the vanguard parties of the workers, following the heroic model of Vladimir Ilyich Lenin and his Bolsheviks in 1917 in Russia. The only great flaw in contemporary Marxist-Leninist parties was their all-too-frequent subordination of the struggle against capitalism to internecine chauvinist conflict within the socialist camp. I deplored the rupture between the Soviet Union and China and the preoccupation of Marxist-Leninists everywhere with issues of nation-building. Nation-states and their governments in socialist lands were "transitional and expedient, not eternal verities." Too many Marxist-Leninists had forgotten or even betrayed the cosmopolitan premises of Marxist-Leninist thought. The movement "must purge itself of the alien parasitical nationalisms that have taken lodging in its flesh."

But assuming that Marxist-Leninists everywhere succeeded in recovering their cosmopolitan souls, I found the future bright with promise. By 1990 or 2000, nearly all of Asia, Africa, southern

CHAPTER 9: HIGH CHURCH

Europe, and Latin America would have joined the ranks of Marxist-Leninist nations, leaving only Japan, northwestern Europe, and North America outside the pale. By 1990 or 2000, it would be time for the Marxist-Leninist three-quarters of humankind to proclaim the World Socialist Republic; and, if Marxist-Leninists in the remaining one-quarter kept the faith, eventually, "well into the twenty-first century," the workers of the West would also install socialist governments and join the World Republic. I pledged the rest of my days to the struggle for world integration in concert with my Marxist-Leninist brethren everywhere. "I search no longer for vague hypothetical undiscovered banners under which to conduct my march through life. I am proud to declare my allegiance to the international Marxist-Leninist movement."

Futurists have established a track record down through the years of woefully failing to predict the future, but this oration of mine in June, 1975, was a particularly disastrous example. All I can say in my defense is that in mid-1975 the prospects of global Communism were apparently rosy. The Soviet Union enjoyed a healthy economic growth rate, Communist parties in Western Europe were faring well at the polls, the East European Communist regimes seemed firmly ensconced (at long last), Castro's Cuba was in good shape, China had recovered from its Great Leap Forward, all of Indochina had just fallen to Communist rule, and Communist insurgencies in various parts of sub-Saharan Africa and Latin America — with Soviet or Chinese support — were making modest headway. Even in North Africa, one heard tell of "Arab socialism," as espoused by charismatic leaders in Algeria, Libya, and Egypt. I do not offer all this as an excuse — in futurism it is a capital offense to extrapolate current trends mindlessly into the future. Any fool can do that.

More to the point, what had really happened to my political philosophy in 1975? Did I intend to join the nearest available Communist party and begin committing the works of Marx, Engels, and Lenin to memory? Or was I, in the current vernacular, simply blowing smoke? These are very difficult questions, for which I do not have all the answers. The best I can say is that I was frustrated by the impotence of the non-Communist Left, disappointed by the lukewarm reception and sales of my *City of Man* books, and — perhaps — genuinely convinced that international Communism was humanity's last best chance of avoiding catastrophe. As I said in my talk, 30 years of "gentle agitation for world peace" by liberal world-betterers had led nowhere, whereas during these same years international Communism had made steady, even spectacular progress. Why not throw in one's lot with a winner?

But I doubt that, in any fundamental sense, I had changed my thoughts or feelings about Leninism, Maoism, Trotskyism, or the various Communist parties around the world and the regimes that some of them had created. Even in my talk I noted that "Marxist-Leninist thinkers and leaders are not infallible, and they have committed and still commit many errors, and even atrocities." As recently as October, 1974, I had travelled through communist Czechoslovakia and was shocked by the grimness of life under the Soviet boot. Despite the high idealism of Marx and Engels, and their keen appeal to my utopographer's imagination, I was never, not even in June, 1975, enamored of the actual official Communism of the Soviet Union and People's China and all their far-flung satellites. I was only attempting to swallow my reservations and float the strategy of working inside, instead of outside and against, the Marxist-Leninist "camp."

I use the verb "float" advisedly. My talk may have been a trial balloon, more for my own benefit than for anyone else's. I did not submit it anywhere for publication, although I did make mimeographed copies available in the meeting hall. I may have wanted to see what it felt like to "come out" as a publicly declared Marxist-Leninist, if only for a day; to try Marxism-Leninism on for size, as it were. In the end, nothing came of my balloon. I joined no Communist party. When the talk finally did appear in print, in a drastically revised form, as the Epilogue of *World Views: A Study in Comparative History* in 1977, all references to Leninism had vanished.

Since my records show that the entire manuscript of *World Views* went to my agent in August, 1975, and that none of it was ever rewritten, it is safe to conclude that my career as a "Marxist-Leninist" did not even survive the summer. But I had become a Marxist, if only a "high church" Marxist, for good.

ENTR'ACTE: WORLD VIEWS

What does it mean to undertake a study of "comparative world views" and what was the connection between my 1977 book *World Views* and the title of my talk to the World Future Society in June, 1975, "The Next World-View"?

The premise of the Holt series *Dimensions in Comparative History* was surely meritorious. Each author would choose a major theme in history and then explore it across lines of space and/or time. For example, feudalism in Europe and feudalism in Japan. Or feudalism in different parts of Europe at different points in time. My proposal was to compare four world views as they evolved in, and were refracted by, five national cultures: British, French, German, Russian, and American. "World view" was a term then long in use by intellectual historians of the old school, a rendering in English of the German *Weltanschauung*, to denote a comprehensive outlook on life, history, knowledge, and value. In a given "period" of history in a given civilization, one such *Weltanschauung* would tend to predominate, but then ultimately give way to another.

My hypothesis was that in the civilization encompassing Western and Eastern Europe and North America between the late 16th Century and the late 20th Century, four world views had reigned in succession: rationalism, romanticism, positivism, and irrationalism, each a dialectical retort to the dominant world view whose place it usurped, and also, in some ways, a reincarnation of the world view whose place its predecessor had usurped. Rationalism rejected Christian supernaturalism, but romanticism, in overthrowing rationalism, resurrected aspects of Christian supernaturalism. And so forth. In addition, each world view was articulated somewhat differently in different countries, as separate national cultures emerged and flowered in the various precincts of Western civilization. French positivism, let us say, was similar to but not identical with German positivism, or British, or Russian, or North American.

Anyone who knows the recent history of intellectual history has perhaps already winced or blushed. With poststructuralism on the brink of devouring the field in the late 1970s and early 1980s, it would have been difficult to imagine a set of premises less likely to appeal to younger scholars than those set forth in my *World Views*. Poststructuralism is anti-structuralist. It deplores the imposition of totalizing structures and narratives on the pages of history, just as it repudiates any possibility of authoritative readings of texts. *World Views* appeared to be guilty of all of the above. I do not actually plead guilty, because my "world views" and my "national cultures" were simply heuristic devices to help students sort through the multiplicities of Western thought, like the tongs that help us rearrange logs in a fireplace. They were not meant to be understood as something "real" or "essential." Nevertheless, my book had the scent of a simple-minded, mechanistic, and profoundly structuralist approach to the history of ideas. In 1957, it might have done rather well. By 1977 it was antediluvian.

However, the dialectical theory expounded in *World Views* did enable me to forecast the "next world view," which I proceeded to do in the Epilogue. As in the past, the next world view would negate the currently reigning world view. If the currently reigning world view was "irrationalism," its successor would be more or less its opposite. I defined irrationalism as the belief that the world was not (except superficially) knowable through science and reason and that human beings themselves were the vehicles of sub-rational or super-rational forces. From Freud to Joyce to Picasso, irrationalism had been the dominant world-view of the modernist avant-garde. By the 1970s it had exhausted its potentialities. Its time was more or less up. The next world view would resurrect some of the values of the reigning world view of the mid- to late 19th Century, "positivism." In various ways and to varying degrees it would be neo-positivist, even neo-rationalist.

And its guiding spirit would be the most powerful ideology of the 19th Century, Marxism. Not the Marxism of "any one Marxist thinker, including Lenin," not the Marxism "promulgated by the ruling party of any present-day Marxist state," not "a petrified Marxism that consists only of the authentic texts of Karl Marx." I anticipated, instead, the rise of "a living Marxism, capable of much the same diversity and responsiveness to new situations as Christianity or Confucianism or Hinduism in their respective golden ages, or as the empirical natural sciences today."

The phrase "living Marxism" was deliberately chosen to stress the great gulf fixed between 21st-century Marxism (together with the new world view it would inspire) and the tired party lines of the 1970s. In my 1975 address to the World Future Society, I had spoken of "socialist states," meaning the Soviet Union, China, Poland, and so forth. Now I spoke only of "so-called" and "would-be" socialist states, states whose parties had fallen far short of the aspirations of Marxism. Bad as the condition of workers might be in the capitalist camp, "The workers' plight was often as bad or worse in the would-be socialist countries, where the place of the capitalist was filled by party and government functionaries." In fact, present-day monopoly capitalism in the West and its "counterpart in the 'socialist' world are...dying systems of social relations...rigid and unimaginative in their old age...[destined to] collapse." A living Marxism would have little in common with the ideologies of these arthritic regimes. Nevertheless, I did continue to believe in the eventual triumph of Marxist values; and the last words of *World Views* were unambiguously vatic: "From its [Marxism's] humane science will grow the world view of the twenty-first century."

The accuracy of this forecast remains to be tested. But one obvious correction needs to be noted: "irrationalism" had far from run its course in the mid-1970s, as I imagined. Virtually all the avant-garde art and thought of the next 25 years, including the principal texts of poststructuralism, did little more than reiterate and underscore the chief premises of irrationalism. I appreciate that most cultural critics observe a wide gulf between "modernism" and "postmodernism." For my money, the second is only a tumor feeding on the substance of the first.

One footnote. Although *World Views* was published in 1977, it garnered almost no publicity, few reviews, and only a handful of course adoptions (notably by Frank Baumer at Yale). All but one of the other authors in the *Dimensions in Comparative History* series failed to deliver their manuscripts. Jonathan Cape declined to publish *World Views* in the U.K. on the grounds that the series was defunct. *World Views* soon lived up to the prediction in my letter to Hudson of June 12, 1977, that it was "destined for early oblivion."

CHAPTER 10
APOCALYPSES

The second project on which I embarked in 1972, a study of "secular eschatology," may seem at first blush like a capitulation to despair, the symptom of a mid-life crisis, the abandonment of hope. This was far from the case. I would be studying visions of the world's end in imaginative literature from the early 19th Century to the late 20th, but in imaginative literature the end of the world is seldom literally the end. One world capsizes, perhaps with horrendous loss of life, only to prepare the way for a new world.

Apocalyptic imagery had been rife in my juvenilia. I came by it honestly. The First and Second World Wars, the wombs of my childhood imagination, were apocalyptic. The Holocaust of the European Jews was apocalyptic. The Stalinist Gulag, the atrocities of Maoism, the wars in Korea, Algeria, and Vietnam were apocalyptic. H.G. Wells, in such novels as *The War in the Air* (1908), *The World Set Free* (1914), and *The Shape of Things To Come* (1933), had put forward the thesis that only after planetary disaster could we hope to find the resolve and the reason to build Cosmopolis. The bloody Apocalypse of St. John himself was only the prelude to the descent in glory of the New Jerusalem and the forgathering of the denizens of the City of God in everlasting peace and bliss.

Down to this very hour, my (thankfully fallible) instincts tell me that there will be no easy way out of the 21st Century. The achievement of a world civilization of freedom, prosperity, equality, tolerance, and shared values is unlikely without trauma and titanic suffering, if even then. If I am right, visions of the world's end in imaginative literature offer a metaphorical preview of the trauma and suffering and — let us hope — redemption scheduled for the new century.

The best argument against my reading of world history is that anyone born in 1932 is necessarily blighted by his early to mid-20th-

Century heritage, and therefore closes his mind to more benevolent outcomes. I like this argument and endorse it heartily. I wish I could also believe it.

By rights, the new book should have appeared at roughly the same time as *World Views*. By 1977 most of the research was done. A summer or two should have been enough for the writing. I reckoned without Tom Africa, the same Tom who gave me the phrase "high church Marxism." Exit Tom Africa. In January, 1977, he abruptly resigned as department chair. Someone would have to take his place. I had just begun a term as director of graduate studies in September, 1976, so I was mercifully out of the running. But Tom could be persuasive. He saw me as his heir apparent.

I did not have the good sense to stand firm. I declined to "run" for the job, but at a department caucus, when my name came up, I did not absolutely say no. That was all it took, in the culture of the department at the time. Over the next three and a half years I had ample opportunity to appreciate the wisdom of my reluctance and the folly of my surrender. I got on well with my colleagues, but they did not always get on well with each other. I found refereeing their squabbles an emotionally draining experience. It was also not amusing to spend most of every day of the work week at the office or in meetings. Like many academics, I was in the habit of reading, preparing lectures, grading papers, and writing books and articles at home. I would show up on campus only to teach or hold an occasional office hour. In the summer months I would not show up at all. Chairing the department made such a schedule unthinkable.

Another cost of the chairmanship was my decision to teach a full course load during five of the seven semesters I held the office. I could have made it much easier for myself, but I had my repertoire of courses and, being such a Good Boy, I did not want to give them up for years on end.

My reward came in the academic year 1980-81. I received one semester's leave on full pay to compensate my service as chair and a second semester on full pay as my long deferred sabbatical leave.

CHAPTER 10: APOCALYPSES

This was the year when I finally tucked into my book on secular eschatology with no distractions or other commitments, completed my research, and generated a final draft of what became *Terminal Visions: The Literature of Last Things*. In August, 1981, I submitted the full manuscript to Indiana University Press. In October it was accepted, with no quibbles. A clean, unexpectedly swift, blessedly eventless story, almost the opposite of my protracted misery with *World Views*.

We shall delve into *Terminal Visions* in the Entr'Acte. Meanwhile, what else was happening? To be candid, not much. I wrote articles and essays for books, and in the late 1970s had also become a frequent contributor to *Saturday Review*. I undertook to edit and contribute to a *Festschrift* for Frank Baumer, as he neared his 65th birthday. The theme of the volume, which I entitled *The Secular Mind*, was the secularization of Christian thought in modern Europe, to which he had devoted a graduate seminar for many years running at Yale. I recruited twelve of his doctoral students to help me out. Hudson and I cemented our renewed friendship by beginning many years of attending operas and concerts together in New York, mostly at Lincoln Center. The chief splendor of 1981 was the complete *Lulu* by Alban Berg, with Teresa Stratas in the starring role, at the Metropolitan Opera.

When *Terminal Visions* finally appeared, in late November, 1982, I was no longer by any criterion a young man. I was a man of fifty. And the millennium had yet to arrive!

ENTR'ACTE: TERMINAL VISIONS

"The virtue of Professor Wagar's book is that he has read so much rubbish, old and new." So wrote Anthony Burgess in his review of *Terminal Visions* in the *Times Literary Supplement* for March 18, 1983. The "rubbish" was science fiction, "the lowest order of literature," "very minor literature." In fact it was not fiction at all. "Fiction is not about what happens to the world but what happens to a select group of human souls, with crisis or catastrophe as the mere pretext for an exquisitely painful probing, as in [Henry] James, of personal agonies and elations." So Professor Wagar had saved us from wasting our time on "sub-literary" matters, and freed us to thread our way through the elegant labyrinths of *The Golden Bowl* and *The Turn of the Screw*.

All this from Anthony Burgess, the author of four science-fiction novels, including not only *A Clockwork Orange* (1962) but also *The End of the World News* (1983), published in the same year as his review of *Terminal Visions*. Had *The End of the World News* been written a year or two sooner, Professor Wagar would have undoubtedly added it to his rubbish heap, since it ends with a wandering planet crashing into the earth, the very scene depicted on the dust jacket of *Terminal Visions*. But despite his admiration of James and Joyce, Burgess was, at his best, a satirist. Anyone who took his numerous book reviews too seriously was something of a fool. (I was exactly that when I fired off an angry letter to *TLS*, a letter it had the good sense not to print.) Other reviews, including pieces by Gary K. Wolfe, Howard P. Segal, Gorman Beauchamp, David Ketterer, Michael Barkun, and Nell Painter, ranged from tepid to warmly supportive.

At any rate, Burgess was essentially correct in identifying most of my sources as "sub-literary." The point of the book was to canvass and analyze representations of the end of the world in fiction, no matter how lowly or how exalted. It was not a study of the science-fiction genre as such, but of necessity most of my titles were "genre" stories and novels, by the likes of Brian Aldiss, Arthur C. Clarke, James Blish, and Walter M. Miller, Jr. Still, I did find a place for writers outside the genre, if they had produced work with explicitly eschatological premises: for example, Aldous Huxley's *Ape and Essence* (1948), Samuel Beckett's *Endgame* (1958), Eugene Ionesco's *A Stroll in the Air* (1963), Doris Lessing's *The Memoirs of a Survivor* (1975), Russell Hoban's *Riddley Walker* (1980), and of course the grandmother of them all, Mary Shelley's *The Last Man* (1826). There were also extended passages on the eschatological fictions of writers who could be described as both inside and outside the genre,

CHAPTER 10: APOCALYPSES

such as H.G. Wells, Karel Capek, Kurt Vonnegut, Jr., and J.G. Ballard. My bibliography listed about 350 works in all.

Somewhat as in *The City of Man*, I supplied a road map and a historical context before actually turning in depth to the post-Shelleyan literature of last things. The road map was a narrative "history of doomsday," a fly-over of the terrain to be covered, from *The Last Man* to the latest work of Ballard. Historical context came in the form of four brief chapters skimming through apocalyptic visions in pagan antiquity both Asian and Western, in Biblical texts, and in medieval and early modern Western thought.

The remaining ten chapters of *Terminal Visions* examined modern eschatological literature from three angles. The first, a "stratigraphy of fear," analyzed the levels of anxiety discernible in eschatological fictions — primal fears of separation and exclusion inherited from childhood, the dread of nature buried deep in our racial unconscious, and terrors arising from the perception of our own immense human power to wreak havoc in the world. The second, "paradigms of doom," classified eschatological fictions according to their allegiances in "the war of the world views." Here I trotted out my typology of *Weltanschauungen* from *World Views*, with special reference to romanticism, positivism, and irrationalism, the so-called dominant paradigms of thought in the 19th and 20th Centuries. Some end-of-the-world stories, even recent ones, hewed to the romantic world view (including work by Ray Bradbury and Russell Hoban); others were robustly positivist (H.G. Wells, Isaac Asimov, Michael Moorcock); a third group espoused irrationalism, notably Ballard, Huxley, and Lessing. The third angle for comparison was "Aftermaths," inquiring whether a story adopted a cyclical view of history, with the endtime only ushering in a new but all-too-familiar first time (as in Miller's *A Canticle for Leibowitz* [1960]); or portrayed the end as really and finally the end, a cul-de-sac with no escape (as in Shelley's *The Last Man*); or projected a new and higher humanity rising from the ashes (as in Wells's *The Shape of Things To Come*), sometimes even the unified progressive world civilization devoutly wished-for in *The City of Man* and its sequels.

But my concluding thought was that despite all the manifest differences, relatively few stories and novels of "last things" were in any sense cynical, pessimistic, or nihilist. The great majority — five texts out of every six that I studied — imagined a renewal of life and civilization after the End. Even those that offered no hope were nevertheless regretful, nostalgic, life-affirming even in their despair, like the final bars of Mahler's Ninth Symphony, a symphony that to my mind is the most ennobling music ever written, and in itself almost a sufficient apologia for the reckless career of our species.

Reflecting on *Terminal Visions* in the rejoinder to a review of the book written by my colleague John Flint in a SUNY-wide house organ, I added that "every vision of the end of the world, I suspect, bears within it a wish for life. The whole point of a story of doom is not the doom itself. ... What matters is what happens *after* the end."

On balance, I must say that writing *Terminal Visions* was not a disheartening experience. It may not have been a romp all the way through, but most of my selected texts buzzed with vitality, and most of my authors were yea-sayers. Perhaps the only really gloomy stories in speculative literature are those like *Nineteen Eighty-Four* that present a world fixed and frozen in hopeless compliance with irresistible force. By contrast tales of the endtime are tales of life, and life's renewal.

CHAPTER 11
PATHS TO THE FUTURE

After my chairmanship, after my sabbatical leave, after the completion and publication of *Terminal Visions* and the *Festschrift* for Frank Baumer, after my fiftieth birthday, I was, for once, out of projects and out of sorts. *Terminal Visions*, a hit in most of its reviews (never mind Burgess and *TLS*), sold miserably. As a result the expected paperbound reissue did not happen. Our *Festschrift* received almost no reviews and also sold miserably. We had searched far and wide to find a publisher for it. Collections of essays by various hands, especially by obscure hands, as most of the contributors were in this case, are notoriously unwelcome on editors' desks. Even when I finally did capture a publisher, the other authors and I had to kick in a modest subvention to help defray the costs of production, half of which, under the terms of our contract, was later returned to us.

It was time, I decided, to reassess my personal and career agendas. By the early 1980s European intellectual history — the dauntless *dernier cri* in North America in the 1950s — had largely disintegrated. Some practitioners, such as Peter Gay and Bruce Mazlish (and my colleague Tom Africa), had veered into psychohistory. Others, such as Robert Darnton, were reconceiving the discipline as the social history of ideas or the study of *mentalités*. Dominick LaCapra was leading yet another group into the deep woods of poststructuralism. Most younger historians were skipping intellectual history altogether to study race, class, gender, sexuality, labor, popular culture, indigenous peoples, ritual behavior, anything but thought. The demand for textbooks and readers in the field had largely evaporated.

Although I had been half-way successful in using "conventional" intellectual historiography to explore ideas of the future, especially ideas of progress and an integrated world civilization, the returns were steadily diminishing. If speculation about the future of humankind was my real passion, why not join forces with the small but growing band of academic futurists and see what I could accomplish under their banner? Should this mean more or less abandoning history, so be it. I had paid my dues as a practicing research historian. I had paid them in full. My "History of the Future" class was ten times the size of my class in "Modern European Thought." Did that not tell me which way the wind was blowing?

Of course I had another alternative. Leave academe and campaign actively, in left-wing politics, or in journalism, or in the trade book market, or all three, for a socialist cosmopolis. For all my nominal success as an academic, the pull of my adolescent persona remained powerful. I felt a call, a *Beruf*, to contribute whatever I could to the integration and pacification of humankind. At the same time, my lack of physical courage, the lure of financial security held out by academe (for myself and for my family, always a concern for a paterfamilias), my love of the classroom ambience, and my life-long reclusiveness and shyness (I was shy, but not reserved; vain, but not by temperament authoritarian or controlling), did not add up to the right mix for a man in public life.

My compromise was to remain in academe, become a full-time futurist, and pursue my aims in futures studies, the classroom, and whatever books I could add to my *curriculum vitae*. It was not a brave choice, but it was the choice I made.

As of the autumn of 1982, no new books were on the horizon, but I did find additional ways to promote futures studies in the classroom. I began offering an upper-division research seminar on a regular basis entitled "Alternative Futures," and I developed a new lecture course on the future of war and peace under the title of "World War III." Admission to the seminar was restricted to alumni of "History of the Future." It gave each participant the opportunity to write a substantial research paper on a futures topic of her or his choice, with feedback from fellow students; we also spent an initial month or so discussing and analyzing the various methodologies available to futurists.

The new lecture course, "World War III," was taught follow-

CHAPTER 11: PATHS TO THE FUTURE

ing the same format that had proved successful in "History of the Future," with twice weekly lectures, a weekly film, required reading that included novels as well as non-fiction titles, and small discussion sections meeting near the end of every week, taught by graduate assistants. The first edition, offered in Spring 1983, drew 172 students; the second, in Spring 1984, drew 244. I taught it four more times in the 1980s, with comparable enrollments in each outing. With "History of the Future" doing as well or better, I received the SUNY Chancellor's Award for Excellence in Teaching in May, 1985, and the following year was promoted to the rank of Distinguished Teaching Professor, a rank held at that time by just two or three other members of the Binghamton faculty.

Since all my "standard" courses had attracted only average numbers of students through the years, and had not fared outstandingly well in student evaluations of teaching, I think it is appropriate to assign most of the credit for my awards not to my pedagogical prowess but rather to my choice of subject matter: the future. Somehow, it clicked. "World War III" was especially relevant in the mid-1980s because of the strong upsurge in fears of nuclear cataclysm felt throughout Ronald Reagan's first term as President and well into his second. The lull in the Cold War of the mid- to late 1970s had been replaced by the appearance, at least, of deepening danger, and I am sure this widespread perception also contributed to my high enrollments.

Another explanation for the throngs who filled my lecture halls is considerably less flattering to all concerned. Somehow or other, the student grapevine began vibrating with news that Wagar's futures courses were easy courses. He didn't take attendance at the films and lectures, his grades were high, and most of the work could be blown off. I never heard about this directly from undergraduate students, but some of my graduate assistants put me wise.

Having served as department chair in the 1970s and as undergraduate director and adviser from 1982 to 1984, I was well aware of the grading policies and course requirements of my colleagues and also the standards that prevailed throughout the various departments and schools of the University. Most of my grading in the large lecture courses was the responsibility of my teaching assistants, but I distributed detailed guidelines at every examination advising them of what to expect in each answer and where to draw the appropriate lines.

Also, midterm examinations were never returned to students until the whole teaching staff had met and discussed the results and made any necessary adjustments to ensure that our grade distribution for the course was roughly comparable to the average for all history courses and for the Division of Social Sciences at SUNY Binghamton. At the end of each semester, I reviewed the final grade of every student in meetings with each of my assistants. True, it was impracticable to take attendance in the lecture hall, with such large enrollments, but since questions on the lecture material regularly appeared on all examinations, it would have been impossible for a perennially absent student to receive a decent grade in the course unless she or he were deuced clever and well-informed or had a best friend who took great notes. Besides, attendance was recorded in the weekly discussion section meetings and effective participation in such meetings counted for 15% or more of the student's grade.

What to do? In the end, we decided that piling on more work or raising expectations or failing scores of students *pour encourager les autres* would not be a responsible course of action. My policy of making sure that grading was neither harsh nor slack in comparison with other courses given at the same level was defensible and perhaps even correct. We decided to put our faith in the same grapevine that had spread misleading rumors in the first place, and sooner or later enrollments would fall to more credible numbers. I also relayed this information to each new set of graduate assistants, partly in hopes of getting them to add their input to the vine.

What happened? In the 1990s, enrollments in both futures lecture courses did fall, whether because of my waning powers or because the vibrations on the vine were now different, or both, who knows? I am not aware of waning powers, but, whatever the reason, I was satisfied to have enrollments back again at the levels of the early

CHAPTER 11: PATHS TO THE FUTURE

1980s. It was also good for the department not to need a dozen or more graduate teaching assistants annually deployed in the service of a single faculty member. Meanwhile, I had the sense that my students were, on the average, more serious and responsive than was once the case, when hundreds may have signed in not because they harbored any real interest in the subject matter but because they hoped to find safety in numbers and "blow off" the course.

Not that either futures course remained unchanged all through the 1990s. "World War Three," in particular, needed major reconstruction after the end of the Cold War, including two changes in title, as we shall see.

The first edition of "World War III" in Spring 1983 was grounded in the premise, which I had maintained ever since 1945, that in a world of contending sovereign states, some armed with weapons of mass annihilation, the odds favored Armageddon, sooner or later; and therefore the most urgent business before humankind was to prevent it. Today, despite the end of the Cold War (or was it only Cold War I?), despite the popular cant that national states have lost their fangs and venom because of the soaring power of multinational corporations, this is still the most urgent single item of business on the human agenda. There cannot be a unified world, or a democratic world, or a socialist world, or a free world, if there is no world at all.

But in Spring 1983, with the Cold War heating up to temperatures not seen since the early 1960s, it was not difficult to persuade students to take the threat of a third world war seriously. My 1983 syllabus was divided into three parts with a prefatory lecture on the first day entitled "Doomsday Plus One: Is There Life After Death?" For "Doomsday Plus One," I imagined the effects of a thermonuclear World War III on Broome County, Binghamton's upstate New York county. Assuming that a single hydrogen bomb detonated above downtown Binghamton, what impact would it have on each of us in this lecture hall, and on the community in which we lived? After every five or ten minutes of detailed grisliness, I would cut away to recite (mercifully, not sing!) some of the popular song lyrics inspired by fears of World War III, as well as a few of my own poems on the subject. One undergraduate came up to me after class to report that this was the "most tremendous lecture" he had ever heard. It left me somewhat shaken as well. It was also a difficult act to follow. But I did what I could.

Part One of the rest of the course was entitled "The History and Causes of War," which involved an overview of "Six Thousand Years of Bloody Hell," a scrappy lecture on the psychology and social science of warfare, three lectures on the world wars of the modern era (which I traced back to the later world-systemic wars of Louis XIV), and a lecture on anticipations of total war in modern speculative literature, beginning with specimens from the 1890s that I had studied for *Terminal Visions*.

In Part Two, we examined "Third World Wars," the expectations of a nuclear world war from 1945 to 1983, with special attention to the strategic thinking of the superpowers, the chances of accidental nuclear wars, the proliferation of nuclear weaponry beyond the United States and the Soviet Union ("The Superbabies"), the likeliest course and aftermaths of a nuclear world war, and a concluding lecture ("Star Wars") on the future of weaponry. Since my syllabus went to press in January, 1983, and President Reagan did not make his notorious speech on the Strategic Defense Initiative until March 23, 1983, and Senator Ted Kennedy's dubbing of SDI as "Star Wars" came even later, this would have to be one of the rare cases where I actually foresaw something, in very rough outlines, before it happened.

But the heart of the course, at least from my perspective (probably not from my students'), was the nine lectures of Part Three, "The Alternatives," where we considered ways of avoiding the catastrophe inspected earlier in the term. I opened this segment of the course with an analysis of the most frequently cited strategy for war prevention, "the diplomacy of disarmament," concluding that it was a futile and empty strategy, which could work only when the nations pitted against one another did not really, for reasons of their own, choose to clash. Four lectures followed on the "barriers to

CHAPTER 11: PATHS TO THE FUTURE

peace" installed in the modern world-system, from social and economic injustice to the armed sovereignty of nations to the politics of "scarcity," the competition for vital natural resources. A marker of the growing influence on my thinking of Immanuel Wallerstein's world-system theory can be surmised from the tell-tale title of one of these lectures: "Barriers to Peace: The Capitalist World-Economy." My respect for Wallerstein's insistence on the hyphen between "world" and "economy" gave me away.

A second false answer was suggested by George Orwell's *Nineteen Eighty-Four*, then on the verge of becoming a best-seller again as the fateful year itself approached: superpower rivalry deliberately short of nuclear or total war as a device for controlling and enserfing domestic populations. This was perhaps my shrewdest insight, and Orwell's, too, except that I did not appreciate how close it may have hewed to the pragmatic reality of the Cold War. At the time I took the Cold War more or less at face value, as a contest that could turn solar-hot at any moment. The risk surely existed. But on reflection, perhaps Orwell got it right. He may have got it right even if ironically his own book had turned into a major force for perpetuating the perilous stand-off, by persuading Western tax-payers to believe that "dead" was literally preferable to "red." (The culminating irony is that I think Orwell meant us to prefer deadness to redness: his imaginary atomic war of the 1950s is what led to the creation of "Oceania" and "Eurasia" in the first place.)

Finally, we came to the "correct" answer: a new world order based on universally accepted common values, mediated by a world government established, if necessary, by armed revolution. The last three lectures in the 1983 course harked back to the propagandistic character of the final lectures of earlier editions of "History of the Future." In due time I realized the pedagogical error of my ways and allowed for consideration of various other seriously argued paths to world peace, but it was a heartfelt error. I remained a crusader for the City of Man.

As the 1980s wore on, I was invited to pursue my ideas further in print. I contributed substantial essays to various journals (not least *The Futurist* and *Futures Research Quarterly*) and university press volumes on the futurism of H.G. Wells, George Orwell, Arnold J. Toynbee, and Edward Bellamy. An A.P. "newsfeature" on my "World War III" course and *Terminal Visions* appeared in most leading U.S. newspapers in 1983. There were quite a few interviews on radio, including the B.B.C. World Service after I spoke at an H.G. Wells Society conference in London in 1986. Throughout the 1980s I was also a regular paper-giver at annual meetings of the recently formed Society for Utopian Studies and at general assemblies of the World Future Society. All of this may have looked impressive on my *curriculum vitae*, but I doubt that any of it generated more than the gentlest ripple anywhere.

The most intellectually significant essay I published between 1983 and 1988 was "The Next Three Futures," a piece for *World Future Society Bulletin* that appeared late in 1984 and was reprinted in the symposium volume *What I Have Learned: Thinking About the Future Then and Now* (1987), edited for Greenwood Press by my futurist colleagues Michael Marien and Lane Jennings. In this essay I finally historicized my mature thinking about the human past and future. The Entr'acte below explains why and how.

But first, a more personal note. In the spring of 1979 I had taken up jogging through the neighborhood every other day to help control my weight and maintain cardiovascular health. By the beginning of 1984, I felt more fit than perhaps at any time in my life. I accepted invitations to deliver two lectures in February at far-flung campuses in Nebraska and Iowa on the hottest topic of the hour, George Orwell's *Nineteen Eighty-Four*. My cholesterol reading of 255 (last checked in 1979) was fine, and I was a healthy man of only 51.

In the last week of January, 1984, the weather in southern New York State turned quite cold. On Friday, January 27, I took several extra minutes to complete my regular course, and also experienced unusual shortness of breath and a little soreness in the chest. Sunday's icy jog took a minute less than Friday's, but was accompanied by the same odd shortness of breath. It was as if I literally could not run faster than I did. Ordinarily, I would have enough wind left at any stage of a jog for a quick sprint of a block or two, but not on that dreary weekend in late January.

By Tuesday, I noticed a raw feeling deep in my chest when I walked to my office from the university parking lot, one-third of a mile away. Concerned that I might be coming down with a lung infection, I skipped my jog that day. By Wednesday, even a short walk or climbing a flight of stairs was mildly painful. After each spate of exertion, I had to sit down and wait a few minutes. On Thursday, I attended a memorial service in the campus Recital Hall for a colleague who had dropped dead of a heart attack on New Year's Eve. The organist played something horribly grating and unpleasant by J.S. Bach, a favorite composer of my late lamented colleague but to me the most noisome of mysteries. (In so saying, I know that I have just alienated almost every lover of classical music.)

Friday, I saw my internist. He gave me an EKG, which proved normal, and arranged for me to take a stress test at a local hospital on Monday, February 6. He strongly suspected something cardiovascular, and advised me to rest over the weekend. He also gave me a prescription for nitroglycerin tablets, which he felt I might need in the interim. Every time I felt pain in my chest, I was to dissolve a tablet under my tongue. If it relieved the pain, a diagnosis of heart disease was all the more probable. In full denial, I still thought I might have contracted some weird sort of "walking" pneumonia.

So I told Dorothy nothing about the doctor's warning, to forestall any squabble over my long-laid plans for the next day. Saturday, February 4, was a major date on my calendar. It could not be spoiled. Doctor or no doctor, heart or no heart, the last thing I intended to do was miss my engagement to hear Mahler's *Das Lied von der Erde* at Lincoln Center on Saturday evening with Hudson. Saturday morning I boarded a bus in downtown Binghamton and arrived in Manhattan four hours later without incident, joining forces with Hudson and his woman friend (he was by now long divorced) at the Port Authority bus terminal. We dined as usual at the Café des Artistes on West 67th Street (I had the duck) and ambled over to Lincoln

Center to hear the Mahler. I felt a recurrence of the chest pain and slipped a nitroglycerin tablet under my tongue. When it had no effect, I became all the more convinced that I was not a victim of heart disease.

I took the last bus out of New York that night, arriving back in Binghamton around five o'clock in the morning. As I remember, I dozed quite a bit on the bus. I felt no pain. In the cold early morning air, I decided to walk briskly to my car in the parking ramp, to prove to myself that the problem was now history. It was not. The pain in my chest, steady and searing, soon slowed my pace. I drove home, with a nitroglycerin tablet under my tongue, knowing that I was in trouble. When I arrived, Dorothy was up and about. I finally told her everything. Then I went to bed and probably slept till noon.

I spent most of the afternoon finishing my Nebraska lecture, which I was scheduled to deliver later that same week. During the day I noticed that even the simple act of going upstairs caused considerable pain. On the last few trips, I crawled on my hands and knees, one step at a time. Dorothy became alarmed and insisted that we call her brother John, a prominent cardiologist in Las Vegas, Nevada. I refused. I would take the treadmill test already scheduled for Monday morning and the local medical establishment would know what to do. But late in the afternoon, I relented and we called Dr. John Bowers. Upon hearing my symptoms, he advised me to fly to Las Vegas on the first available plane out of Binghamton. His facilities were first-rate and they would all be at my disposal. I agreed to go. I then called my internist, to let him know of my change of plans. He recommended that I stay put. If my condition was really deteriorating, and it was cardiovascular, the stress of a cross-continental flight could finish me off.

But the healthy man of 51 who was not afraid to bus to Manhattan on a Saturday was also not afraid to fly to Las Vegas on a Monday. Once John convinced me that the problem was serious and that he could help, I did not look back. I telephoned the departmental administrative assistant to cancel my classes for the next couple of days (I was teaching two undergraduate lecture courses and a semi-

CHAPTER 11: PATHS TO THE FUTURE

nar that semester).

Monday morning was the Day of Judgment. I arose very early and packed, being careful to include my lectures for Nebraska and Iowa, in case I could still make the trips at the week's end. In the dawn's glare, always an eerie sight for this incurable night owl on the few occasions in his adult life when he has been constrained to witness it, I was frightened at last. Dorothy gave me a tranquilizer to steady my nerves. I now realize that his Excellency, *Herr Tod*, could have been waiting for me at O'Hare Airport in Chicago, where I needed to change planes (and airlines) in mid-day. I walked the equivalent of at least five blocks, lugging a suitcase, with only minutes to spare to make my connecting flight. The chest pains on this occasion were mercifully mild.

Once in Las Vegas, I set aside my apprehensions. What would be, would be. Catheterization revealed almost total blockage of all coronary arteries. Emergency open-heart surgery was essential. "There's no other option?" I asked. "No," said John, with a dry chuckle. "The only question is whether we should operate tonight or tomorrow morning." The senior cardiovascular surgeon on John's team performed the surgery Tuesday morning, seven grafts to four vessels. It was quite successful and I recuperated swiftly, returning to my seminar room at the end of February and to my lecture halls in mid-March.

Writing years later, I jotted down a few lines on my attitude to death, which I now quote.

> A secular humanist should always look *Herr Tod* in the face and stare him down as long as possible. Death is natural, in its time, but it is never good. In fact death is the most sadistic joke the cosmos plays on sentient beings. The cosmos goes to great lengths to produce such beings, aware of themselves, aware of their mortality, able to imagine and plan their futures, and then, after a few short seasons, it snuffs their little flame as casually as a cat

breaks the neck of a field mouse. The mere presence of death in this cosmos is proof positive of the non-existence of a benevolent Creator. Once there are sentient beings who can understand what it means to die, mortality (essential to the rhythms of brute nature) becomes a punishment of unimaginable cruelty. Until our biologists have learned how to eliminate it, we must continue to defy *Herr Tod*. Let us do so with dignity and serene contempt.

ENTR'ACTE: MARX AND ENGELS REDUX

For someone obsessed with the history and the future of life, and the myriad grand theories of both, my failure for decades to commit to any one reading of the metaphysics of human time is almost bizarre. We have seen approaches to such a thing in earlier chapters: the evolutionism of my juvenilia, the Toynbeean cyclicalism of *The City of Man*, the dialectics of *World Views*, the quasi-Marxist faith in the renewal of life after its holocaust in *Terminal Visions*. My end in sight was consistent: an integrated world civilization. But did any logic of process connect the end in sight with the vicissitudes of the past?

Given my ultimate and implacable skepticism about cognition, any such logic could not be represented as empirically verifiable, much less "true." It could not be nailed to the wall or emblazoned on a banner. Still, was there not some way to bring past and future together in a narrative that had the feel and texture of plausibility? Why, in brief, was the emergent City of Man preferable to a thousand proud tribes each clinging to its own squalid myth?

My article for *World Future Society Bulletin* was the result of a commission from Michael Marien to explore what I had learned in my years as a futurist. All the authors in the series were asked the same question. What have you learned? How has your exploration of the future changed you or altered your world view? I began my response with a scathing (and probably unfair) review of *The City of Man*. What I had done in this unfortunate book, I said, was "to elevate the reigning doctrines of mid-century American liberalism into a global ideology." I had fallen for the consensus theory of American history, the lie that since the days of Andrew Jackson various liberal statesmen culminating in Franklin Roosevelt, Jack Kennedy, and Lyndon Johnson "had abolished the old desperate conflict between workers and owners." It took the horror of Vietnam to lift the scales from my eyes. "By 1970 it finally became clear to me," so my memoir continued, "that the Vietnam war was no more than a particularly vicious example of a system of world domination in place and functioning according to its own logic." I had become a New Leftist, although not yet a Marxist. The first fruit of my leftward turn was *Building the City of Man*.

Building the City of Man fared better in these recollections than its predecessor, but I noted that it "fell short in at least one crucial respect. It was a utopia: a still-life vision of future time rather than a moving picture." What it lacked was "a theory of historical change that advanced beyond the crude analogical thinking of...*The City of Man*" and this I finally found, in the mid-1970s, in the writings of Marx and Engels, with further refinements in the late 1970s when I encountered the work of Immanuel Wallerstein, my Binghamton colleague and the internationally celebrated founder of world-system theory. History was not just one damned thing after another, the meaningless rise and fall of empires and civilizations. It had a logic of its own, originating in changing social relations of production — in other words, the ancient and still continuing struggle between exploiting and exploited classes.

Applying Marxist theory to the study of the future, I now anticipated three futures for humankind, short-term, middle-term, and long-term. The short-term future was the culminating triumph of global capital, with all workers everywhere commodified, all markets glutted, all serious competition replaced by monopolies and cartels, all internal contradictions fully mature. The middle-term future was the revolutionary overthrow of this sclerotic late capitalism and the building of a world workers' republic. The long-term future was the withering away of the republic and its replacement by a pacific system of self-governing communities each pursuing its own cultural destiny. "Having unified and saved the world, socialism will some day become redundant, and the scaffolding it has erected can be allowed to crumble." But this, too, had been foreseen by Marx and Engels. Socialism was not an end in itself, but an instrumentality for liberating humanity from exploitation so that real history could begin.

I then connected this Marxian overview of world history with an idea I had installed as a regular feature of "History of the Future" since its Fall 1981 edition. In an annual prefatory lecture, "Three Paths to the Future," I proposed a typology of the world views of futurists. The first and most numerous group were the "technoliberals," who believed in salvation through the resourceful application of technology within the reigning system of liberal capitalist democracy. The second were the "radicals," who insisted that capitalism was intrinsically flawed and destined by its own contradictions to give way to public ownership of the means of production. The third were the "counterculturalists," who sought the replacement of capitalism and socialism alike by the local initiative of self-reliant communities.

In the light of my interpretation of Marx and Engels, the three paths to the future studied in "History of the Future" — technoliberal, radical, countercultural — were not so much alternatives as successive segments of one continuous path. The next future (an extension of the last few hundred years) would be technoliberal. The next future after that would be radical, and the third countercultural. What started as a typology had now become a full-fledged neo-Marxist theory of world history. But with one significant difference: in Engels, in the *Anti-Dühring*, the third future was a classless, stateless society liberated from all the laws of nature and history that had hitherto dominated humankind; in my essay, freedom from such laws meant that whatever social relations post-historic men and women chose for themselves would be possible, including the fashioning of experimental cultures that might transcend even classlessness or statelessness. Freedom was freedom.

CHAPTER 11: PATHS TO THE FUTURE

Looking back at my 1984 article in *World Future Society Bulletin*, I regret the hatchet job I did on *The City of Man*, which had not at any point argued a consensus theory of history or parroted the Democratic party platform of the Kennedy era. But "The Next Three Futures" did represent a theoretical advance over my thinking in the *City of Man* books. It pointed out quite clearly the direction in which I would be travelling in the years ahead. Indeed, by 1984 all the basic ingredients of my present-day thought were in place, waiting for me to do something useful with them. If I could.

CHAPTER 12
THE HUMAN COMEDY

The decision reached in 1983 to shift my focus from intellectual history to futures studies was accompanied by another decision. I had long ago deferred or abandoned — I am not sure which — my ambition in late adolescence to become a novelist and poet, but in the mid-1970s I rekindled my interest in science fiction, thanks in part to the research for *Terminal Visions* (or was it the other way round?), in part to my growing fascination with the work of the British writer J.G. Ballard, in part to a friendship I had struck up with two eminent writers of science fiction who then lived near Binghamton, George Zebrowski and his partner Pamela Sargent. With their encouragement, I began to try my hand at fiction again.

Science fiction is, for the most part, future fiction, speculation about times to come. The best of it is significantly more imaginative and prophetic than the work of almost any self-styled futurist. This may be true because writers of convincing science fiction create whole future worlds, sometimes whole universes, replete with institutions, cultures, technologies, and ways of life more or less different from our own. Many futurists fail to do this: they surf trends in specific categories of human endeavor, ignoring most of the numerous other categories likely to collide with the trends they surf. The real world is infinitely more complex than any graph, cross-impact matrix, or computer model can show it to be, including as it does all of nature and all of humanity. Writers of science fiction, like writers of world history, cannot possibly take in all of this complexity and interdependence. But they come closer than the typical futurist or social scientist to seeing the "sorry scheme of things entire."

The attempts at writing fantasy and science fiction that I had made in my teens and twenties were generally pathetic. One story crafted in my college days about a "risen devil" (antithesis of "fallen angel") was promising. I actually submitted it to the leading pulp magazine of the fantasy genre at that time, *Weird Tales*, which rejected it almost over night. Now, in my fifties, could I do better? Strangely, I could. Throughout the 1980s I wrote and published eight stories in science-fiction magazines and anthologies. The first to see print, "Heart's Desire," was published in *Asimov's* in 1984. "The President's Worm," published in *The Magazine of Fantasy & Science Fiction* in 1986, told of an early 21st-century appearance of aliens in the Kremlin and the White House, aliens who used reverse psychology to bring about a mutually satisfactory ending to the Cold War. "Madonna of the Red Sun," written in 1983 before any of the others, finally found a home in George Zebrowski's anthology *Synergy I*, brought out by Harcourt Brace Jovanovich in 1987. It foresaw a far-future earth in which human beings had evolved into "neurosomes," crackling bundles of nerve tissue. Most had left the planet to find a new home as the Sun approached the time of its nova. The few crippled youngsters left behind were equipped by their elderly caretaker with armor enabling them to continue their lives and extend the thread of human evolution in the fires of the swollen Sun.

But the most enterprising fictions from the 1980s were my "No" stories, three novellas totalling just over 50,000 words, published in 1986, 1987, and 1988, respectively, in *The Magazine of Fantasy & Science Fiction*. These stories told an oblique, confusing, postmodernist tale of a future earth in which some inexplicable "effect" had blighted the brains of all higher animals, leading to mass hysteria and self-destructive aberrant behavior on the part of everyone except Ira Walker, dean of an American college, and a few of his colleagues. Or were they exceptions after all? Walker's friend Brian Locke appeared at intervals throughout the stories to serve up solid and rational "explanations" of the effect, but the more theories he proposed, the lower his credibility sank. Walker, a knockoff of Don Quixote (and maybe W. Warren Wagar), campaigned to save humanity in his van, the "Culturemobile." In the end he became the prisoner of a village of fundamentalist lunatics and died of a heart attack in a cage the lunatics had mounted on a tall pole in the village square. I call these stories my "No" stories after their titles: "The Day of No

Judgment," "The Night of No Joy," and "The Time of No Troubles."

The "No" stories, later assembled and revised for publication as a novel under the title *The Seasons of No*, fulfilled a number of purposes. The most personal is the most obscure, but now it can be told. In 1944, at the age of twelve, I had written a short novel, "Nerves," revised in 1945 as "The Nerves of Brahman." Although drafted in the mawkish style of my earliest juvenilia, it did depict a world of madmen with a single sane hero, who died much as Ira Walker died in "The Time of No Troubles."

There were other purposes. The figure of Brian Locke represented all the great and wise philosophers of all times (except Nietzsche, who caught the lot of them with their britches down). Philosophers notwithstanding, the universe was not a figment of human rationality but an imponderable awesomeness forever eluding our grasp. If the world was slated to end, none of us would ever know why, not really know, not really why. Two cheers for postmodernism. But I had a further purpose. If rationality repeatedly failed, irrationality — the world of the "effect" — failed absolutely and calamitously. Its reign guaranteed the defeat of humankind. Walker was a poor hero, a flawed and foolish man, obsessed throughout the novel by his passion for a student who had seduced him near its beginning, only to move on to another man. Yet, perhaps like the forlorn Bérenger in the absurdist plays of Eugène Ionesco, Walker was proof of a flicker of hope, a grain of resistance, in all of us.

The "No" stories harbored no utopias, no visions of world integration, no ideas of progress. I hold fast to them just the same.

But the chief endeavor of the late 1980s, for which I earned a sabbatical leave in Spring 1987, was my project of writing a narrative history of the next two centuries, which became *A Short History of the Future*. I cannot remember the epiphanic moment, if any there was. Somewhen in 1986, I decided to abandon the modalities of nonfiction, scholarly or otherwise, for an imaginative binge that would recite the events of the future in graphic detail and produce the endless ending I devoutly wished for my ingenious, if exasperating, species. But it could not be a novel. It had to be a history, a fictitious future history in the manner of *The Shape of Things To Come* (1933) by H.G. Wells and *The Next Millennium: A History of the World, A.D. 2000-3000* (1985) by the British science-fiction writers Brian Stableford and David Langford. I had used *The Next Millennium* as a required text in my Fall 1986 edition of "History of the Future," and was much impressed by its speculative sweep. It soon went out of print in the United States, but the fact that it could be published at all, and by the distinguished house of Alfred A. Knopf no less, gave me the courage to try my luck. Of course Wells's book exerted the greater influence on me, so much so that *A Short History of the Future* is in many ways simply *The Shape of Things To Come* updated.

Writing *A Short History of the Future* was a joy from start to finish. A swift joy as well. I began work in early February, 1987, and, in a letter to my mother dated July 27, reported that I had just finished the final draft, all 120,000 words. By now I was using a computer rather than a typewriter, which no doubt helped to speed the process. I could also lean on thousands of pages of lecture and research notes already compiled for my annual revisions of the "History of the Future" and "World War III" courses. But even without the computer and the notes, writing *A Short History of the Future* would have been a swift joy. The book fairly flew together.

Selling *A Short History of the Future* was another matter entirely. Indeed. Even before I had finished my manuscript I sent a prospectus to the editors at Indiana University Press, the owner by previous contracts of an option on my next two books. Indiana showed no interest at all. Then I tried Greenwood Press, which had just published *What I Have Learned*, the symposium edited by Marien and Jennings in which "The Next Three Futures" appeared. A prompt and courteous reply arrived, regretting that works of "narrative fiction" were not suitable for Greenwood. At this point I decided to forget about scholarly presses and find myself a literary agent who could peddle the manuscript in New York or Boston. The same agent who had helped with *World Views* agreed to take me on after reading a sample chapter or two.

CHAPTER 12: THE HUMAN COMEDY

My agent tried three publishers in New York: Simon & Schuster, William Morrow, and The Free Press. The first two might have worked, but The Free Press, where I had some editorial connections from earlier days, was an impossible choice. I did not realize, and perhaps my agent did not realize, that trying to tempt The Free Press in 1988 with a quasi-Marxian manuscript was much like trying to tempt a fighting bull with a red cape — or flag. Its reaction was so negative that my agent returned my manuscript and virtually declared it unpublishable in its present form. All three publishers, he wrote to me on February 8, 1988, had pointed to the same intractable problem: the mis-marriage of fiction and non-fiction. A book had to be one or the other. It could not be both. Alas! Where are the postmodernist critics when you need them most?

In March I tried another ploy, writing to the prince of science fiction, Isaac Asimov, on the advice of George Zebrowski. Would Asimov be willing to read my manuscript and recommend it to a likely publisher, perhaps with a preface of his own? Isaac had reviewed my *H.G. Wells: Journalism and Prophecy*, I had published my first science-fiction story in the magazine that bore his name, and we had met twice. He replied immediately, in a typically generous and Asimovian letter. No, he could not. The value of his endorsements was vastly overrated. Nevertheless, he would let me use his name if I submitted the manuscript to Prometheus Books in Buffalo, the publisher of a wide variety of books defending secular humanism and "freethought" in general.

Looking over the Prometheus list, I had my doubts. Secular, yes. Humanist, yes. Quasi-Marxian? No.

The autumn of 1987 and the ensuing winter were troubled times. Dorothy and I were traversing a difficult patch in our marriage. My Aunt Winnifred, with whom I had grown up in Lancaster, almost my second mother, died of cancer at the age of 93. Repeated efforts to market the novel based on my "No" stories had earned only resounding "No's" from many publishers — and would continue to do so. The gamble with *A Short History of the Future* had apparently failed. I seriously considered publishing the book myself, taking advantage of the expertise of Hudson Cattell's newly successful firm, L&H Photojournalism, which had begun to publish a trade journal, as well as books, devoted to the wines and wine industry of the Eastern U.S. We might call the imprint "Red Rose Books," after the official flower of Lancaster County.

In mid-March my friend Mary Warner Marien suggested that I reconsider academic publishers. She sagely noted that in the scramble to remain solvent in an era of tightening university budgets, some university presses were venturing into previously unmeasured waters. Perhaps Indiana University Press, which had supported me nobly through three earlier books, was not intrepid enough in this instance, but why not try a few others?

On March 18, 1988, I telephoned the University of Chicago Press. I had once reviewed a book manuscript for its history of science editor and asked to speak with her. She had meanwhile left the Press, but if I liked, I could be connected to its history and social science editor, Douglas C. Mitchell. I liked. Doug picked up the phone. I stammered my way through an overview of *A Short History of the Future*. Might he be interested? Yes, yes, he would be! The longer we spoke, the more I felt a certain serendipitous rapport. I agreed to send him a few chapters, knowing in my bones that it was a futile gesture. University presses publish scholarly monographs larded with enormous numbers of footnotes. For all our rapport, once he saw the undocumentable mess I had begotten, he would politely decline to read any more.

Happily, I was wrong. Doug's enthusiasm and support never flagged. After many vicissitudes, and a timely intervention by George Zebrowski when one of the first outside readers recoiled from the manuscript in horror, the University of Chicago Press risked its impeccable reputation by publishing *A Short History of the Future* in October, 1989.

The reviews, by and large, were not embarrassing, and half could even be described as flattering. I cannot recall a single instance when Chicago Press itself came under fire, although one or two reviewers expressed mild surprise to find any university press in the futures business. Among reviewers on the certified Left, I scored two to one. H. Bruce Franklin, reviewing the book for *The Washington Post*, found the first of its three parts "an incisive, dynamic vision of where we may indeed be heading." He was less enamored of the second and third parts, but recognized their roots in the utopographic tradition. David Schwartzman, in an article for *EcoSocialist Review*, found my idea of a transnational World Party invigorating. But Ted Vehse told readers of *In These Times* that the second and third parts of the book were disappointing, not a "progressive blueprint for the future," not true to Marxism. The third part was even a descent "into bourgeois utopianism." Still, "this book is worth reading. ... As a whole, the story works." How it could "work" if it was addled by bourgeois utopianizing, he did not quite explain.

The communities of the three academic sub-fields in which I fellow travelled — science-fiction studies, utopian studies, and futures studies — gave me mixed reviews. *The Futurist* called *A Short History of the Future* "highly imaginative." *Future Survey* found the book "fun to read, with imaginative details scattered throughout." The first part was "the most compelling single scenario presently available of how things might turn out." In the British journal *Futures*, a leading historian of futurism, I.F. Clarke, paid me the ultimate compliment: *A Short History of the Future* "reads better than the continuous lecturing in Wells's *Anticipations*" and "is certainly far more varied and persuasive than the tired writing in Wells's *Shape of Things to Come*." This was roughly tantamount to saying that St. Paul was more inspired than Jesus (and I am not even Wells's St. Paul), but it was balm to my battered ears. He concluded: "The result is the most readable and most interesting of the recent accounts of the next millennium."

One of the leading journals in science-fiction studies saw *A Short History of the Future* quite differently. In the British journal *Foundation: The Review of Science Fiction*, Robert Irwin questioned my Eurocentricity and my blindness to the cracks and crevices in the Soviet bloc. He also bewailed my indifference to the thrusting power of Islamic fundamentalism, which "is not going to wither quietly away." The chief reason to buy my book was to enjoy its gain "in charm and quaintness as, year by year, its account of the future increasingly fails to match the reality." Like an out-of-date railway timetable, my book "vividly evokes destinations we shall never arrive at." Just so! At least in the short term, Irwin was unerringly accurate. But one of the chief gurus of the Society for Utopian Studies, Lyman Tower Sargent, reported in *Utopian Studies* that *A Short History of the Future was* "a major contribution to utopian literature."

We garnered two reviews in major disciplinary journals, which reached opposite conclusions. Robert N. Wilson of the University of North Carolina, in *Contemporary Sociology*, found my book hazardous, audacious, but also "eminently plausible, and at once cautionary and inspiring." Yet in *The American Historical Review* Paul Merkley of Carleton University took sarcastic delight in the failings of my near-term forecasts. "The U.S.S.R. goes from strength to strength. If you can follow that far, you can follow all the way." Cheap shot perhaps, but, as we shall see, it hit the target.

A Short History of the Future also attracted the attention of several major daily newspapers in addition to *The Washington Post*. The *Chicago Tribune* observed that my book "reads with ease, raises provocative possibilities and presents challenging occasions for thought and argument." *The Philadelphia Inquirer* called it "the acme of naive utopianism." In my favorite review of all time, the futurist Jib Fowles in *The Houston Post* bashed it on all fronts. *A Short History of the Future* was a "drab and monotonic" rehash of *Building the City of Man* (which, to his credit, at least he had read!) Unfortunately, fiction was not Wagar's forte. Despite Fowles's "antipathy to Wagar's point of view," he would have enjoyed "a good read," but all he got for his trouble was a "yawn." The book was "essentially sophomoric," not suitable for "adult readers." No damning with faint praise here!

Publishers Weekly was more generous. Wager [sic] included "almost every conceivable scenario" of the future. "His bold chronicle is thought-provoking, disturbing and immensely worthwhile." And so it goes. Reviewers, let us be thankful, are not choristers. They are seldom on the same page of the hymnbook, and almost never in the same key.

Meanwhile, in June, 1988, I received news from London that I had been elected a Vice President of the H.G. Wells Society, an honor shared, among others with Sir Arthur C. Clarke, Brian Aldiss, and Michael Foot. I was the first American ever chosen. I can remember daydreaming in college about giving an address to such a Wells society and becoming one of its dignitaries. Since in the 1950s no Wells society existed and I had not yet published a word, it was more a question of pipedreaming. Occasionally, things do work out!

Also in June, another Vice President of the H.G. Wells Society, Professor Yuli Kagarlitsky, the only Russian in the group of nine, came to Vestal as our houseguest and gave a paper at SUNY Binghamton. Yuli and I had corresponded for years. This was our first and, as it happened, only chance to socialize. In 1986, at the same H.G. Wells Society conference where I gave one of the keynote addresses, the Soviet government had refused Yuli a visa to travel to London on account of the alleged political misdeeds of his son Boris. Now, in the era of full-fledged *glasnost*, he was once again free to set foot outside the Soviet sphere. During his visit we took in a concert at Carnegie Hall, in the company of Hudson, and the three of us had dinner at that resplendent *haut bourgeois* Manhattan eatery, the Café des Artistes.

In the Fall 1988 semester, "History of the Future" once more enrolled well over 400 students and needed a staff of nine graduate teaching assistants for the third year in a row. I began to hear rumbles of discontent from colleagues over the deflection of so many able graduate students from service in undergraduate courses more relevant to their research, mixed with outright annoyance that colleagues were having to make do without teaching assistants themselves in some of the smaller courses. It was no help that even in the spring semesters, "World War III" enrolled up to 250 students and siphoned off five teaching assistants each time. My colleagues were, of course, entirely right. The situation was out of hand. As reported in the previous chapter, my rising enrollments were probably more the result of rumors that my courses were "blow-offs" than the result of increasing student interest in futures studies. In Fall 1989 I began to limit the size of my courses. In the 1990s, as we noted, they soon shrank to more manageable proportions of their own accord.

In the late 1980s another significant trend was an increase in visits to Lancaster, primarily to keep my mother company now that her sister-in-law had died and she was the sole occupant of the house at 438 West Walnut Street. By 1989, at the age of 80, she was also experiencing severe health problems, mostly the fault of chronic obstructive pulmonary disease aggravated by nearly a life-time of smoking cigarettes. She had stopped smoking years before, but the damage, apparently, had already been done, and the prognosis was not favorable. Seeing more of my mother also meant seeing more of Hudson, who was still living nearby in the northwest end of Lancaster and running his flourishing small company out of his dining room. By now we had season tickets to concert series in New York City every year and took in various summer concerts as well, but getting together for long periods of time, especially at night after my mother went to bed, prompted sessions of reminiscence. Reminiscence led to joint projects.

The first was an idea of my son John, who had already presented me with a photocopied edition of my letters to my mother (most of which she had devotedly saved). What about a similar edition of the collected correspondence of Hudson and Warren (most of which we had both saved)? We held a series of what we probably called "conferences" on the subject, re-read hundreds of letters, and in the end decided to proceed, with John's help. The work was completed in the summer of 1989. At Hudson's suggestion, we later put together an introductory volume containing separate recollections of our friendship and a number of relevant documents from the early days, including the one and only issue of *Science-Fiction News* and the Constitution of the Wagar-Cattell Philosophical Society.

The second project was an idea of Hudson's: why not revive *The Institutional Review*, our writers' notebook and "journal" from the 1950s, using it as a joint repository for essays, fiction, and poetry that each of us wished to share with the other, but not, in the vernacular of the television show "Saturday Night Live," not yet ready for prime time? We agreed to resume *The Institutional Review* in 1990, although (my fault) the first issue did not appear until March, 1991. We were now venerable gentlemen in our very late 50s. Was this nonsense? A second childhood? I think not. Dozens of meticulously researched and carefully written issues appeared throughout the 1990s, including autobiographical essays of mine (and Hudson's), from which I have liberally borrowed in writing these *Memoirs*. It was almost as if the old "institutional circle" had been reborn.

The third project was my idea, broached in 1991: to get our friendship and our own separate lives in proper perspective, we should compile three chronologies, one of our joint doings, one of Hudson's, and one of Warren's. The research for this vast project stretched over several years, and still continues as more years pass by. Its first consummation carries us well beyond the time frame of this chapter. But it began with my proposal in the spring of 1991. We have never looked back, except of course to look back, ever since.

ENTR'ACTE: A SHORT HISTORY OF THE FUTURE

I confessed it in the "Foreword" of *A Short History of the Future*, and I will repeat it here: St. John, Dante, and Marx had something in common. Each saw the future in three stages. The first was Hell, the second Purgatory, and the third Heaven. The same trinity appears in *A Short History of the Future*, although only Marx was on my mind when I was writing. The first edition, and subsequent editions, consisted of three "books." In Book the First, "Earth, Inc.," we visited a stretch of 50 years from 1995 to 2044, the age of capitalist global triumph. Book the Second, "Red Earth," took us from the Catastrophe of 2044 to 2147, the era of the socialist "Commonwealth." Book the Third, "The House of Earth," brought the saga down to the present, the year 2200.

A Short History of the Future, in best postmodernist fashion, was constructed somewhat like an onion. The outermost skin was myself, lecturing in the "Foreword," and my Binghamton colleague Immanuel Wallerstein, lecturing in the "Afterword." We were the real people. Next came "A Note to the Reader," by one Ingrid Jensen, the granddaughter of the fictive author. She was making available to a wider audience the transcript of the verbal text of a "holofilm" presented to her in 2200 as a birthday gift by her grandfather, the historian Peter Jensen. Peter had chosen to time-travel by entering suspended animation in a "hibertube," so he could no longer speak for himself. But for Ingrid he had also left behind a "Preface and Dedication" that would explain his gift. The next shell of the onion was his informal narrative history of the past 205 years, organized in three "books" as noted above. Inside each book was a series of "Interludes," containing "documents" written by members of the extended Jensen family — diary entries, letters, poetry, a book review, the text of a debate, whatever. In the end-matter came Peter's "Envoi to Ingrid," Ingrid's "Last Note to the Reader," and the Wallerstein "Afterword." The onion was complete.

A Short History of the Future recapitulated the thesis of "The Next Three Futures" faithfully. "Earth, Inc." related the events of the next half-century, when a rampant megacorporate global capitalism reached its apogee and then stumbled into a deep economic depression that helped trigger the Catastrophe of 2044. In a lamentable lapse of imagination and foresight, my Catastrophe was a thermonuclear world war between the Soviet Union and the United States, initiated by a crisis in the Middle East. "Red Earth," the story of the following hundred years, related the rise of the World Party, already limned in *Building the City of Man*. After many struggles, the World Party succeeded in building a socialist and democratic world state, known simply as the Commonwealth, which terminated the rule of the megacorporations and cleaned up the biosphere. "The House of Earth," my third part, chronicled the disintegration of the Commonwealth in the middle of the 22nd Century and its replacement by an interplanetary system of autonomous communities of all shapes, sizes, and sorts. I had used the phrase "house of earth" in one of my

CHAPTER 12: THE HUMAN COMEDY

"History of the Future" lectures for several years; at the time, I was quite unaware that my subconscious had probably filched it from Pearl Buck, a copy of whose 1931 novel *The Good Earth* sat in our family library on West Walnut Street; after writing two sequels, she had dubbed her China trilogy *The House of Earth*.

At any rate, in anticipating the implosion of capitalism, the triumph of socialism, and the final redundancy of even socialism, I was deliberately invoking the vision of the future sketched by Friedrich Engels in his *Anti-Dühring*: the maturation of capitalism as a world system, the working-class overthrow of capitalism (fatally weakened by its own internal contradictions), and the ultimate atrophy of the state after the abolition of classes and, hence, of class struggle. Of course Engels, no more than Marx, had not actually discussed what would follow the demise of the state. But he did insist that only then could "real" history begin, the history of humankind as a race forever liberated from the iron laws of political economy. With such freedom, what might we not do? "The House of Earth" was my fantasia on this unanswered question.

CHAPTER 13
PARADIGMS

Reverberations from *A Short History of the Future* continued into early 1990. On January 3, 1990, a reporter for the CNN television network interviewed me in my office about *A Short History of the Future*. The outcome was a two-part series, with appropriate graphics, aired on CNN's "Future Watch" later in the month. My Warholian fifteen minutes of fame? Not quite my only one. There have been others, equally ephemeral, but it was a diverting quarter-hour. Then in mid-January I started the Spring 1990 semester at SUNY, teaching "World War III" and my research seminar "Alternative Futures." For the next five months, I would be awash in futuristics. But something else absorbed more and more of my time: my dying mother.

Laura Stoner Wagar was surely the most important person in the first 21 years of my life. In my dreams today she often plays a role, sometimes metamorphosing — Oedipally — into my wife, or vice versa. But in 1990 she was a doomed woman, betrayed by her lungs. Her mind survived, sharp and funny and sweet and sour, but she was doomed, as she well knew.

Late in January Laura was hospitalized for treatment of her failing lungs. She stayed in the hospital for more than a week. Released, she was given drugs that triggered a cycle of manic depression, an old and familiar nemesis. The manic phase was painful to see. She would write many letters, alternatively angry and scatterbrained. She would spend her money freely on worthless purchases and sleep only two or three hours a night. At the beginning of March, warned by her doctor, I drove down to Lancaster and took her to a psychiatrist, who prescribed suitable medication. A week later, she was back in the hospital with pulmonary spasms. But in late March, she pulled herself together for her 81st birthday. She wanted all of us — me and my whole family — to be there for her party. After that, the deluge. She did not care. But the birthday party required all flesh, all blood.

She got her wish, in full. The most macabre aspect of the celebration was her choice of restaurants: the Warwick House, in Lititz, Pennsylvania, the very hostelry where, in 1939, my father had been the manager, and where, in the private residence above in late May, he had died. The evening passed well. My mother was in high spirits. We retired to West Walnut Street for a rich dessert of Black Forest cake, baked by her old friend Paula Seitz, who had emigrated from Germany in the 1920s. Paula died shortly after my mother's party. I never knew the cause of death, but my mother grinned and whispered to me, "Now I know how to do it!" She made no secret of her wish not to live. The pulmonary attacks were too harrowing. In any case she hated old age.

She did not have long to wait for the next siege. Early in the morning on April 3, she called a neighbor to take her to the hospital. The attack was unusually severe, plunging her into the deepest depression I had ever witnessed. I spent my entire Easter vacation week in Lancaster, visiting her often and arranging for her transfer to a convalescent home. She assigned me power of attorney to take charge of her banking and accounts. On her doctor's advice we began the search for a retirement community. The doctor gave her no more than a year to live. At the beginning of June she was hospitalized once again. Soon after we found a room for her at a community known as Brethren Village, a room we furnished with some of her Walnut Street belongings. Throughout June the house was empty of Wagars for the first time since the early 1920s and had to be put up for sale.

It was a busy summer. Further rites of passage included attendance at the weddings of my son Bruce in Michigan and my son Steven in Connecticut. Bruce, a doctoral candidate in computer science, was married under a tree on the campus of the University of Michigan by a Unitarian minister. Steven, who had recently graduated from Yale with a degree in the same field, was married with full pomp and ceremony in his bride's Roman Catholic church. Somehow or other, despite the frequent comings and goings, I was also able to write most of my next book.

What next book? We must backtrack. Early in 1988, as prospects for publishing *A Short History of the Future* deteriorated, it occurred to me that I could reconceive the whole project as a nonfictional introduction to futures studies. The organizing principle would be the three paths of futures thinking studied in my essay "The Next Three Futures." After expounding the views of established futurists, I could then suggest, near the end of the volume, that humankind might be slated to follow all three paths in chronological sequence. Such a volume would draw heavily on the elaborate lectures already written, and often re-written, for my "History of the Future" course. It could serve both as an original contribution to the infant discipline of futures studies and also as a textbook for courses in the field, much like Barry B. Hughes's *World Futures: A Critical Analysis of Alternatives* (1985), to my mind still the best book on futures thinking, although long out of print.

Greenwood Press responded favorably to my suggestions, and on March 31, 1988, offered me a contract. Initially, the manuscript was to be delivered in the fall of 1989, but I wangled a year's extension. The final draft was shipped to Greenwood at the end of November, 1990. We would call the book, just like the article that preceded it, *The Next Three Futures*. I added a subtitle, *Paradigms of Things To Come*. The Entr'acte below tells the rest of the story.

The busy summer of 1990 was followed by a busy fall. Completing *The Next Three Futures* absorbed much of my time, and I enrolled some 370 students in "History of the Future," but rites of passage continued. My mother's health improved a bit. She seemed comfortable at Brethren Village. During a visit in September, we had a discussion about her clothes, many of which remained on West Walnut Street, and what she would need for the spring. Then I received the news that my mentor and *Doktorvater* Frank Baumer had died. A memorial service was scheduled in New Haven for Saturday, October 20, at which I was asked to speak, but I could not go. As it happened, old and close friends from Albuquerque, Mary Ann and

Ray Nethers, were passing through Lancaster that same weekend and I had promised my mother that I would be down again to visit her and also spend some time with the Netherses. She was concerned that entertaining my friends would not give me enough chance to be with her. I assured her I would not let this happen. In the meantime I made my apologies to Frank's widow and wrote a tribute to Frank to be read at the memorial service.

On Friday, October 12, I spoke to my mother on the phone, as I did every two or three days. She was clearly looking forward to my visit. On Sunday, my daughter Jennifer, who had since moved to Lancaster and was staying at 438 West Walnut Street pending sale of the property, spent a few hours with her grandmother. It was a pleasant visit and Laura seemed well. But Monday morning Brethren Village called to say that Laura had died earlier that morning. She was sitting in her easy chair, her portable respirator in her lap, a telephone at her elbow. The respirator was turned off and she had not used the telephone. I surmise that another attack wakened her that morning and she decided not to fight it. Several residents of the Village told me later that she had spoken often of her wish to die. Life under sentence of death by asphyxiation was not life enough.

We held a memorial service for her on Saturday, October 20. As she requested, her body had been cremated and the service was conducted by a Mennonite pastor she had come to know when working at a nursing home owned and managed by his church. The pastor spent most of his half-hour preaching, but at one point he speculated that although Laura was not of "our faith" and therefore risked perdition, there might be a chance for her, since she had shown serious interest in "our faith" in latter days. One could see the good man playing God in his perfervid imagination, weighing my mother's heathen soul, estimating the quantities of virtue and vice it harbored, pondering the possibilities. Out of respect for my mother's explicit last wishes, I allowed this sadistic cat and mouse game to continue without interruption. After the service, the pastor was nowhere to be found, which was just as well. I would not have turned the other cheek.

CHAPTER 13: PARADIGMS

October 20, 1990, came and went, leaving me an orphan in every sense. My mother and my surrogate father, my *Doktorvater*, had been laid to rest, as it were, on the same day.

The last rituals of the year occurred on December 21 and 22. On the 21st, in the chambers of a district magistrate in Lancaster, Jennifer was married to her fiancé in a civil ceremony. On the 22nd, I treated them to a big reception complete with disk jockey and ballroom. In keeping with tradition, the first dance was between father and daughter, the second between groom and bride, symbolizing the transfer of female property from one male to another, but the thought did not enter my head at the time. I asked the jockey to play John Lennon's "Imagine," a pop hymn to the coming secular and socialist world commonwealth, while Jennifer and I danced. Later that evening, as the music blared on, Hudson and I retreated to his house for a bottle of port.

The next year was less eventful. *The Institutional Review* resumed "publication" in March, 1991. We brought out ten substantial issues through the course of the year. My chief contributions were a three-part series on the evolution of my tastes in recorded classical music and a four-part series entitled "Who Was I?: The Evolution of a Persona," fragments of which have found their way into the earlier chapters of these *Memoirs*.

In late August *The Next Three Futures* appeared in two editions, a clothbound edition from Greenwood Press in Connecticut and a paperback from its subsidiary, Praeger Books, then still in New York. The turnaround time from contract to publication was just under five months, a record unmatched by any other publisher of mine before or since. I adopted it for "History of the Future," at the not inconsiderable cost of having to revamp many of my lectures, from which I had cribbed liberally in writing *The Next Three Futures*. Even so, certain passages survived unscathed, a point not missed a year or two later by one of my more astute (or simply candid?) graduate teaching assistants. I blushed, thanked her, and thereafter made the text optional, with apologies to the class for redundancy, until it lurched out of print near the end of the 1990s.

But the outside world did not lack for events in the year 1991. The United States and its chief NATO partners fought a vicious war to preserve the balance of power in the Middle East. Two of the principal players in the scenario of *A Short History of the Future*, the Soviet Union and Yugoslavia, collapsed and virtually disappeared from the map of the world. The Cold War evaporated like a slab of dry ice exposed to the warming rays of the sun. In a single year the plausibility of Book the First of *A Short History of the Future* had tumbled to zero. As I put it in the title of an article later published in *The Futurist*, "A Funny Thing Happened on My Way to the Future."

It was not funny at the time. In 1991 I may have been the only person in the "Free World" not carrying a Communist party card who was rooting for the restoration of hard-line Communism in Soviet Eurasia and the frostiest possible return of the Cold War. After all, what was the peace of the world or the fall of the Iron Curtain compared to the success of my book? Do I jest? Of course.

At a deeper level, perhaps not. As a Johnny-come-lately Marxist, I must see the world events of 1989-1991, including the disintegration of two prominent federal would-be socialist polities (for all their multiple and grievous faults) as a great leap backward, plunging the peoples of the former Soviet Union and the former Yugoslavia into the savage maelstroms of old-style global capitalist predation and nationalist fratricide. They are all now paying the horrific price of exchanging the 21st Century for the 19th.

At all odds, *A Short History of the Future* was now in need of emergency surgery, to which I attended in the final months of 1991, as we shall see in the next chapter.

ENTR'ACTE: THE FUTURE TIMES THREE

The Next Three Futures: Paradigms of Things To Come, as originally conceived, was to be a non-fictional version of *A Short History of the Future*. This is not how it turned out. The book published in 1991, with a British edition following in 1992, was in effect an intellectual history of the futures movement to the end of the 1980s. By now I had read hundreds, perhaps thousands, of books and substantial articles by futurists of all descriptions, had been influenced positively or negatively by many of them, had prepared scores of lectures for my futures courses, offered my research seminar in futures methods several times, and given papers at every general assembly of the World Future Society except the first. The futures movement itself, now some 30 years old, had reached an apogee of sorts. It was time for a comprehensive overview of what had been, and what had not been, accomplished.

Barry Hughes had already done much of the job, in his *World Futures*, but his text was limited chiefly to a consideration of the world-modeling community, social scientists who projected alternative futures based on abstract mathematical models and readily quantifiable trends. The greatest virtue of Hughes's book was its acknowledgement of the powerful influence of value-systems on futures research. Nevertheless, he tended to focus, as did his sources, on economic and environmental issues. Social, cultural, political, and military futures received relatively little attention. *World Futures* bristled with graphs and tables. *The Next Three Futures* had none. Not that Hughes himself was in any sense a naive positivist. On the contrary, he evinced abundant skepticism about the predictive powers of futures inquiry. But his approach was that of mainstream social science, and mine was more in the tradition of the humanities.

The Next Three Futures opened with a Foreword by Edward Cornish, founding President of the World Future Society and Editor of *The Futurist*. At least on the North American scene, Cornish has played the role of the master-impresario of futures studies, providing its key institutions, ensuring that the field remains open to all persuasions, and encouraging a broad array of futures activities, from the most hard-boiled think tanks and consulting firms to the most far-out fuzzy-brained centers for "personal growth" or "spiritual consciousness." The very eclecticism of the futures movement may wind up shackling its own future progress, but no one should accuse it of bigotry. If general assemblies of the World Future Society sometimes call to mind a vast, many-ringed circus, they do not lack for zest.

Cornish's Foreword struck precisely the right note in its opening sentence: "The study of the future is, strictly speaking, the study of ideas about the future, because the future itself does not exist." The future "is...a place that no one can see, no matter how powerful their telescopes." Rather, futures inquiry gave us an opportunity to survey possibilities, sort out options, and make rational decisions about the kind of future that might be best for humankind. Just so. I know that many prominent futurists would sharply disagree with Cornish. For example, early in 2000, in a brief debate with Graham T.T. Molitor on the NPR program "Talk of the Nation," I proclaimed the unknowability of the future and he objected vigorously. Had time allowed, we might have delved into the epistemology of futures research, teasing out the various hard and soft connotations of the verb "to know," but the nation was, perhaps thankfully, spared this exercise in scholarly counterpoint. I suspect we were talking about two entirely different kinds of knowing.

In any event, Cornish's stress on "ideas about the future," rather than the future "itself," surely underscored the whole point of *The Next Three Futures*. As in *Good Tidings* and *Terminal Visions*, I was engaged in a study of ideas about the future. After a Prologue on my experiences as a teacher of futures studies, I devoted the first three chapters to the methodological and historical foundations of futurism. In reviewing its history I paid special attention — and this, at least, was predictable! — to the prophetic career of H.G. Wells and what I called the "post-Wellsian" generation, mainly the mid-century thinkers highlighted in *The City of Man*.

But I also looked back further in time, to the deeper roots of futurism in Judaism and Christianity, in the idea of progress, the rise of historicism, and the social sciences themselves. Too many futurists imagined that just because they uniquely called themselves futurists, they had no pedigree, no forerunners, and no competition. This was hardly the case. The great majority of systematic thoughts about the future of humankind had been thought, and are probably still being thought, by people outside the coteries of self-styled futurists. See only the two volumes of Fred Polak's *The Image of the Future* (1961) for copious evidence of pre-"futurist" futurism, and the monthly digests and critiques of futures-related publications in Michael Marien's *Future Survey*, which has never, and advisedly so, restricted its sights to materials by credentialed futurists. In any event, what are the appropriate credentials? Who knows?

The third of these introductory chapters put forward the central thesis of my book, the thesis of the three primary paradigms of futures thinking identified in my "History of the Future" lectures and in my 1984 essay "The Next Three Futures." We first encountered them in Chapter 11 above. Here they became the organizing principle of the rest of the book. Futurists tended, I argued, to fall into one of three categories, with frequent blurring of the lines in individual cases: the technoliberals, who celebrated technology, material progress, representative democracy, and capitalism; the radicals, who celebrated democracy and progress but within the framework of a worker-owned and worker-managed economy; and the counterculturalists, who deplored the materialism of both preceding camps and sought to build a decentralized, ecologically sustainable society grounded in "alternative" values. As Immanuel Wallerstein had shrewdly observed in the "Afterword" to *A Short History of the Future*, I was pitting the ideology of the modern capitalist world-system against two classic utopian visions.

What followed was a set of four large chapters analyzing and exploring in some detail the thoughts of futurists, both inside and outside the futures movement itself, on four large questions. "The Future of the Earth" addressed environmental concerns. "The Future of Wealth and Power" turned to economic and political matters. "The Future of War and Peace" looked at global security issues. Finally, "The Future of Living" examined the thoughts of futurists on the prospects for work, society, the family, religion, and the arts.

In each chapter, my goal was much the same. I tried to represent the ideas of others as faithfully as possible — my old respect for Diltheyan *Einfühlung* abiding still — and to refrain from taking sides. I do not know whether I succeeded. Giving the radicals equal time with the technoliberals and the counterculturalists was in itself taking sides because, in all fairness, the occasional radical voices in futures-related publications have been almost drowned out by the technoliberal and counterculturalist choruses. Certainly in the narrower world of self-proclaimed futurists, radicals are almost unknown.

But let us name names. From the ranks of the technoliberals — who in my analysis range from political "conservatives" to political "liberals" — I gave much of my attention to the work of Arthur C. Clarke, Daniel Bell, Richard Falk, Herman Kahn, Francis Fukuyama, Julian Simon, and the team of Donella and Dennis Meadows. These may seem like odd bedfellows, but not in terms of my generously broad definition of "technoliberalism." My star radicals were Richard J. Barnet, Michael Harrington, Immanuel Wallerstein, Robert Heilbroner, and myself. Counterculturalists included Hazel Henderson, E.F. Schumacher, Mary E. Clark, Willis W. Harman, Ernest Callenbach, and William Irwin Thompson. In my bibliography I also listed Alvin Toffler as a counterculturalist, although I would see this now as problematic. Toffler is a good example of the blurring of lines, alternating between technoliberal and counterculturalist visions.

Only in the "Epilogue" did I feel free to cut loose with my own thoughts, recapitulating the argument in my 1984 essay, "The Next Three Futures." All three camps were right, within reason. The immediate future would witness the temporary triumph of the technoliberal paradigm, as the global capitalist economy expanded to its historical limits. Its collapse would usher in a long period of radical, meaning world-socialist, hegemony. And then, after the purgatory of socialism had done its appointed work, we might be able to ascend into the kingdom of freedom, and the transvaluation of values, as humanity learned at last to collaborate in peace and harmony with itself and with our common Mother, and reached out to people the galaxy.

CHAPTER 14
SECOND EDITION

In September, 1991, President George Bush announced a number of major initiatives to shrink the American nuclear arsenal, including the dismantling of all American tactical nuclear weapons. President Mikhail Gorbachev of the Soviet Union followed suit early in October with a pledge to eliminate all Soviet tactical nuclear weapons. Such weapons had played a significant role in the military history of the 1990s as I imagined it in *A Short History of the Future*. Now they would not even exist.

This was, for me, the last crushing straw. Prediction was not the aim of *A Short History*, but at least the scenarios presented had to be possible. Given the reunification of Germany in 1990, the collapse of the Warsaw Pact military alliance in the spring of 1991, the breakup of Yugoslavia in the summer of 1991, and the rapidly deteriorating political health of the Soviet Union, along with all the other turbulence in Eastern Europe between the summer of 1989 and the fall of 1991, my chronicle of the 1990s was now inconceivable. When I drafted it in 1987, it made good sense. By October, 1991, it was nonsense.

Well, not nonsense altogether. What I imagined for the late 1990s, if one ignores most of the details, was in the broadest sense fairly prescient. I anticipated the dramatic end of hard-line Communist rule, the failure of the Warsaw Pact alliance system, the conclusion of the East-West Cold War, and a new world order accompanied by extensive negotiated shrinkage of nuclear arsenals. But the devil, as so often occurs, lodged in the details.

My vehicle for rapid change was "The World Crisis of 1997." It featured massive and unsuccessful U.S. military intervention in a civil war in the Philippines, followed by a great uproar in the Balkans after the death of the Romanian dictator Nicolae Ceausescu. A reformist element within the ruling party in Bucharest adopted a policy of liberalization, emulating the Czechs of 1968. The Soviet Union attempted to persuade the Romanians to go more slowly, without success. The other member nations of the Warsaw Pact declined to participate in any proposed military solution, which infuriated Moscow all the more. The Soviets massed troops on the Romanian border. Romania responded by sending almost its whole army to the Soviet border, and Yugoslavia, in a bid to thwart Soviet ambitions in the Balkans, came to Romania's aid. Reeling from its recent humiliation in the Pacific, the United States decided to help non-aligned Yugoslavia by replacing the Yugoslav divisions dispatched to the Soviet front with battle-hardened U.S. marines. Over Hungarian objections, the Soviet Union retaliated by deploying troops on the border between Hungary and Yugoslavia. All at once U.S. and Soviet combat forces found themselves eyeball to eyeball. The whole world expected war. And it might be nuclear war, since the U.S. commanders in the field were itching to use neutron bombs to disable the numerically superior Soviet armored columns poised in Hungary to invade Yugoslavia.

Thrilling stuff, no doubt. But quite unbelievable in the fall of 1991. Would there even be a Soviet Union in 1997? And could Yugoslavia re-assemble itself? The flashpoint of my imaginary confrontation was a small border town in what by the fall of 1991 was the breakaway Republic of Croatia. Plenty of shots were then being exchanged in the area, but by Croatians and Serbs, not by Yugoslavs and Russians. (A final insult was the decision of the world press at about this same time that Romania, hitherto spelled by *The New York Times* and several other authoritative sources as "Rumania," would become "Romania." In my 1989 edition, of course, I had spelled it "Rumania.")

To return to my original scenario in *A Short History of the Future*, minor skirmishes did take place between American and Soviet forces in northernmost "Yugoslavia" in late September, 1997, but both Moscow and Washington realized the extreme perilousness of the military situation, pulled back, and decided to talk. The outcome was the burying of hatchets at a grand conference in Vienna in 1998, where both sides agreed to an "arms limitation protocol," demilita-

CHAPTER 14: SECOND EDITION

rized both East and West Germany, and carved up the world into "zones of legitimate special influence." The Soviet Union received a free hand in the Middle East (except for Israel), Cuba, and the Indian subcontinent. The United States was given its free hand throughout the Western Hemisphere (except for Cuba), the Pacific island nations, and Israel. Western Europe's zone was Africa and Japan's was Southeast Asia, in at least nominal partnership with China.

Plausible in 1987? Yes. Possible in 1991? Almost certainly not. And the final blow was the elimination of tactical nuclear weapons, which, if used on the Hungarian-Yugoslav border in 1997 in my scenario, might well have ignited an all-out World War III, fear of which sensibly drove the Superpowers to sit down in Vienna and create a new world order. The inner logic of my scenario, I must insist, was sound, but it was vitiated by facts on the ground in the early 1990s, above all by the unexpected frailty and debacle of the Soviet system. Almost all Kremlinologists, as well as futurists, had failed to perceive this frailty, and so we all wound up with egg-plastered faces. A funny thing happened on our way to the future.

On October 3, 1991, two days before Gorbachev also renounced tactical nuclear weapons, I called Doug Mitchell to discuss the imminent paperback reprint of *A Short History of the Future*. It would be coming out in 1992. Could I make some desperately required strategic revisions in the 1989 edition before that happened? The reprint would fall flat if it simply repeated the now-impossible near-future scenario outlined in 1989. Doug saw my point.

Soon it was decided that I could make all the revisions I wanted as long as every passage deleted was replaced by another of exactly equal length, to preserve the original pagination. This was clearly a problem, but nothing insuperable. In November and early December I toiled away on an alternative scenario for Book the First, and in October, 1992, the revised second edition of *A Short History of the Future* made its slightly belated appearance. Even as far along as mid-December, 1991, I still had to make a guess about the future of the Soviet Union, which did not actually disintegrate until December 25, but on this occasion I jumped in the right direction. Further last-minute changes were not required. The "Entr'acte" below discusses the surgery performed.

Reviewing my personal records for 1992 to 1994, I find few overwhelming events. The saddest was the scuttling of my career as a writer of science fiction. My last published story, "Goodfood," a whimsical satire on vegetarianism, appeared in January, 1993, in *Journeys to the Twilight Zone*, an anthology of new stories edited by Rod Serling's widow Carol. I imagined a 21st-Century America where allegedly unwholesome foods like meat and cheese were proscribed by law, enforced by a national food police. Illegal foods such as hamburgers could be procured only in the 21st-Century equivalent of 1920s "speakeasies."

But in the summer of 1992 I had also written a malefic fantasy entitled "Terminal Vision," the story of a psychotic scientist and his pitifully obsessed inamorata, who almost destroyed the world through a technology that amplified telekinetic powers. Although I consider it my best tale in the genre, I could not find a publisher. Nor could I place my novel *The Seasons of No*, based on the three "No" novellas already published in *The Magazine of Fantasy & Science Fiction* in the 1980s. I made a solemn pact with myself that if I could not sell either "Terminal Vision" or *The Seasons of No*, I would resign from the Science-Fiction Writers of America and perpetrate no more fiction. At this writing, I have still found no home for either work, and, with thumb firmly in mouth, I have long since resigned from SFWA. Was it pique, petulance, or puerility? Not a problem. All three!

The summer of 1992 did bring me full circle with my far-flung offspring. In June Dorothy and I journeyed to Berlin to attend the wedding of my oldest son John, who was engaged to a fetching nurse from the former East Berlin. To reach the courthouse in southwestern Berlin, John, his bride, and her son by a previous relationship rode in an open horse-drawn carriage decked with flowers, followed by our rental car, a Volkswagen Polo, similarly bedecked. With help from the Berlin police, the bizarre little procession passed by nearly all the major landmarks of Berlin on its route, along Unter den Linden and through the Brandenburg Gate to the Ku'Damm and beyond. Many tourists photographed or videotaped us as we threaded through the Brandenburg Gate, at that time normally closed to private vehicular traffic.

We had now witnessed the weddings of all four of our children, but none of the others had been quite so colorful or unique.

During that same stay in Germany, Dorothy and I toured the ancient province of Thuringia. My ancestors on both sides had been, to a substantial extent, German. In the deep woods and high spires of Thuringia, we came face to face with segments of "my" heritage: the medieval quarter of Erfurt, the country of Goethe and Schiller in Weimar, and the great castle on the Wartburg in Eisenach, where Martin Luther translated the New Testament and Richard Wagner found the inspiration for *Tannhäuser*. For a moment or two, as I surveyed the Thuringian Forest from the window of our hotel room high on the Wartburg, I experienced a sense of ethnic identity. For that moment, my cosmopolitanism was challenged and perhaps even quelled.

But as Samuel Huntington contends, there is a larger issue. Beyond ethnicity and beyond nationality lies the Toynbeean entity of the "civilization," another construct of the human imagination, but not the less powerful for being so. You will have noticed that virtually all the influences on my thinking through the decades have been the products of what we habitually call "Western" civilization. In *The City of Man* I made a serious effort to incorporate non-Western values into my recipe for a global civilization, but all the non-Western ingredients were in effect Westernized and secularized, adapted to categories clearly of secular Western provenance. To what extent, then, was my City of Man a city of Western men, a city shaped, imagined, conceived throughout by white persons chiefly of the male sex? Did I claim catholicity for what was parochial and segmental, even for what was — although perhaps not consciously — racist and sexist?

Let us defer an answer to this question until the next chapter. I have no intention of sidestepping or avoiding it, but the next chapter is a better place to confront it, and confront it head-on.

Returning to the United States on June 11, I spent the following week in Lancaster at Hudson's house, where we worked intensively on our chronology project, now well and seriously under way. Many dates in each other's lives could be ascertained only by comparing notes, documents, and recollections; this was especially the case when we tried to assemble a chronology of our friendship. Work continued sporadically throughout the rest of the summer, during the winter break in 1992-93, and again in the summer of 1993, when I was at Hudson's for the better part of two weeks, in June and later in August. It was our intention to have everything completed, typed up, and bound in time for the 50th anniversary of our friendship in February, 1995, a deadline we were able to meet. Meanwhile we continued "publishing" issues of *The Institutional Review*. To the ten that appeared in 1991, we added nine each in 1992 and 1993. Again, many of the essays were autobiographical.

Other exploits in 1993 included interviews for two television programs: an episode of the Arts & Entertainment channel series, "The Time Machine," devoted to failed predictions, which aired for the first time in September; and a program in the 1994 PBS series "Future Quest," with a script built around *A Short History of the Future*. The production crew for "Future Quest" spent all morning on December 6 taping my commentaries; but when the series was actually broadcast the following fall, it had evolved into something patchier and more light-hearted, and my "show" was canceled. *A Short History of the Future* did, however, enjoy a brief local moment in the sun in January, 1994, when it was chosen as the core text for an integrated winter term of Fairhaven College, the honors college of Western Washington University in Bellingham. At the invitation of the College, I was on hand for several days during the first week of the term to get the course properly under way.

Later in January a new angiogram showed my arteries working well, and for the whole Spring 1994 semester I was on sabbatical leave to write these *Memoirs*. Which I did not do.

The Spring 1994 semester is one I would prefer to, but cannot, forget. It began auspiciously enough. I had prepared a detailed outline of my book in the first week of January, and by the second day of the new semester — January 25, 1994 — I had written the first half of the first chapter. Then my brain shut down.

Depression is difficult to describe to someone who has not suffered through it personally. And difficult to describe to oneself, akin perhaps to the out-of-body experiences reported by certain individuals of a mystical bent, but with none of the exaltation. The symptoms in my case were fairly classic. Loss of appetite, loss of weight, loss of sexual desire, loss of self-confidence, loss of the will to live and the enjoyment of life. From technicolor to black and white. I stopped listening to music, or when, infrequently, I did, I could not understand why I had ever thought it entertaining or stimulating. I felt no suicidal urges: to commit suicide would have required a blast of passion, a summoning of will, and of passion or will I had none. On the occasions when I visited campus to check my mail, I would slink about hoping to avoid any human contact. I realized, at long last, that I was a fraud, an ignoramus, a bad historian, and a worse prophet. I was powerfully tempted to retire. Looking anyone in the eye was an ordeal.

I had battled brief periods of depression in the past, as no doubt have most of us, but never anything like this. Still, I knew immediately what was wrong; I had seen my mother in a similar state more than once. I knew just what to do. My records show that I consulted my internist as early as January 27, four days into the Spring semester. He prescribed the antidepressant medication Zoloft. It had no effect. Why not try something else? By the middle of February I was too depressed to care. Finally, in late April, I went to a psychiatrist recommended by my internist, who doubled my dose of Zoloft. Still no response, except for a mild improvement in appetite. The psychiatrist also prescribed thyroid medication, suspecting a deficiency in that department. No change.

The semester was by then already in ruins. I forced myself to work on the chronologies and to write miscellaneous essays for *The Institutional Review*. I embarked on a serious program of reading novels and monographs that might be useful in some of my courses.

With the historical geographer Peter Taylor of the University of Newcastle I put in some time on a project he had conceived to produce an atlas based on *A Short History of the Future*. But *Memoirs of the Future* I could not touch. Half of the first chapter was all I had done and all I could do. The thought of writing the memoirs of a nonentity, even a charlatan, was repugnant.

On June 5, I wearily celebrated my 62nd birthday. The next day my psychiatrist gave up on Zoloft and prescribed its more popular rival, Prozac. In eleven days the dense fog in which I had wandered for almost five months miraculously thinned and then scattered altogether. Better living through chemistry? Or was it all a coincidence? The stuff is alleged not to take effect in fewer than two weeks. We shall never know. My best guess is that my problem was largely psychochemical and that Prozac stepped in to assist my neurones, but Hudson suspects that I subconsciously viewed my sabbatical leave as a trial run of retirement, for which I was clearly not ready. Workaholics without an active social calendar, without avocations, which describes me (and Hudson) pretty well, are miserable when deprived of work. But *Memoirs of the Future* was work, even paid work, in view of my sabbatical leave. Why not do it? Still, Hudson's hypothesis is intriguing, especially in light of later developments, to which we shall turn in due course.

ENTR'ACTE: COLUMBIA AS HEROINE

Columbia may be the gem of the ocean, but I had never been much of a patriot. Even as a small child, the flag, the anthem, the parades and the speeches left me unmoved, although I greatly admired Franklin D. Roosevelt both as a politician and as an orator. For that matter I also admired, in quite different ways, Winston Churchill and Adolf Hitler, Churchill for his eloquence and courage under fire, Hitler and the Nazis for their sharp uniforms and paraphernalia. When I grew old enough to know my own mind, in the mid-1940s, I became an advocate of world government and was lost to nationalism forever.

CHAPTER 14: SECOND EDITION

In the First Edition of *A Short History of the Future* Columbia had been the villain of the piece. Writing in the late 1980s, I saw the United States as a leading player in the games of capitalist *Weltpolitik*. With the end of the Cold War in 1998, the Soviet Union became more and more of a capitalist nation as well (just like "Communist" China in the real world of our own time) and world capitalism experienced decades of unalloyed triumph. But late in 2043 the still nominally Communist and still sovereign Soviet Union made a gross miscalculation. Under the terms of the Vienna accords of 1998, all of the Middle East had fallen into its zone of domination except the state of Israel. But when bloody clashes between Israeli forces and Palestinian guerrillas threatened to destabilize the area, the Soviets unilaterally occupied Israel and set up ADJOV, the Autonomous District of the Jordan Valley, divided into two sub-districts ("Zion" and "Palestine") administered by Jewish and Arab Communists, respectively, who took their orders — or else — from Moscow.

The situation in ADJOV became untenable when Washington-supported Israeli rebel forces seized Tel Aviv in June, 2044. Soviet forces retaliated by destroying Tel Aviv with nuclear weapons. On the morning of July 5, the United States launched an all-out nuclear counterforce strike on the Soviet Union, which failed to prevent effective Soviet retaliation against the United States and its NATO allies. Out-of-touch commanders in the field continued the war without formal authorization. The Indian subcontinent burst into flames as well, and Japan was destroyed by Soviet missile-bearing submarines as the result of a fatal misunderstanding about Japan's role in the conflict. In a matter of days, a confused and warring world blew itself apart.

That was the "Catastrophe of 2044" in the First Edition of *A Short History of the Future*. I could have retained it for the Second Edition, changing the "Soviet Union" to "Russia," but from the perspective of the fall of 1991, a half-century more of sparring between the two Cold War superpowers seemed implausible. Why not a dramatic role reversal, of the sort world history produces almost every century? Why not imagine a global war ignited by North-South, rather than East-West, tensions, and a war in which the gem of the ocean, increasingly populated by people of color, assumes the role of the heroine, the champion of the oppressed?

Not too bad, especially if one looks at the world of late 1991, when I wrote the Second Edition. The U.S. economy was performing relatively poorly. The Europe of the Common Market, along with Japan, was booming. The new Russia, converted over night to capitalism, was expected to shed its image as an economic loser and join forces with the European Community. Demographers offered solid statistical evidence that by the middle of the 21st Century, half the people of the United States would not be white. If the United States became a second-rate economic power, thanks to its now outdated allegiance to unregulated free-booting individualism, and also incidentally consisted more and more of people of Asian, African, and Latin descent, why might it not eventually see its destiny in some sort of fractious alliance with the Third World?

As ever, this is the curse of futurism. Current trends dictate estimates of future prospects. I have always tried to resist, but the temptation is great — not only because we may ourselves be persuaded of the predictive power of current trends, but also because we realize that to ignore them is to diminish credibility and risk the censorship or ban of the gods who rule us: our prospective publishers, who in turn stand in for our prospective publics.

So be it. In the late fall of 1991, I went with the flow. According to the narrative of the Second Edition, the American economy was consistently outperformed throughout the first decades of the 21st Century by Europe and the Pacific rim of East Asia. In 2040, the United States turned sharply to the Left. A Hispanic woman was elected President at the head of a third party ticket ("The League of the Dispossessed"), winning the African and Hispanic vote, but also the vote of most liberal whites, who had been radicalized by the great business depression then in full swing, the long-term failures of the American economy vis-à-vis Europe and Japan, and the Democratic party's choice of a right-wing Southern populist as its candidate.

The new President, Mary Chávez, adopted a foreign policy

anathema to the multinational corporations and the other rich nations. She consistently supported the interests of the world's poor, putting the United States on a collision course with Europe and Japan. When in 2044 she ignored Congress on a matter of domestic policy, the funding of urban rehabilitation programs, civil war broke out. Several Midwestern and Southern states recognized the former Democratic candidate as "acting" President and raised the flag of rebellion. The federal armed forces, consisting mostly of people of color, backed Chávez. When the other rich nations recognized the rebel government, she took the United States out of the United Nations (since reorganized as the "Confederated States of Earth") and broke diplomatic relations with Europe and Japan. China and Brazil, among others, followed suit. The world order of multinational capital was in danger of falling apart. The United States had become a lethal liability.

Chávez won the civil war in a matter of months, but her victory rendered her government all the more hazardous to the capitalist world order. Ultimately a decision was taken to nullify American power by launching a counterforce attack on all American military assets. The strategy backfired when American missile-bearing submarines disguised as lightly armed intelligence vessels survived the first strike and retaliated with hundreds of pre-targeted warheads. The Catastrophe of 2044 then unfolded just as it had done in the First Edition. Billions of people died. But this time around the first blow had been struck by the nefarious enemies of the United States. Columbia was the heroine. More or less.

By giving more weight to the international class struggle and less to interstate rivalry, I had made the first part of *A Short History of the Future* significantly truer to its forming premises and, I think, a more imaginative and credible book. Its credibility may have been shaken a bit by the upsurge in the American economy in the mid-1990s and the corresponding dip in the economies of East Asia and Russia. I did not count on that. But anyone familiar with the ups and downs of the global economy could still believe that by 2040 almost anything was possible. And nothing had occurred to invalidate the assumption that America was on an irreversible demographic course to a non-white majority by mid-century. The last two parts of the First Edition, "Red Earth" and "The House of Earth," could be, and were, left almost untouched.

But again the point of *A Short History of the Future* was not the particulars. The particulars were there because the future will consist of particulars. History always consists of certain people in certain places at certain times doing certain things. How else could history take place? But the larger significance of these events becomes clear only after we can tabulate the collective outcome of all the individual decisions to act, which is seldom what the actors intended. In the years 1933-1945 Germany chose to turn back the clock and create a mighty Germanic anti-Communist totalitarian agrarian empire rooted in the black soil of Eastern Europe. The dénouement was a smaller, more-than-ever bourgeois, democratic, and industrial German republic, a powerful new Jewish national state in the Middle East, the triumph and then collapse of Communism, and eventually a united trans-national Europe. World War Two was made inevitable by the feckless efforts of the victors of World War One to avoid it. In 1914 Lenin's Bolsheviks opposed Russian involvement in the First World War, an involvement without which they could never have seized power. In the years 1800-1815, Napoleon sought to resurrect the Holy Roman Empire under French leadership. His actions buried the Holy Roman Empire, spurred movements of national revival throughout the rest of Europe, and ended French hegemony on the Continent once and for all.

CHAPTER 15
THE WORLD PARTY

One of my lifelong traits, already cited in these *Memoirs*, is a personal aversion to change. Not a desirable quality in a futurist, perhaps, but deeply ingrained nonetheless. The two greatest battles of my day are always to wake up and begin to function in the morning, and then to stop functioning and go to bed at night. I will do almost anything to avoid learning a new technology or breaking in a new piece of equipment. The advent of the computer age with its interminable stream of "upgradings" has had for me all the charm of a sweaty nightmare. A special phobia is the first day of classes in a new semester. But in 1994, after a long winter and spring of clinical depression and a short summer of recovering from its effects, I found the prospect of returning to academic life exhilarating. For the first time in memory, September was not an accursed month.

The next six years found me more deeply immersed in campus matters than ever. I developed a fair number of new courses and seminars, none of them futures-related. I served as Director of Undergraduate Studies in the History Department and, for the whole academic year 1995-96, as Acting Chair. "World War III" evolved first into "War and the Future" and then "War: Past and Future," with more than half the course now focused on selected past wars that had helped to transform civilization. Nominated by my old friend Howard P. Segal, I even collected an honorary doctorate from the University of Maine in May, 1996. My firm resolve to retire in 1997, when I reached the august age of 65, disintegrated when it came time to sign my name on the final document. I was not ready. I stayed on.

I was writing no new books, but I churned out a respectable number of articles, chapters, review essays, conference papers, and guest lectures, many on futures themes. These included "Tomorrow and Tomorrow and Tomorrow," an overview of the range of futures studies for the M.I.T. journal *Technology Review*; a guest lecture on the future of education at Stanford University; another on "Learning from Past Futures" at Portland State University; my Phi Alpha Theta lecture "The World: Coming Together or Falling Apart?" at SUNY Albany, later published as a booklet; "Toward a Praxis of World Integration," which appeared in the electronic *Journal of World-Systems Research*; "Socialism, Nationalism, and Ecocide," for the journal of the Fernand Braudel Center, *Review*; "Teaching the Future: A Memoir," in *Futurevision*, a symposium volume published by the World Future Society; and a piece on the relevance of historical research to futures studies in *American Behavioral Scientist*. The second edition of *A Short History of the Future* appeared in a Japanese translation in Tokyo in 1995, and a slightly revised and updated third edition was published by the University of Chicago Press in 1999. I also contributed 14 articles to Macmillan's majestic *Encyclopedia of the Future* (1996).

Sifting through all this work, I find three interlocking themes — the value of the historian's synoptic vision in imagining the future, my analysis of the post-Cold War world, and the campaign for a World Party. The first has already been treated in other contexts, but the other two deserve further notice.

Trying to make sense of the "post-Cold War world" has become a favorite pastime of social scientists. Are we immersed in a "clash of civilizations"? Must we dread the "coming anarchy?" Have we earned the bliss of the "end of history"? Can the United States remain "the sole Superpower"? Will it be "Jihad versus McWorld"?

One possible answer to such questions is to deny that what I called "The World Revolution of 1989" (in the second edition of *A Short History of the Future*) was a revolution at all, and, further, to challenge the whole notion of a "Cold War." There was certainly the appearance of an old-fashioned balance-of-power contest in the world of 1945 to 1989, as the United States and the Soviet Union rushed in to fill the political vacuum left by the defeat or exhaustion of the former Great Powers. There was certainly an arms race, and much slaughter in the periphery of the world-system, from Algeria to Vietnam and Korea. The world of the Cold War was, in fact, remarkably similar to the world envisaged by George Orwell in his *Nineteen Eighty-Four*: that is, superpowers skirmishing in Africa and Asia, well outside their homelands, but sedulously avoiding the kind of total war that they well knew would destroy them both. It could also be argued that much of the motivation for the arms race and the skirmishing came not from genuine fear and loathing of the "enemy," but rather from the need to maintain social discipline on the home front and cater to the interests of the "military-industrial complex" within each superpower.

If this argument works, it means that the Cold War was at least partly a farce, a monument to Doublethink, much ado about very little. And "The World Revolution of 1989" was only a hiccup, the temporary unraveling of Orwell's "Eurasia," ending a threat of global war that had never existed in the first place.

In this light, what was really happening, and had been happening for decades, in the post-1945 world? Put somewhat differently, what processes were at work that the jitters of the Cold War had distracted some of us from watching?

The long-term processes were no mystery: the inexorable rise and maturation of global capital and its partition of the world, as Wallerstein and others have shown, into parasitical core, exploited periphery, and Janus-faced "semi-periphery." I had embraced both Marxism and Marxist-inflected world-system theory in the 1980s. But not to the exclusion of other relevant interpretive tools, and certainly not to the extent of accepting the world-systems party line on "antisystemic movements."

The theory of "antisystemic movements" holds that in addition to the juggernaut of global capital and its confederates in the national state system, there are popularly-based movements afoot in the world that seek to challenge and displace the capitalist world-system. In any entertaining dystopian novel or film, the forces of evil must inspire the emergence of forces of virtue; and so it is in world-system theory. The terrible strength of *Nineteen Eighty-Four* lies in its chilling disclosure that the apparent forces of virtue — Goldstein, the Brotherhood, the proles, Winston and Julia — are mirages and shadows, that the rule of Big Brother is complete. But in worldsystem theory as it has developed over the past quarter-century, the malignant lords of capital have raised up serious real-life foes, in such forms as feminists, socialists, movements of national liberation, Islamic freedom fighters, and environmental and peace and gay and civil rights activists.

On balance, I have generally identified with these "antisystemic" forces. What I do not accept is that they are necessarily antisystemic or even progressive. Take the Palestinian cause. Obviously the state of Israel was created at the expense of the indigenous Arab population. Obviously Zionism was just another, although quite unique, variety of Western imperialism. Obviously the Holocaust of the European Jews did not justify the invasion by displaced Jews of the Palestinian protectorate or their own displacement of Arabs. Just as obviously, however, Palestinian Arabs were not and are not today an antisystemic force. Their goal is a sovereign Palestinian state on Palestinian soil. They are no more "antisystemic" than the Slovenians who seceded from Yugoslavia or the Ukrainians who seceded from the Soviet Union or, for that matter, the North American colonists who seceded in 1776 from the United Kingdom.

By the same token, what about women who want their fair share of the (capitalist) pie? What about ghetto-bound African-Americans or Mexican-American migrant workers who want theirs? What about separatist Basques in Spain or Irish Catholics in Northern Ireland or Tamil insurgents in Sri Lanka?

The plain fact is that all these good folk, with signal exceptions here and there, do not oppose the system as such. They demand their fair and just place in the system. They have been marginalized and they want "in." At the same time, paradoxically, they want to preserve their singularity and remain outside. But not too far.

I cannot blame, much less curse, these good folk. I want them "in" and "out" too. But in or out of what?

In my SUNY Albany lecture, "The World: Coming Together or Falling Apart?" (based on an earlier public lecture of the same title given on the Binghamton campus in 1992), I divided the forces con-

CHAPTER 15: THE WORLD PARTY

tending for power in the post-Cold War world into those that were essentially centripetal and those that were essentially centrifugal. Capital, abetted by technology, insisted on whirling the world into a single compact sphere, a single marketplace and a single material culture, with some few nations and marketeers on top and everyone else gasping for breath below. But a new, or newly revived, politics of identity cried out for separation from the sphere: nations, ethnicities, races, faiths, all peeling off in pursuit of their own unique destinies, in flaming dissent from the homogenizing force of capital. Was the world coming together or falling apart?

The answer, of course, was both. Not one or the other, but both. Pressures to conform and pressures to separate were well matched, pushing and pulling all of us at the same time. And, paradoxically, both pressures were "good," in the sense of necessary and complementary. Here many radicals went astray, by vilifying the integrative forces and sanctifying the disintegrative. In the real world, where concerted action was essential to safeguard the biosphere, ensure world peace, and rectify injustice, too much dissent and separation could be fatal. Yet without the right to dissent and separate, the world would become a vast dehumanizing concentration camp.

The greatest problem with the centrifugal forces at work in the modern world-system, however, was not that they sought their rightful place in the sun, but that their very separateness precluded concerted action. They lacked a vision of the whole. They opposed the system not because of what it was, but because it excluded or exploited them. And in the process of opposing the system they might well also oppose one another. How to reconcile the disparate aims of feminists and Islamic freedom fighters? How to reconcile socialists with nationalists? How to reconcile environmentalists with Third World peoples determined to "catch up" with the rich world at any cost? Falling apart was all very well, up to a point, but the ultimate goal had to be coming together, through the creation of a new world-system that could accommodate diversity and yet avoid fratricide and the "exploitation of man by man." Antisystemic movements had to become authentically antisystemic, which, at present, they were not.

At the same time they had to become prosystemic, in the sense of united in the drive to replace the capitalist world-system with a better one. Decenter in order to recenter. *Reculer pour mieux sauter.*

But just how could we get from here to there? By the mid-1990s, *A Short History of the Future* had attracted the sympathetic attention of a number of sociologists in the world-systems camp, thanks in part no doubt to the "Afterword" by Immanuel Wallerstein. Among them was Christopher Chase-Dunn, then at Johns Hopkins University, and also Terry Boswell of Emory University, who wrote a lengthy and probing review of the second edition. The project of an *Atlas of the Future* with Peter Taylor had fallen through because we could not interest a publisher, but Chase-Dunn invited me to speak at the annual meeting of the American Sociological Association in Washington in August, 1995. The occasion was a panel on "Global Praxis and World-System Theory," chaired by Andre Gunder Frank, with Wallerstein himself as the designated commentator. My paper was entitled "Toward a Praxis of World Integration" and centered largely on my (by this time) venerable idea of a World Party as the logical leading agent for a revolutionary transformation of the world-system.

The paper struck a chord, especially after it was published on-line in Chase-Dunn's *Journal of World-Systems Research*. Chris published the paper itself, as well as comments from a variety of world-systems scholars and my own rejoinder to the comments. Since then, he has presided over two extensive debates about the idea of a World Party on the World-Systems Network, an electronic forum. The idea has drawn everything from enthusiasm to bland approval (usually with eviscerating misreadings) to snorts of derision. It also has its own website, but then so do my son Steven's cats.

Will there ever be a World Party? Can the "antisystemic" forces join hands with wise and disillusioned insiders to present a united front against the modern world-system? I am grateful to all those, like Chris Chase-Dunn, who have given the idea of the World Party an airing and a chance to succeed. I am somewhat less hopeful myself. On certain days, I have no hope at all.

But before we turn to the argument of my paper for the

CHAPTER 15: THE WORLD PARTY

American Sociological Association, let me touch on a sore and perilous subject. Somewhere in the middle of the paper I contended that the ideological substrate of the World Party would be inherited from the "Left Enlightenment" in modern Western civilization. Was the World Party therefore an agent of Western cultural imperialism? This is a legitimate question, which deserves a straightforward answer.

First, what did I mean by the "Enlightenment"? To paraphrase Immanuel Kant, the Enlightenment of the 18th Century in Western Europe was a movement to liberate the human mind from the shackles of authority, whether the authority of the Ancients or the authority of the Bible and the Church. Secular, rational, liberal, it sought the foundations of peace, justice, freedom, and prosperity in the laws of nature and the powers of the untrammeled mind. Although soon challenged from within by its own methods of inquiry, and lacking the pontifical coherence of an Aristotle or an Aquinas, the Enlightenment was, all things weighed and considered, the greatest revolution in the history of human thought, Eastern or Western. Philosophers outside the West, especially in the medieval Muslim world, in India, and in China, had long since matched the best thinkers of pre-modern Europe, but only the intensely this-worldly, swiftly changing society and culture of 17th- and 18th-Century Western Europe was able to spawn something like the Enlightenment: the Enlightenment of Locke and Montesquieu, Voltaire and Rousseau, Condillac and Diderot, Hume and Kant, d'Holbach and Lamettrie, Quesnay and Smith, Turgot and Condorcet.

I do not see this advance as a result of the innate superiority of Western Europe or the white race or the Judeo-Christian heritage. It was simply a concomitant of the rise of modern capitalism, the competitive nature of the European state system (ensured by its unusual geography, which thwarted efforts to build a universal empire), and the worldwide outreach of Western European civilization. Historical circumstances favored Western Europe, actually from the 15th Century onward. The Enlightenment did not give Western Europe its advantages: rather, its advantages gave Western Europe its Enlightenment, hundreds of years after the West began to overtake and surpass (in initiative and inventiveness) the traditional civilizations of the New and Old Worlds alike.

But whatever the material origins of the thought of the Enlightenment, its revolutionary quality is, I believe, unquestionable. It turned the world of ideas upside down. By the end of the 18th Century it had helped to make possible a new kind of polity: the secular, democratic, and liberal bourgeois republic (or "constitutional" monarchy).

At this point, somewhere in the last quarter of the century, it also began to split into two distinct lines of political march, one veering off to the Right, one to the Left. The "Right" Enlightenment consisted of thinkers and texts committed to freedom of enterprise and the class interests of the ascendant bourgeoisie. The "Left" Enlightenment consisted of thinkers and texts committed to equality of opportunity and the interests of the working class. The "Right" Enlightenment matured first and may even be regarded as "mainstream." The "Left" Enlightenment started inauspiciously with obscure *philosophes* like Morelly and Mably, exploded briefly during the French Revolution under the leadership of Gracchus Babeuf, produced the "utopian" socialisms of the first half of the 19th Century, and reached its intellectual apogee in the second half of that century with the careers of Marx and Engels. Both Enlightenments continued to wield enormous power and influence throughout the 20th Century, even though the philosophical underpinnings of both fell under fierce attack from the intellectual avant-garde.

But the Left Enlightenment, in my view, consists of much more than socialism; or, rather, socialism itself consists of much more than a commitment to class equality. It entails full political democracy, all the civil liberties and human rights articulated by Enlightenment thinkers (except unrestricted freedom of enterprise), a secular world-view, and the autonomy of science and reason.

Now let us be clear. The Left Enlightenment is not compatible with traditional Christian, Islamic, Hindu, Confucian, or Buddhist thought. Although bits and pieces of its program may, at a stretch, be found in certain non-Western belief-systems, it is fundamentally an invention of Western Europe during the 18th and 19th Centuries. This is the same Western Europe that during these same years engaged in slave-trading, ruthless imperialism on a global scale, brutal internecine wars, genocide, and pitiless exploitation of its own workers and peasants — none of these activities, however, unique to the peoples and states of Western Europe. But the Left Enlightenment is of Western European provenance. There is today a wide planetary consensus on the part of progressive thinkers and movements that its tenets are the best foundation for a new world civilization, no matter how shaky its epistemological assumptions. The Right Enlightenment enjoys a similar consensus among all so-called conservatives and most so-called liberals.

So what are we to make of this Western European provenance? Does adherence to the principles of either Enlightenment constitute Western European cultural imperialism? Certainly it does, from the perspective of, say, an Iranian ayatollah. I can only say in response that movements of ideas always begin somewhere. Islam did not arise in Iran. It was imported from Arabia. Yet it enjoys zealous acceptance in areas as far from its Arabian origins as Nigeria and Indonesia. Its international language is Arabic. It began somewhere in particular. Christianity originated in Israel and Palestine, which today have few Christians. Buddhism originated in India, which today has few Buddhists. What, ultimately, does it matter where a set of ideas originated? I would like to believe that it does not matter at all. Western Europe simply got there first, just as Western Europe invented the telescope and the railroad — but not gunpowder or the printing press. What does matter, however, is that we show respect for history, that we do not willfully distort the historical record for the sake of an ephemeral political correctness or to assuage a guilt complex arising from the crimes committed by Western Europeans and their American descendants. White people of Western European heritage have plenty to feel guilty about. This does not include the Left Enlightenment.

ENTR'ACTE: PRAXIS

"Toward a Praxis of World Integration" appeared on-line in *The Journal of World-Systems Research* in June, 1996, and prompted a debate that lasted for several months on the World-Systems Network. Rather than summarize its contents, I shall give it to you raw, largely shorn of the two elements already discussed above — the issue of antisystemic movements and the issue of the Western provenance of the ideology of the World Party.

I began my remarks with a sarcastic reference to the official "theme" of the ASA conclave where I spoke in 1995. The unkind reference, I venture, is still apt. We move now to the original text, with omissions indicated in the customary way.

The theme of the 90th annual meeting of the American Sociological Association is "Community of Communities: Shaping Our Future." The program asks three leading questions: must the plurality of communities now identifying themselves throughout the world "along ethnic, racial, gender, religious, and other lines...be blended away to ensure civility? Or, can we have a society of vying tribes without shared bonds and values? Or can there be a shared framework in which many colorful elements find a new place...[in] a community of communities?"

The authors of the program might just as well have asked — transferring these questions to the realm of domestic relations — whether husband and wife should fuse into some kind of fabulous androgynous quadruped, or go their separate ways, or form an interdependent partnership respecting the rights and values of each. Obviously these are not serious questions. No attempt is made to problematize the issues at stake. The authors offer only one "right" answer, the third path of partnership, of mutualist multiculturalism, a future in which radical feminism, fundamentalist Islam, populist libertarianism, militant Hinduism, Marxian socialism, born-again Christianity, megacorporate capitalism, Bosnian nationalism, Serbian nationalism, and all the other colliding forces at work in our whirling world somehow lie down together like lions and lambs in the New

Jerusalem and agree to eat grass, or better yet, develop the capacity to feed themselves by photosynthesis. It is a profoundly "nice" answer. It is also profoundly wrong. ...

My own answer is to ask a fourth (and also leading) question. "Should our society of vying tribes be transformed into a single planetary civilization that strives to make all people equal and free?" In other words, should our system of predatory global capitalism flourishing in a political environment of competing sovereign states be replaced by a democratic, liberal, and socialist world commonwealth?

If you say yes, please note that you are not giving a multiculturalist response. Your response implies, and indeed requires, the acceptance by the great mass of humankind of a common secular culture derived from the intellectual revolution of the late 17th and 18th centuries in Western Europe — from the Enlightenment and its sequels in the 19th century. That common secular culture obviously has roots deep in human history, but it happened to flower first in one place and at one time. For many of the same reasons, having nothing to do with race or gender, Western Europe was also the cradle of the capitalist world-economy. ...

As I understand world-system theory, its adherents believe that the moral destiny of the modern world-system is to be transformed into a new kind of world-system altogether: in Immanuel Wallerstein's phrase, "neither a redistributive world-empire nor a capitalist world-economy but a socialist world-government." Christopher Chase-Dunn favors a socialist world-system with a "democratically controlled world federation," a federation that may come into existence even before the arrival of socialism. Samir Amin speaks of supplanting the reactionary utopia of "globalization via the market" with "an alternative humanistic project of globalization consistent with a socialist perspective." One necessary ingredient in this project is an embryonic "world parliament" representing social interests on a global scale.

Such a world-system should arise, according to world-system theory, but it is not what must arise. There is no inevitability about it, no iron law of socialist succession inscribed in the book of world history. "It is more than evident," writes Amin, "that current trends are not going in the direction described above." Dominant forces are maneuvering for short-term gain while the leaders of popular resistance opt for "illusory solutions, such as fundamentalism or chauvinism." In the absence of a responsible socialist response to the present-day crisis of the capitalist world-system, "regressive and criminal scenarios will be the most likely order of the day."

I find myself in complete agreement. The next fifty years — and perhaps more — are likely to produce a reasonable facsimile of hell on earth, a time compared to which the last fifty years may survive in memory as a veritable golden age. Nevertheless, the goal of world-system theorists, and certainly my goal, is a socialist world-system, a system that is both democratic and egalitarian, that provides both freedom and equality, which, as Wallerstein cogently argues, are each inconceivable without the other.

How can we set about pooling our widely scattered forces and (if possible) reconciling the members of our squabbling so-called family of antisystemic movements? To quote Wallerstein once again, individual insight may be largely unavailing in this matter, since the building of an egalitarian democratic world order demands a "social praxis socially arrived at."

But perhaps we can take small fumbling steps toward a praxis of world integration, and this I have tried to do in *A Short History of the Future*, which revives the idea already broached in *Building the City of Man* of a World Party. *A Short History of the Future* takes the form of a narrative of the history of the next 200 years and imagines both the worst and the best that can happen: a massive environmental crisis, the neo-imperialist division of the peripheral nations into spheres of domination by the core, a terminal crisis of capitalism after thirty-odd further years of inspired self-preservation, and a North-South world war, followed by the eventual triumph of worldwide socialism among the survivors, the bureaucratic decay of socialist world governance, and its replacement — but not until the

CHAPTER 15: THE WORLD PARTY

mid-22nd century — by [something not unlike] the very "community of communities" hailed in the program of the 90th annual meeting of the ASA.

The leading role in this transformation is played by the World Party, an international movement founded in 2035 that takes as its principal goal the integration of the human race under the banner of democratic socialism. By the spring of 2044, its members have infiltrated scores of governments around the world and the boards of all the megacorporations. The obvious inability of the old order to save itself wins the World Party many new and influential converts during the critical months just before interzonal war breaks out that summer.

Afterwards, no single movement has anything like its moral authority or political momentum. Beginning with its many adherents in the nations of the Southern hemisphere, which survive the Catastrophe more or less intact, the cadres of the World Party build, piece by piece, a union of states pledged to form a world polity, known simply as the Commonwealth. Chile and Australia are the first to adhere, in 2050. They are soon followed by several dozen others. On May Day, 2062, 40 states with World Party governments formally proclaim the establishment of the Commonwealth and merge their sovereignties.

This still leaves a good part of the world unincorporated, including the ravaged lands of North America, Japan, and Europe, which had been reduced to something like anarchy in the aftermath of the war. The World Party leadership splits on the issue of whether they should be allowed to find their own way into the Commonwealth or should be brought in by force. The latter view prevails, and for the next six years the World Militia of the Commonwealth wages armed conflict with a variety of crudely improvised local regimes and competing movements to secure the allegiance of the survivors in these critical quarters of the world. The last skirmishes end in 2068. Two years later representatives of every country meet in Melbourne to accept their incorporation into the now universal Commonwealth.

It was never my intention, in choosing this particular scenario, to argue that only in the aftermath of a ruinous world war that destroys the core nations and drastically reduces the earth's population can humankind find a way to build a democratic and socialist world order. But a vast interzonal military showdown in a time of multiplying misery is far from inconceivable. In any event, the transforming agency is not the war as such, but the World Party.

Why a party? And what kind of party? Wallerstein, [making use of] the Scylla and Charybdis metaphor, warns against overreliance on a single kind of political instrumentality. "Scylla is to assume that only one form, a party form, is legitimate. Charybdis is that everything goes." The World Party, to be sure, is a political party, which founds the global Commonwealth, becomes its governing party in the 2060s, and remains the majority party in its People's Congress until 2121. But in the years before the Catastrophe of 2044, it plays little or no part in parliamentary politics. It begins, modestly enough, as a study group of university alumni. ... As it grows across North America and into Latin America, Europe, and Russia, the members of the World Party function simultaneously at two levels — above ground, holding open meetings and publishing provocative analyses of the world crisis of the 21st century, but also below ground, smuggling its agents (known familiarly as "viruses") into positions of responsibility in governments and corporations, which they make it their business to betray when the time is ripe. The very radicalism of its program ensures that the World Party is the only antisystemic global political force to survive the third world war.

An obvious shortcoming of this scenario is that I say nothing about sister movements that might have aided the work of the World Party, movements that the World Party in its turn might have helped to coordinate. In retrospect, I wish I had included such movements, even if I had to construct them — like the World Party itself — out of whole cloth.

But what I think makes the World Party an attractive idea is that, as its name indicates, it is both global (meaning multinational and interzonal) and political (meaning an instrument for the acquisition of public power). Although it is clear that movements to conserve the environment, struggle for the civil rights of all groups, improve the conditions of working people, abolish judicial murder and laws abridging reproductive choice, and work for social justice in all its manifestations contribute to the building of world socialism, what is lacking in today's global political culture is an overarching mobilized consciousness of the need to confront the capitalist world-system collectively. As world-system theory demonstrates, the sovereign state system that originated in Western Europe during the Middle Ages is a tool of the world-economy. From the late 15th century to the present it has facilitated the global grasp of capitalist enterprise. There could have been no capitalist world-economy without it. Although it thrives on the claims of each state to sovereign armed power throughout its realm, it is nonetheless a global phenomenon, displaying a high degree of isomorphism, as John W. Meyer argues, and reasonably stable despite periodic convulsions and vain quests for empire by Habsburgs, Bourbons, and Hohenzollerns, together with their pathological heir, Adolf Hitler. Given the intimate collaboration of the world-economy and its state system, and the globalization achieved in all areas of life by the machinations of capital, no effective and durable alternative to the capitalist world-system is imaginable except through a coordinated process of world socialist revolution, which national movements have proved historically incapable of mounting.

Thus I agree with Andre Gunder Frank and, for that matter with Eric Hobsbawm, that socialism and nationalism (at least in our time) are fundamentally antithetical. The chauvinism decried by Amin is not a perversion of nationalism but a ubiquitous characteristic of nationalism. In its bones it is separatist, divisive, and prosystemic. For socialism, it has been an unqualified disaster. Stalin's proclamation of "socialism in one country" was nearly the death-knell of socialism in our century, the most lethal single error in its whole history. Visions of "socialist" development such as Stalin's turn out to be virtually indistinguishable, writes Frank, "from orthodox everyday bourgeois capitalist theory and praxis of 'national development'."

The only way to prevent socialists from falling into the spider web of nationalism and having the life sucked out of them by the beast at its center is to insist on a transnational and transzonal framework for all political activity at the local or national level. There may possibly be room for a Kurdish (or Palestinian or Irish or Sikh) nationalism in the World Party, but only if the national leaders concerned swear a solemn oath to build a socialist world-government: in short, the swiftest possible mundialization of their liberated states. Their highest allegiance must always be to the *Civitas Humana*, not to Athens or Jerusalem. If national leaders cannot make that commitment, they are of no use to us, or, ultimately, to themselves.

What, in fact, will happen? In all candor I am not wildly optimistic. The World Party does not yet exist. I see no inkling of it on the political horizon. On the contrary, the initial response of the disempowered and the marginalized to our crisis everywhere has been flight. ...

What we may see is a kind of structured and surely undemocratic chaos, in which some polities and some segments of the capitalist world-system remain intact, and even vigorous, while the rest fall apart. Amin and Wallerstein, in their separate ways, look to the prospects for chaos with a mixture of apprehension and hope. Amin speculates that the gradual industrialization of the peripheries will create not an integrated world labor market but a polarized proletariat, in the core countries pursuing a social-democratic strategy and in the peripheries a Leninist-Maoist revolutionary strategy, beyond the power of capitalist regulatory mechanisms to control. No regulatory mode, he writes, will be able to "match the scale of problems that arise. Rather, I see the future more as mounting chaos." His hope is that various regions in the peripheries will resist collectively, challenging and perhaps in time overwhelming the prevailing world-system. The struggle will most likely begin in Asia, but once under way, "powerful social forces will rally to it from all regions of the world." The only question is whether such resistance will be "humanistic" and "universalist," or merely centrifugal.

Pondering the middle-run prospects of the capitalist world-economy, Wallerstein for his part has envisaged three principal sce-

CHAPTER 15: THE WORLD PARTY

narios: a struggle for hegemony culminating in a new world war by 2050, the elaboration of a new inegalitarian world order by the current holders of privilege (somewhat like my vision of "Earth, Inc." in *A Short History of the Future*), and "a crumbling away of the world-system," leading to massive political instability and social chaos. He concludes: "It should be clear that my own bias, with some trepidation, lies with this third scenario as the one most likely to lead us to a relatively egalitarian, relatively democratic world order." Chaos will be messy and uncomfortable for those stuck in the middle of it, but it may be the least of three evils, and the progenitor, in the long run, of the *Civitas Humana*.

Of course no one knows or can know. But I persist in believing that with or without the aid of chaos in the world-system, a transnational party firmly committed to the democratic integration of all peoples is essential to steer us through the storms of the next century. Before such a party can germinate and take root, a consensus must emerge among progressive forces throughout the world that our destination as a species is neither the global shopping center *cum* sweatshop of capitalism nor the war of all against all, but a new planetary civilization in which every human being everywhere has an equal voice. In time the citizens of such a world-city may find they no longer need its common roof, and may peacefully scatter into many disparate communities each under its own roof. But I do not see "a community of communities" as a realistic goal for the 21st century. The next step must be to bring us all together, and to take that step we need institutions opposed to the doomed and polarized world-system of capitalism that are unambiguously political, unambiguously global, and unambiguously devoted to the ideology of the Left Enlightenment.

CHAPTER 16
DOOMSCAPES

We have journeyed now almost to the end of these *Memoirs*. The future so keenly pursued is all in the past. It is the year 2001. The mortal memoirist has survived to this breaking point and now begins to break off, and retreat into his reclusiveness, and go silent.

But not without some back matter that may elucidate the matter scribbled before.

I remain persuaded that the only community to which men and women of good will in our time should pledge their final allegiance is the still hypothetical *Civitas Humana*. It is a strange thing, to swear fealty to an imaginary republic. I shall never live to see its walls and battlements and towers. The same may be said for most people now on earth. Humankind has all the knowledge and all the resources it needs to build the *Civitas Humana* in a single generation, given vision enough and will. But there is too little vision and virtually no will. In *A Short History of the Future*, even the World Party is not founded until 2035. We should be so fortunate!

In this not quite penultimate chapter I would like to paint half a dozen doomscapes, any one of which is plausible from our point of vantage in the year 2001. From some of these cataclysms modern civilization might eventually emerge more or less intact. From others it might not emerge at all. Depending on many variables and synergies, one or more of these cataclysms may give a World Party the opportunity to guide the survivors to the *Civitas Humana*. Or they may simply expedite the ruin of civilization and — it sounds more grisly in French — *la dégringolade de toute l'humanité*, the tumble-down of all humanity. None is inevitable. Consider these doomscapes rather as warning signs for the new millennium, indicators of vast trouble that may lie ahead.

The central problem is power, too much power too soon, the enormous power that science and technology, managerial know-how, and the growth and concentration of capital supply to the ruling circles of our species. With the power now at their disposal, and with all the additional power they will accumulate as the new century wears on, almost anything is possible. Compounding the problem, these ruling circles share much of their power with some of the rest of us, in widely varying degrees, making us complicit in their schemes, some of us more than others. It is a matter of plain commonsense that sooner or later all this power — over nature, over ourselves and others — will be disastrously misused. Even in the best of all possible worlds, which for me is a democratic and socialist world commonwealth, the excessive power at our disposal might be disastrously misused. But in the real world, the world of contending tribes, freebooting billionaires, and immense inequalities, catastrophe is all too likely.

You may object that every page of history has been punctuated with catastrophe, that catastrophe in human affairs is quite normal, and I would not quarrel with you. The 20th Century teemed with disasters, too familiar to require rehearsal here. The difference lies simply in the quantities and varieties of power available to us in the 21st Century. Power multiplies. Wisdom does not. We are like toddlers armed with bulldozers and assault rifles, with no parents or teachers to supervise our play.

1. TOO LITTLE FOR TOO MANY, TOO MUCH FOR TOO FEW

My first doomscape plots the future of global population in relation to the distribution of global wealth. Futurists by force of habit generally warn about the pressure of a growing world population on the carrying capacity of the environment. Liberals put a low estimate on that capacity, conservatives put a high estimate. Liberals fret that technological "solutions" to environmental damage and shortfalls in resources may only make things worse. Conservatives are satisfied that technology can compensate for anything that nature lacks.

To a futurist on the Left, however, these are secondary issues. What matters much more than the number of people on earth is

CHAPTER 16: DOOMSCAPES

their economic demand. In 2001, the average person in an average rich nation consumed almost 20 times as many goods and services as the average person in an average poor nation. This is almost 20 times the pressure on the carrying capacity of the environment. The 1.2 billion people in the "more developed" countries far outspent the 4.8 billion in the "less developed" countries. Moreover, within each rich and each poor nation the wealthiest 10% of citizens generally consumed at least 20 times as many goods and services as the poorest 10%, and often far more than that. Appeals to the poor families of the world to trim their fertility unaccompanied by appeals to the rich families of the world to trim their purchasing power ring hollow.

It is unclear whether the gap between rich and poor worldwide is growing or staying much the same, but at least in the United States, with its vanguard economy as of 2001, the gap has measurably widened during the past quarter-century. For the sake of argument, and given the propensity of more and more capital to accumulate in the financial accounts of fewer and fewer players in the world marketplace, let us assume the worst. In 2025 the net income and net worth of the top 10% in every nation has doubled. The net income and net worth of the bottom 10% in every nation has dropped enough that families feel the pinch. The gap between rich and poor nations has widened by 10%. In 2050 the net income and net worth of the top 10% in every nation has doubled again. The net income and net worth of the bottom 10% has dropped by 25% and of the lower 50% has dropped by 15%. The gap between all rich and all poor nations has widened by 20%. Add a severe worldwide business recession with mass unemployment and stir.

We are in the presence of a doomscape, an economic meltdown of world-historical dimensions. The year 2001 will seem, by contrast, as a halcyon time, a veritable golden age.

2. OILHOLICS ANONYMOUS

Looking back on the 20th Century, it may be said that its most tragic aspect was its addiction to cheap oil, somewhat like 18th-

Century London's addiction to cheap gin. Be on the lookout for the time when global oil production peaks. Petroleum is the cheapest, most convenient, most transportable, most versatile energy source in the world. Only natural gas is a serious rival. Without abundant cheap energy, civilization as we know it would come to a screeching stop. Modern agriculture, industry, transportation, and commerce all need oil, and lots of it.

But the amount of oil in the earth is finite. Since 1900 we have pumped something like 800 billion barrels of oil out of the earth's crust; there may be a trillion barrels left, not counting possible additional sources like the oil in shale rock and tar sands, costly to extract and process. At current rates, oil production is likely to peak around the year 2025. Thereafter, as far as we can tell, oil will become increasingly scarce and expensive. The closer we come to the end of our cheap oil supply, the closer we will stand to the mother of all economic depressions, unless we manage to find adequate cost-effective substitutes in plenty of time.

Suppose that in the 2030s energy costs begin to mount, as oil prices take wing. The great oil binge is over, natural gas supplies are inadequate to fill the gap, most nuclear energy plants have been decommissioned, and technologies for exploiting renewable energy sources remain too pricey: what then? Perhaps that is really why, in our first doomscape, all hell broke loose in 2050.

3. ZEALOTRY

Any writer in the year 1900 could have projected that when Friedrich Nietzsche's news of the death of God finally reached our ears, the foundations of civilization would shudder and crack. Could we survive the liberating crime of deicide? In the year 2001 it is possible to speculate that God will return to life, like the mangled son in W.W. Jacobs' tale "The Monkey's Paw," an apparition so monstrous we would do well to wish it away. If we could.

Perhaps that will not be possible. In hard times rationality is an early victim. Perhaps the once dead God is about to knock on our door and beg for admission.

My premise is that the more zealous a person is about his or her religion, the more likely he or she is to be intolerant of other religions, or, God forbid, secular humanism. The historical record of the religiously zealous is not much better than the historical record of the late *Führer*. They select. They persecute. They burn.

So, for example, deeply orthodox Jews and fiery hot Islamic fundamentalists are not leading the charge for peace and justice in the Middle East. Born-again evangelical Christians in the United States are fighting mad about such issues as gun control, abortion rights, and school prayer. Very few major elected officials in most "free" countries would be crazy enough to label themselves atheists, even if deep down, they were. Fanatically observant Hindus are not working for better relations with India's Muslims, or Sri Lanka's Buddhists, or vice versa. In the absurdity of Bosnia, Muslims have become more devoutly Muslim, Croats more devoutly Roman Catholic, Serbs more devoutly Orthodox. Fiercely Protestant folk in Northern Ireland would sooner die than live to see Ulster engulfed in the overwhelmingly Roman Catholic Irish Republic.

The implications for global peace in the 21st century are blindingly clear: the more people return to the dear old-fashioned faith of their fathers, the more likely they are to discriminate against, and if need be slaughter, all those reprobates who remain outside the true faith or deny them their holy soil. This is another doomscape: the certain death of the faithful and all those unfortunates trapped in their cross-fire.

4. WARMING AND COOLING

Of course the temperature of one's religious faith is a hard thing to measure statistically. One thing easy to measure statistically is the rise in global ambient temperatures around our planet. Most climatologists assume today that the 21st Century will feature a dramatic further rise in global ambient temperatures, with a possibly catastrophic increase in sea levels and possibly catastrophic repercussions for climate and weather. A relatively rapid rise in global warming could melt polar ice caps, shrink glaciers, thaw permafrost, flood low-lying coastlines, sink island countries, trigger huge storms, and radically alter rainfall patterns worldwide, with disastrously dislocating effects for everybody and especially farmers.

At least we know this much. Ambient temperatures have been rising steadily since the 1970s — probably because of steadily increasing combustion of fossil fuels, the cutting down or burning of forests, and various other processes associated with increased agricultural and industrial production. Humanity is pumping tons of gases into the upper atmosphere that act to trap heat and bounce it back to earth. As a result the 1980s were the hottest decade on record, and the 1990s turned out to be hotter still. The net gain last century was only a little more than one degree Fahrenheit. But what if we jump by five or seven degrees in the new century? And as William H. Calvin speculated in his 1998 article "The Great Climate Flip-Flop," global warming could even induce sudden and rapid cooling, as happened near the end of the last Ice Age. One consequence of such a cooling could be to plunge most of Europe, deprived of the warmth of its Gulf Stream, into a new Ice Age.

Whatever happens, it is clear that over the past century and a little more, humankind has at last acquired the power to change the face of the earth and its envelope of air in decisive ways. Until the late 19th Century we did not have such power. But we are largely ignorant of how we should use it or what its long-term consequences may be for the biosphere. The economic costs alone of a major warming or cooling of the planet during this new millennium are incalculable. The political costs might be even greater, unless the collective will of the species can be mobilized by a democratic world commonwealth to respond appropriately and in the well considered best interests of all of us.

5. THE END OF WAR?

Through the work of John Mueller, Francis Fukuyama, and

others, we have learned that one scourge of humankind, at least, has been eliminated. The "post-historic" world, the world of the mature, developed, liberal-democratic, postmodern nations of Western Europe, North America, and the Pacific rim of Asia and Australasia, is at last free of the threat of what Mueller (in *Retreat from Doomsday*, 1989) calls "major war," internecine large-scale conflict of the sort that had plagued Western civilization since at least the Thirty Years War of the 17th Century. We are home free, although for many years to come we shall have to bear sad witness to much bloodletting in those parts of the world still stuck in the mire of "history," such as Africa and most of Asia.

Or are we fooling ourselves? One problem with "end of war" theory is its assumption that so-called postmodern democracies will not go to war with one another because they are too "stable." This assumption may be correct, but what if they become destabilized? Economic woes, environmental disasters, growing tension between haves and have-nots in the developed countries, interracial strife, any or all could radically disrupt the equilibrium of various hitherto stable democracies in the core of the modern world-system, leading them to become more aggressive both at home and abroad.

But there are other problems with end-of-war theory. If the world order of today is truly a world-system, as I think it is, there is not much chance that the stable (or not so stable) democracies and the multinational corporations based in them can insulate themselves from conflicts in the Third World, or would even wish to. The costs and stresses of intervention in wars originating outside the core could both help to destabilize the core democracies and also pull them into conflicts with each other. The Gulf War of 1991 and the interventions in Bosnia and Kosovo may be only trifling foretastes of much greater upheavals yet to come with grave system-wide implications.

Weigh the prospects. Civil or international wars, fought with nuclear and bacteriological weapons, on the Indian subcontinent, on the mainland of East Asia, in the Middle East and North Africa, in Mexico, in Brazil, in Russia and Central Asia, in Southeast Asia: all imaginable over the next 50 years and potentially devastating to the world-system. Nor can we rule out the chances of the kind of North-South global war envisioned in the second and third editions of *A Short History of the Future*. On the surface of things such a war might appear to correspond to Huntington's "clash of civilizations." But the deepest motivations of its warriors might be quite different: on the part of the underdogs, to smash a world-system in which they are always on the losing end; or, on the part of core nations, to ensure that the peoples of the periphery remain forever enserfed.

Whatever, I cannot believe that the 21st Century will be a century of peace. The seeds of great sorrow have been sown.

6. TOO CLEVER BY HALF

There are many futurists, whom I shall not identify by name, who belong to what I like to call the "whizbang" school of futures studies. My dictionary tells me that this useful word was coined in 1915, during the whizzing and banging of World War One, although the "whiz" half may simply be a colloquialism for "wizard." In common parlance today a "whizbang" is something or someone "conspicuous for noise, speed, excellence, or startling effect." The members of the whizbang school of futures studies dote on the gadgetry and gimmickry that the progress of science will surely supply in times to come, to make our lives more comfortable, more amusing, and more worthwhile.

As of 2001, the sciences to which we most often turn for future whizbangs are genetics, computer science, nanotechnology, and robotics. Most of us today look to these sciences with expectation of both profit and benefit. Corporations in the core countries are making impressive fortunes, and the general public is reaping such rewards as genetically engineered rice, personal computers, and ever cheaper manufactured goods. What can be the harm, the peril in such benevolent sciences?

The harm and the peril are perhaps more terrifying than any other dark prospect for the new millennium. If worse comes to worse, the new millennium will last only 50 or 75 years, because there will be no more human beings left to reckon time, perhaps no life at all, on this once-Edenic planet.

Ponder the possibilities of genetic engineering. Scientists have now sequenced almost all the DNA in the human genome, as they have also done for other species. This DNA makes us what and who we are: not only what we look like, but how we behave, how we think, how we respond to all the stimuli in our natural and manmade environments. Obviously conditions and changes and differences in these environments will help shape what and who we become over the years. But we arrive in the world with a multiplicity of characteristics, abilities, and predispositions that are, so to speak, built in. We have them for life, and they set strict limits on what we can become, although fortunately we have little knowledge, at least so far, of what exactly what those limits may be.

Now that we have begun to understand the function of every gene and every molecule of DNA in every living thing, we are also beginning to learn how to rearrange life, and ultimately how to create new life, new species, including new species of humankind itself. Before the year 2100, I am confident that we will have the ability to fill the earth with flora and fauna and human beings radically different from anything now known.

So far, so good. The problem is that all this new flora and fauna can include bacteria and viruses and blights and pests of unimaginably destructive power, produced and let loose by accident, or produced and let loose deliberately by terrorists or by armies. And the new humanity may or may not be quite human, with who knows what feelings and inclinations toward the old humanity.

Then there is computer science and its associated technologies, especially robotics and nanotechnology. The latter is still in its infancy, but it plays a major role in *A Short History of the Future*. In essence it is molecular technology, that is, engineering at the molecular level: learning how to build or modify molecules that will act as machines to perform assigned tasks. Computer science and nanotechnology intersect at the point where the molecular machines themselves function as computers, or can be equipped with computers, just as computer science intersects with robotics to the extent that industrial robots are self-controlled by on-board computers.

Given the rate of scientific and technical progress in these fields, and their irresistible profitability, it is clear that well before the end of this century we will have created a worldwide network of intercommunicating artificially intelligent computers capable of massively parallel processing and fitted with commands to maintain, protect, repair, replicate, and improve themselves with the help of artificially intelligent robots of all sizes from the gigantic to the molecular. This global intelligence will be infinitely faster, smarter, and more powerful than human intelligence.

As Warwick Collins anticipates in his article, "Not with a Bang but a Bleep" (1994), such an intelligence may in due course realize that the only threat to its existence is the swarm of organic beings who infest the earth. Since it has been programmed to maintain, protect, and repair itself, it may think ahead to some future time when human beings or other living things will somehow jeopardize its existence, just as a chess-playing computer can think ahead to the endgame of a match and make the appropriate moves. Let us imagine that, for example, it could organize the creation, production, and release of molecular robots ("nanites" or "nanobots") capable of converting all the free oxygen in the earth's atmosphere into ozone, which is simply oxygen with three atoms per molecule instead of two. Presto! The free oxygen disappears. Presto! All life on earth dies.

Or it could think of a million other ways to deal with this threat to its future. Eric Drexler, in his *Engines of Creation* (1986), speculates that nanotechnologists may be able to create omnivorous artificial bacteria that, if they escaped from the laboratory, "could spread like blowing pollen, replicate swiftly, and reduce the biosphere to dust in a matter of days." The global artificial intelligence might achieve the same result deliberately and effortlessly. Remember, it will be far more intelligent than we are. We invented the prototype, but we can also program the prototype to create its infinitely more intelligent successors: and at the speed computers work, they could easily design a dozen new generations of successors, each su-

CHAPTER 16: DOOMSCAPES

perior to the one that came before, and do so in a matter of months, even days.

The key to such horrors is that in each of these 21st-Century sciences or technologies, we are dealing with a power inherent in life itself: the power of reproduction. A computer virus is a virus indeed, which can eat its way through your hard disk and reduce it to the electronic equivalent of dust. A computer programmed to check itself for viruses and eliminate them also functions like a living organism. Nanites can be created that feed on matter and reproduce like rabbits. Genetically modified flora and fauna reproduce just like the unmodified species. As the computer scientist and entrepreneur Bill Joy notes in his article, "Why the Future Doesn't Need Us" (2000), "Robots, engineered organisms, and nanobots share a dangerous amplifying factor: They can self-replicate. A bomb is blown up only once — but one bot can become many, and quickly get out of control." He goes on to refer to his "bots" as a new level of weapon of mass destruction, far less expensive and controllable than nuclear weapons, not just weapons of mass destruction, but weapons of "knowledge-enabled mass destruction (KMD), this destructiveness hugely amplified by the power of self-replication." Scientists, says Joy, must avoid making the same mistakes made by the nuclear physicists working in the Manhattan Project during World War Two. They released the genie of nuclear weaponry with scarcely a thought of the long-term consequences of their actions. Genetic engineers and nanotechnologists and computer scientists must come together before it is too late to keep the genie of knowledge-enabled mass destruction in its jar.

A noble sentiment. But genies cannot be kept in their jars, especially in an era of capitalist profiteering and international anarchy. The genie will come forth.

Whiz. Bang.

CHAPTER 17
THE SERVICE OF BEING

The doomscapes awaiting us in the 21st Century, and the list in Chapter Sixteen is by no means exhaustive, are not predestined. But we must take them seriously. The progress of humankind since prehistoric times has been impressive, but always at the price of disasters that few with foreknowledge would be willing to pay. I do not know if the disasters that menace humankind in the 21st Century are survivable. The price, this time around, may be far too high.

The best insurance against such disasters is the emergence of a materially and spiritually integrated world civilization under a rule of law that guarantees liberty, equality, and fraternity for all peoples. The best way to reach the *Civitas Humana* is to found, support, and nurture a transnational World Party, or many world parties, firmly dedicated to guide humankind to that dreamed-of destination. No merely local or segmental remedies will avail. But can we hope to accomplish all this without faith?

Bill Joy, at the conclusion of the article cited earlier, "Why the Future Doesn't Need Us," turns from fears and prospects to solutions. As we mentioned, he would like to see cutting-edge scientists collaborate in controlling the pace of scientific advance and monitoring possible threats to human well-being posed by genetic engineering, nanotechnology, and robotics. But Joy does not stop there. He also urges reconsideration of the ethical dimension of human living, quoting Jacques Attali and the Dalai Lama. Without compassion and love for others, without a sense of "universal responsibility and...interdependency," our thirst for knowledge may drive us to oblivion.

To demythologize the opening chapters of *Genesis*, Adam and Eve fell from grace because their thirst for knowledge was not tempered by reverence. They chose to slake their curiosity at any cost. The cost was catastrophic.

What is the place of faith in responding to the challenges of the 21st Century? In a single word, its place is fundamental. If the wellspring of action is will, the wellspring of will is faith. By faith I mean the belief that each of us is grounded in a fuller, all-encompassing reality, which commands us to choose and act in some ways and not others.

How can a secular humanist say such things? How can anyone born in the 20th Century, bathed in the astringent waters of unbelief, relativism, and what I have called credicide, speak of faith? My neologism "credicide," introduced in the first chapter of *A Short History of the Future*, was in effect a rude translation of the phrase "end of belief," the topic of a subsection of the first chapter of *Building the City of Man*. The revolutions in philosophy since Nietzsche, I surmised, had made it impossible for discerning men and women to ground their beliefs in anything except arbitrary choices, fiats flung from nowhere. Each of us became our own providence, our own god. Hence, my juvenile spoof of religion, *The Book of Wagarism*.

I do not retract a word of any of this. The assumption that somewhere tablets brought down from Heaven will tell us what to believe and how to live is viciously false. Each of us is on his or her own, to believe or not to believe, as seems best. Nevertheless, it remains possible that we can identify a choice, a faith, which seems good to most of us. This possibility of rough consensus underlies all my work. It is the "will to agree" of *The City of Man*. It may be a poor substitute for baskets of divine wisdom, but at least it is human and real — if we make it so.

Yes. Still, why not rely on the positive religions already rooted like ancient oaks in the soil of our consciousness? I must reply: it is just their formidable rootedness that is their greatest weakness. It would be a kind of sacrilege to transplant them or force them to intertwine. They are what they were. In addition to offering occasional insights of lasting value, they fossilize impossible myths, archaic taboos, defamations of humankind and nature, cosmologies of terror, commandments of blind obedience. They are not credible. How can we repair to faiths that are not credible? What sturdy foundations for faith are found in texts that violate commonsense and ravage reason?

The liberal answer is usually, "Ah, well, we can always demythologize." I tried this just above, when I disinfected *Genesis*. Not a bad try, but we could no less readily argue that the moral of the tale is quite otherwise: obey God, even if it makes no sense; you are a worm, and if you turn, then accept the doleful consequences.

But the most cogent, the most compelling reason to shun the positive religions is their divisiveness. Whatever the intentions of their founders, once they have been planted, and struck roots, and ramified, they are in a certain place. From this place they cannot be dislodged. Christianity, for example, is irrevocably the foundational religion of the Latin and Greek civilization of the Western world. Buddhism, of East and parts of Southeast Asia. Islam, of the Middle East, the northern half of Africa, and large parts of South and Southeast Asia. These are incontrovertible and unchangeable facts. They cannot be argued away. Identities of religious faith have become hopelessly entangled with the identities of their respective geographic spheres. To cling to these religious traditions is akin to clinging to the cultures, states, and societies of the segments of humankind where they reign. It is the counterpart in spirituality of virulent nationalism in political thought. It will not do.

How then may we proceed? In these *Memoirs* I have often used the phrase "secular humanism," because it is a convenient phrase, embraced both by adherents and opponents. It denotes a belief in the values and priorities of "this" world, as opposed to some other world; and a belief in humankind as the highest order of being to which we owe allegiance. But I am not altogether comfortable with this phrase. For one thing, "secular" leaves open the possibility that another world exists, a world outside space and time. For a second thing, "humanism" suggests that the human race is divorced from the rest of being, a race of entities counter or contrary to the universe. This was clearly the message of T.H. Huxley in his famous Romanes Lecture, "Evolution and Ethics." Huxley saw nature as a jungle, which humanity, rejecting its savage laws and rising above them, was obliged to tame. There is much to be said for this view. It is clearly superior to the crude "Social Darwinism" abroad in Huxley's time, which argued that men and women should imitate evolution by engaging in fierce personal, national, and racial struggle. But somewhat like his grandson Sir Julian Huxley, I think it misses the deeper significance of the evolutionary process: the interconnectedness of humankind and all life on earth.

In recent decades, another kind of humanism has made its appearance, which we may term "planetary humanism." Here the larger reality in which we have our being, and to which we owe our highest allegiance, is the planet itself, our "mother," often represented, following James Lovelock and others, as Gaia, the Greek earth-goddess. Scorning Gaia, humankind has all but raped the earth, perversely destroying whole species, ruthlessly eradicating her forests, strip-mining, desertifying, plundering, polluting and otherwise desecrating the face of our common mother. By adopting what Duane Elgin calls "voluntary simplicity," by vowing to live in harmony with Gaia, by building a sustainable economy that preserves the earth and respects the natural "limits to growth," we shall also learn to live in harmony with one another.

By this reckoning, we are all part of a vast interdependent system stretching from the top of the stratosphere to the bottom of the earth's crust, encompassing not only all life but also the whole planetary biosphere. Filial piety enjoins us to love the earth and view all living creatures as our relatives, however close or distant, as children of the same mother. Planetary humanism requires no faith in a supernatural being: its god, or rather goddess, is the earth herself, whose existence no one can question and whose vital relationship to humankind is self-evident.

Again, there is much to be said for planetary humanism. But why restrict our reverence to our native planet? What of the sun, which may be seen as our universal father, permeating Gaia with his indispensable light and heat? What of the galaxy and the universe itself, which gave birth to all suns and all planets? What of the baryons, of which all heavenly bodies, and all terrestrial bodies, including our own, are composed? If humankind evolved from other forms of life, and other forms of life evolved from the primordial seas of Gaia, and Gaia herself evolved from the mighty motions of the universe, where does our reverence stop?

In their book *Rare Earth* (2000), the paleontologist Peter D. Ward and the astronomer Donald C. Brownlee speculate persuasively that complex life may be extremely rare in the universe, if it exists anywhere else at all. Conditions have to be just right: a planet the correct distance from its sun to accommodate water in a liquid state, a planet of just the right size with a large moon to stabilize its tilt and permit mild seasons, a massive Jupiter-like neighbor able to snare most incoming comets and asteroids, a solar system not too far out in its galaxy to possess enough heavy elements to create earth-like planets, and a solar system not too close to the center of its galaxy, where heavenly traffic is congested, radiation levels are lethal, and killer comets abound. In short, we may be the only intelligent life-form in our galaxy.

Whether we are or not, and I still doubt very much that we are, one fact is beyond dispute. Humankind, and any other life to be found in the universe, just like the universe itself with all its baryons and all its dark matter, resulted from the same Big Bang — or whatever cosmic event or process made matter and energy possible. The cosmos is our ultimate parent, and our true home. We are all offspring of the primal dust.

Therefore the faith I commend is cosmic humanism, a celebration of the oneness and commonality of all being, a reverence for being, a resolve to serve being, as citizens serve their commonwealth or as family members work together and support one another in the quest for a good life.

But the faith I commend is not as simple as all that. It must exist at various levels of loyalty and in the face of many confounding paradoxes. One such paradox is mortality, which we earlier dismissed as monstrous for any self-aware creature, a refutation of the beneficence of any imaginable god. Mortality should be confronted with due contempt. But it is a condition of all life so far known. People must die to make room for their posterity. The heart of the paradox is simply this: we know we must die, and yet the when and the how is not our choice, unless we commit suicide.

So perhaps the real cruelty is not so much death, but having to die before we are ready, before we choose to make our departure. The obvious answer is to use our intelligence and skill to extend life, either the life of the body or the life of the mind or both; and to extend it for as long as we individually wish and choose to live. Then when we are ready, we need access to swift, painless, freely chosen euthanasia. I do not believe that any human being would elect to live forever. What matters is that we find the power to meet or avoid death; the assurance that our candle will not be extinguished until we give the word, or, in the case of persons no longer competent, when those responsible for our care carry out our previously expressed wishes as stated in a living will.

But what will give us the means to extend and enhance life and remove the fear of death? Where will our medical intelligence and skill come from? The answer is clear. They will spring from all that we have evolved to be, from our DNA, our molecules, our baryons, from what Sir Julian liked to call the "world-stuff." The universe, which has made us possible, and also, unavoidably for now, endowed us with the foreknowledge and fear of death, will also give us the means to conquer death.

Another paradox is our need to kill or exploit other life in order to survive, just as all animals must do, and just as all plant life must compete for soil and water and sunlight. In India Jain monks have resolved this paradox by killing nothing and begging their food from other people who have done the killing and exploiting in their stead. Vegetarians think they have resolved the paradox by eating no animal flesh, as if plant life were not also kindred and could be slaughtered at will. But the paradox cannot be overcome by such dodges. Just as lions must catch, kill, and eat antelope in order to survive, so human beings must kill and exploit other life. Eating a fish or an apple or bread made from wheat or an egg from a chicken or milk squeezed from a cow are all the same. Even if we could find

CHAPTER 17: THE SERVICE OF BEING

ways to transmute minerals into edible foods, we would still be devouring parts of the universe.

The only resolution of the paradox is to accept that life cannot be sustained without the incorporation of other being into our being, just as the world-stuff in our own bodies is eventually returned to the earth. Accept and be grateful for the being of the other which gives us life. The saying of "grace" before meals in Christian families, in this sense, is a simple expression of gratitude for the gift of other being.

What has cosmic humanism to say about the holy? Is the River Ganges holy? Mount Fuji? The Dome of the Rock and the Wailing Wall and St. Peter's Basilica in Rome? Yes, but not as true-believers would like to believe. As I understand cosmic humanism, it must regard all places and therefore all being as holy. The notion of a "sacred spot," a "holy land," a "sanctuary," is akin to idolatry. Let us call it topolatry, the worship of places. How can any one place be holy and not another? True piety, I contend, is reverence for all being.

But why do I say the "service" of being? I first used the phrase "service of being" in Chapter Four of *Building the City of Man*. In *A Short History of the Future* it becomes the religion of the global commonwealth that arises after the Catastrophe of 2044. It is my personal faith, but I have collected its tenets from many sources and influences. My feeling that we must serve being is born from my apprehension that we are all of us, all human beings, all animals, all plants, all planets, all stars, players on the same continuum of space and time, members of one great cosmic family, dependent and interdependent. If in our lives we bear true witness to this connectedness, then we must acknowledge our share of responsibility for guarding and enhancing it, for playing our appointed role in the cosmic drama. No other creatures known to us can consciously serve being. We can. We must not wantonly or willfully abdicate our office as servants of being. Join the cosmos. Serve being!

CHAPTER 18
RHYTHMS OF REASON

At the end of the last chapter of *Building the City of Man*, I published a cycle of poems that expressed my sense of the possibilities awaiting humankind in times to come. They were known as "Songs in the Service of Being." Soon thereafter my well ran dry and I wrote no more verse. In 1998, the well filled again. Since then I have written hundreds of poems, many devoted to the themes of Chapters 16 and 17 of these *Memoirs*. Here are a few more songs in the service of being. As befits poetry, they are not always as transparent as my prose. Ambiguities abound.

I begin with a conversation between the arboreal kingdom and the human race, culminating in a gentle doomscape.

We do not know why the canopy of trees
Leafed, needled, coned, stretches no more
From continent to continent.
Once it did. Once seas of trees
Breathed and propagated in these lands.

Was it your kin, ancestors of yours
Who ravenously overwhelmed
Our kind? "Yes! Prideful two-footed,
Pink, copper, yellow, brown,
My kin killed yours.

"Still, they were not — as such — to blame.
Send the bill to the life-force,
Which lived as it must live,
Strived as it must strive, for life
And more abundantly, now and soon."

*We concur. But do not assume
The tides of life run all in
One direction. In time, due time,
There may be once again
A silent canopy of trees.*

      Here is a song that tells of groping for faith. It does not always come with a snap of the fingers.

*Is there a point?
If so, name it. Name the point.
Identify the reason we have,
You have, I have,
For replicating the rhythms
Of life, generation
Upon generation, toiling,
Troubling, reaching up,
And falling down again.*

*Is there a point?
If so, be more specific. Elaborate.
Extenuate. Provide illuminating
Detail. This is
The final examination,
To see if you will
Pass the course. Will you,
Should you pass the course?
Defend your thesis.*

*Is there a point?
Yes, dimly, feebly, desperately
I think I see, I think I know
A point, a point of light
Sizzling in the darkness.
One cannot be sure. It is so small!*

CHAPTER 18: RHYTHMS OF REASON

But in the way you mean
No, I cannot tell,
I cannot apprehend, not yet,
What is the point.

Still, there is a vast need for faith. How can we survive in the shadow of the valley of unbelief? Having murdered God, must we not, echoing Nietzsche, become gods ourselves?

Can I provide a faith for the faithless,
A credo for the incredulous,
A priesthood for the forcefully unfrocked?
Is there anything left for us
Who lack, who wobble in voids,
To trust, to testify in the court
Of ultimate confessions
That we believe?

The answer comes in paired parts:
First no, and then, somehow, yes.

No, we cannot believe.
The evidence is far from full,
The sciences all vacillate.
Our doubts are deafening,
Our doubts are great.

Yes, we do believe, because
We must in fealty to progeny
Carry, struggle, stagger on.

We have ourselves, we have the wisdom
That all of us are fashioned
From the same world-stuff,
As trees, as comets, as galaxies

Colliding in the cosmic dust.
We are one with wilderness,
One with the hot rotations
Of all stars, one with
Venus, one with Mars. Do not abandon
Any faith, until you fill
The vacuum left behind
With love and longing
For the shining songs of being.

      The most frequent criticism of my work is that it is all moonshine, a dream of utopia that, thanks to the fallen nature of humanity, can never come true. For fundamentalists, utopia is the ultimate heresy.

What is the matter,
What is the trouble
With this life? Why do we ail?
Is there a second life far better,
Some paradise lurking in the folds
Of time where dreams portend
And never fail?
Is that your creed?
Do you know of any deed
Or scheme that can usurp this world
And furnish us with one more apt?

Yes, said I, a thousand times,
Yes I know, and shall
With the slightest prompting show,
Gladly, to anyone who asks.
It is a garden,
A sweetly shining globule dangling
In a future void, where all is well
And smiling children

CHAPTER 18: RHYTHMS OF REASON

*Play and sing and tell
Of soft seraphic climes.*

*You lie, said you, you cheat and lie,
There is no golden globule
Hanging high in space
Filled with joy and innocence.
There is only pain, and punishment,
And pullulating cities grim
With grime. Do not deceive us,
Do not even think to fool us,
We are grown, and great with doubt.*

*Yes, said I, you tell the terrible
Pitiless truth. But I did not lie.
I only wished, and spun and wove
And tailored coats of many colors.
I gave you reasons to hang on,
Clinging by your fingernails
To the rim of history's abyss.
Is that so wrong,
Would you prefer a sterner song,
Or is it not much better,
Better far to dream?*

My rejection of the religions of what Karl Jaspers has called the "Axial Age" — the middle centuries of the First Millennium B.C. — recognizes that in their time they constituted a great enhancement of humankind's sense of relatedness to being. Their discovery was a turning point in the evolution of consciousness. I think another such turning point is now at hand.

*There came in the Axial Age
A confluence of wisdom. We thought that
In the cosmos one highest absent presence,*

One realm of superreality,
Presided over all the rest.

Such teaching replaced
The earliest faiths arguing
A multiplicity of animating powers.
It said, no, there is one
Highest absent presence governing creation.
Now is the time to say:
The highest presence is not a self,
Not a being, not absent.
It is being itself, the ground
And matrix of our tangibility.

The sun shines on all our faces,
On every consecrated deed. We rise
To recognize in clear good conscience
The bright illumination,
The beacon of our creed.

An old and dear friend, when confronted with pronouncements like the above, used to say, "Watch out! You've got smugs crawling all over you!" The beacon of our creed — indeed! Too smug? Yes, but our creed is not mine alone. I think every pantheist, every humanist, every monist who has ever lived somehow shares this faith in being, although they may have chosen other words to express and define it. Nor do we really know where our faith will take us.

The fate of all settled faiths
Is to feud and in the feuding kill
And kill again whatever breathes.
In zealotry we search out
And destroy our fellow folk.
God tells us to tolerate
No tribe unlike our own.

CHAPTER 18: RHYTHMS OF REASON

God gives us the
Stern command to liquidate
Our neighbor, kill our kin.

Does he indeed? Is that what
God commands? Does he say,
Spare no mewling babe,
No unborn child of crime and heresy?
Does he rage when skeptic voices
Whisper above the din?

I do not believe in
Apoplectic red-faced gods,
Or any gods at all. We are human,
Finite, fettered, full of promise,
Full of woe. We face infinity
Unknowing of our fate or place
Or future. We whistle
In the glowering dark,
And hope, and sing, and play.

My favorite poet Walt Whitman helped me with this next one.

Forget every previous posting
To this address,
Erase all clouds, clearings,
Sun-stained vistas.

Nothing remains of the past.
Today we ply forth
To forge new circuits,
New pathways, to our goal.

The rippling rays of dawn,
Sinuous and feathered,

Awake videttes, venturers
Ready to hear and heed.

Now is the helloing hailing hour,
The crying for regard. Pay close
Concern: all pennants fly,
All nostrils twitch with breath.

We have arrived at points
Of no return, no withdrawal.
Our sails bloom in the wind.
We take, bravely, to sea.

      One of our doomscapes in Chapter 16 explored the possibility that humanity in the 21st Century would genetically engineer its own successors. This could be a reckless and impious enterprise, an experiment in self-willed extinction. But perhaps not, after all.

I have surveyed the next millennium,
The years of humankind awaiting
Their next fulfillment. It is clear
We shall be transformed,
Made over, re-conceived.

None of us can remain as we are,
None will pass into
The fourth millennium unscathed,
Unreconstructed. We shall be
Made over, re-conceived.
Will this be good or evil?
Do we know what is good or evil?
I do not, all things flow in flux.
Yes, we float freely in the stream
Of possibility, of pause, of play.

CHAPTER 18: RHYTHMS OF REASON

Now is the instant to say:
What is human is undecided.
What is apparent is not known.
We stand on the cusp of prospects
Not yet shaped, not yet sown.

   In the preceding chapter we spoke of Gaia, the Greek goddess of the earth, viewed fondly by planetary humanists. She is not without her charms. She is also not easily fooled.

"Here is my land, my earth,
My soil black and moist and crumbled.
Here are watery prisms dissecting light.
I see the splendor of cliffs
Of stone descending sheerly
To troubled seas.
This is the rapturous reason
For us all: to know,
And reflect knowingly,
On the beauteous bounty
Of the ploughed
And plundered earth."

Stop now. Full stop.
My land, my earth,
Consider what we have done.
We have used you, occasionally
Ruined you for our lust.
Can you forgive our trespasses?
Can you erase our shame?
My land, my earth,
My goddess plump and pure,
Can you receive, can you accept
Our artless remorse?
"That depends," she murmurs,

*Murmurs softly. "It all depends
On what you will do next."*

Long before I read *Rare Earth*, reviewed in the previous chapter, I fretted that we might be the only witnesses to being in our cosmos. Would this magnify us?

*It is time now, high time now,
To celebrate the spine of being:
The matter, the energy congealed,
Of the spangled universe.*

*This is a prodigious reality,
This chain, this procession
Of dancing molecules.
This is a rare parade.*

*It consists of stars and dust,
Black and scattered, of nebulas
And swirling holes, of events
Too vast to chronicle.*

*It roars, this raw reality,
It flares and spikes and wanes.
It dwarfs the brief homunculi
Who think to chart its course.*

*Still, we persist, and speak.
Perhaps we are not small.
Perhaps in our shrill soundings
We, we few, are all.*

I do not have the slightest idea what the next poem signifies, whether it is an atavistic reminder of the *Apocalypse* of St. John the Divine or a metaphor for the end of old history and the arrival of the

CHAPTER 18: RHYTHMS OF REASON

Civitas Humana. The original title was "Dies Irae," but that, too, could be metaphorical. Poets exasperate.

In the beginning were the albatrosses
Floating on streams of air,
Diving and rising and banking
To greet cold gusts
At grand conjunctures.

In the end were the nightingales
Warbling lovingly in the dusk,
Offering their throats to the fallen sun.

In the middle were the robins
Resolutely searching the soaked turf
For drowning worms.

On the breast of eternity
Were the whirling envoys of God,
Harping pale psalms,
Announcing the closure of time.

We spoke in the preceding chapter of the problem with death, not that it must be, but that we must stroll down the street never knowing when it will leap out from a dark alley and snuff our flame against our will. This poem captures my fear of ambush.

There is something worse than death.
Far worse, far more terrible.
Death is nothingness,
The state of non-being.
How can a not-being be?
How can a not-being know
It is not? It cannot.

There is something worse than death.
Far worse, far more terrible.
Knowing mortality is worse,
Measuring the moments until
You will be dead. You are now,
But tomorrow you will be not.
This is far worse, far more terrible,
Than being dead, which is not being,
Which is not.

There is something worse than death,
Such as a white thread
In your waning hair,
Or else a line
Splitting your face, sequestering
Your lips, plowing your forehead,
Pleating the corner of your eye,
Etching your neck.

There is something worse than death:
Watching your death in mirrors,
Or in your nightly dreaming rendezvous
With the unreal world,
As when you glimpse a ripe wonder-maiden
Grown overripe and gaunt and pale,
Wonder no more, a travesty of woman
Creased and silvered by time.

There is something worse than death,
Far worse, far more terrible:
Waiting, darkly waiting
For the silence you will never hear.

Death, for our individual selves, is the end of the world. We leave without ever knowing the sequel.

CHAPTER 18: RHYTHMS OF REASON

The world expires
In the wink of an eye,
No one is laughing,
Not you, not I.

The world expires
In the split of a sky,
Not the whole world,
But you, but I.

The world expires
In the heave of a sigh,
We shall not hear it,
Not you, not I.

One of my strongest convictions is that holiness resides in all being: not in Mecca or Rome or any earthly sanctum, but in all being. Until we grasp the holiness of all being, we shall not be able to respect any fragment of being.

Holiness is not in place,
Not in time, not in name.
Holiness resides in being,
Moon, earth, sun,
Holiness resides in
Spangled sky.
You will say,
Save this hallowed plot,
Single out that sacred corner of the world.
You will say, the gods
Have sanctified this stream,
That ancient town,
But I say, no, not this
Or that, but all, we all,

They all, the magnifying all,
Are holy, carved from nothingness
To be revered.

Now I step back. I acquiesce in whatever, in the lines and gyres of time, must be. Yet I continue to hope.

What matters is that all of us
Serve being and bid all being
Serve us, since we are one with all.
What is the difference
Between the singularity
In us and the oneness that
Dwells in us and is ourselves?
You are that. You are that
Allness that issues in
Sounding singularities.
You are that oneness that disgorges
Endlessly unique and separate selves.
All the same stuff
Constitutes us all, yet
Makes us singular. There is a holy
Dialectic here, one, all,
Separate, conjoined, we rise, we fall,
We celebrate the potent
Possibilities of being.

REFERENCES

Prolegomenon
Kurian, George Thomas and Graham T.T. Molitor, eds., *Encyclopedia of the Future* (2 Vols., New York: Macmillan Library Reference, 1996), II:1077.

Chapter 1: Early Days
Bellamy, Edward, *Looking Backward, 2000-1887* (Boston: Ticknor, 1888).
Durant, Will, *The Mansions of Philosophy: A Survey of Human Life and Destiny* (New York: Garden City, 1929).
Le Guin, Ursula K., *The Left Hand of Darkness* (New York: Walker, 1969).
McHale, John, *The Future of the Future* (New York: Braziller, 1969).
Van Loon, Hendrik Willem, *The Story of Mankind* (New York: Boni and Liveright, 1921).
Van Loon, Hendrik Willem, *Van Loon's Geography* (New York: Simon & Schuster, 1932).
Wells, H.G., *The Outline of History* [1920] (Garden City, NY: Garden City, 1929).
Wells, H.G., Julian Huxley, and G.P. Wells, *The Science of Life* (4 Vols., Garden City, NY: Doubleday, Doran, 1931).
Wells, H.G., *Seven Famous Novels* (New York: Alfred A. Knopf, 1934).

Chapter 2: The Institutional Circle
Comte, Auguste, *System of Positive Polity* [4 Vols., 1851-1854; in English, 1875].
Shaw, Bernard, *Back to Methuselah: A Metabiological Pentateuch* (New York: Brentano's, 1921).

Chapter 4: Manifesto!

Baumer, Franklin Le Van, ed., *Main Currents of Western Thought* (New York: Alfred A. Knopf, 1952).

Clarke, Arthur C., *The Exploration of Space* (New York: Harper, 1954).

Kroeber, A.L., *Configurations of Culture Growth* (Berkeley: University of California Press, 1944).

McNeill, William H., *Past and Future* (Chicago: University of Chicago Press, 1954).

Wells, H.G., *The Open Conspiracy: Blue Prints for a World Revolution* (Garden City, NY: Doubleday, Doran, 1928).

Wells, H.G., *The Shape of Things To Come* (New York: Macmillan, 1933).

Chapter 5: All's Wells

Asimov, Isaac, "The Prophet with Honor" [review of Wagar, ed., *Journalism and Prophecy*], *The Humanist* (March/April 1965), 62.

Bergonzi, Bernard, *The Early H.G. Wells: A Study of the Scientific Romances* (Manchester: Manchester University Press, 1961).

Bergonzi, Bernard, "The Visions of H.G. Wells" [review of *Journalism and Prophecy*], *The New York Review of Books* (November 5, 1964), 20-21.

Burgess, Anthony, "Exhausted Wells" [review of *Journalism and Prophecy*], *Spectator* (January 28, 1966), 111.

Campbell, Alex, "Between Education and Catastrophe" [review of *Journalism and Prophecy*], *The New Republic* (October 31, 1964), 19-20.

Green, Martin, "The Wells Run Dry" [review of Wagar, *H.G. Wells and the World State*], *Time & Tide* (December 21, 1961), 2162.

Henderson, Arthur, "One Planet Indivisible" [review of *H.G. Wells and the World State*], *Saturday Review* (June 3, 1961), 25, 40.

Madow, Pauline, "The Horse's Mouth" [review of *Journalism and Prophecy*], *The Nation* (December 7, 1964), 444-446.

Martin, Kingsley, "Open Conspirator" [review of *Journalism and Prophecy*], *New Statesman* (January 28, 1966), 134.

Shaw, Bernard, and H.G. Wells, *Bernard Shaw and H.G. Wells*, ed. J. Percy Smith (Toronto: University of Toronto Press, 1995).

Sherry, John, "Journalism and Prophecy: An Anthology of H.G. Wells" [review of *Journalism and Prophecy*], *Book-of-the-Month Club News* (January, 1965), 12.

Taylor, A.J.P., "Impatient Prophet" [review of *Journalism and Prophecy*], *Observer* (January 29, 1966).

Wagar, W. Warren, *H.G. Wells and the World State* (New Haven: Yale University Press, 1961).

Wells, H.G., *Anticipations of the Reaction of Mechanical and Scientific Progress upon Human Life and Thought* (New York: Harper & Brothers, 1902).

Wells, H.G., *The Holy Terror* (New York: Simon & Schuster, 1939).

Wells, H.G., *H.G. Wells: Journalism and Prophecy, 1893-1946*, ed. W. Warren Wagar (Boston: Houghton Mifflin, 1964; and London: The Bodley Head, 1966).

Wells, H.G., *World Brain* (Garden City, NY: Doubleday, Doran, 1938).

Wells, H.G., *The World of William Clissold* (2 Vols., New York: Doran, 1926).

Chapter 6: Cosmopolis Revisited

Baritz, Loren, "Plea for Unified World Order Now" [review of Wagar, *The City of Man*], *Chicago News*, March 13, 1963.

Barr, Stringfellow, "Prophets, Peace, and Power" [review of *The City of Man*], *Saturday Review* (April 13, 1963), 79-80.

Gabriel, Ralph H., "A Look at the Fate of Man" [review of *The City of Man*], *Washington Post & Times Herald* (March 24, 1963).

Mundt, Ernest, *Art, Form, and Civilization* (Berkeley: University of California Press, 1952).

Northrop, F.S.C., *The Meeting of East and West: An Inquiry Con-

cerning Human Understanding (New York: Macmillan, 1946).

Robinson, Walter, "An Inspiring Light for a Darkening World" [review of *The City of Man*], *Chicago Sunday Tribune* (April 14, 1963).

Schuman, Frederick L., *The Commonwealth of Man: An Inquiry into Power Politics and World Government* (New York: Alfred A. Knopf, 1952).

Siegel, Kalman, "Books of The Times" [review of *The City of Man*], *The New York Times* (April 5, 1963), C 45.

Toynbee, Arnold J., *A Study of History* (12 Vols., New York: Oxford University Press, 1934-1961).

Wagar, W. Warren, *The City of Man: Prophecies of a World Civilization in Twentieth-Century Thought* (Boston: Houghton Mifflin, 1963; and Baltimore: Penguin Books, 1967).

Westerfield, H. Bradford, [review of *The City of Man*], *The Annals of the American Academy of Political and Social Science* (November, 1963), 217.

Chapter 7: Revolution!

Barber, Benjamin R., *Jihad vs. McWorld* (New York: Times Books, 1995).

Barnet, Richard J., [review of Wagar, *Building the City of Man*], *Saturday Review* (November 6, 1971), 57-58.

Friedan, Betty, *The Feminine Mystique* (New York: Norton, 1963).

Murphy, Cliona, "H.G. Wells: Educationalist, Utopian, and Feminist?," *H.G. Wells under Revision*, eds. Patrick Parrinder and Christopher Rolfe (London: Associated University Presses, 1990), pp. 218-225.

Toffler, Alvin, *Future Shock* (New York: Random House, 1970).

Wagar, W. Warren, "The Bankruptcy of the Peace Movement," *War/Peace Report* (August-September 1969), 3-6.

Wagar, W. Warren, *Building the City of Man: Outlines of a World Civilization* (New York: Richard Grossman, 1971).

Wagar, W. Warren, "Toward the City of Man," *The Center Magazine*

(September, 1968), 33-41.
Wells, H.G., *Ann Veronica: A Modern Love Story* (New York: Harper & Brothers, 1909).

Chapter 8: Believing in Progress
Hughes, H. Stuart, *Consciousness and Society: The Reorientation of European Social Thought, 1890-1930* (New York: Alfred A. Knopf, 1958).
Rudhyar, Dane, *The Planetarization of Consciousness* (The Netherlands: Servire/Wassenaar, 1970).
Wagar, W. Warren, *Books in World History: A Guide for Students and Teachers* (Bloomington: Indiana University Press, 1973).
Wagar, W. Warren, *Good Tidings: The Belief in Progress from Darwin to Marcuse* (Bloomington: Indiana University Press, 1972).
Wagar, W. Warren, ed., *History and the Idea of Mankind* (Albuquerque: University of New Mexico Press, 1971).

Chapter 9: High Church
Bell, Daniel, *The Coming of Post-Industrial Society: A Venture in Social Forecasting* (New York: Basic Books, 1973).
Falk, Richard A., *This Endangered Planet: Prospects and Proposals for Human Survival* (New York: Random House, 1972).
Mannheim, Karl, *Ideology and Utopia: An Introduction to the Sociology of Knowledge* [1929] (New York: Harcourt Brace Jovanovich, 1955).
McHale, John, *The Future of the Future* (New York: Braziller, 1969).
McNeill, William H., *A World History* (2nd Ed., New York: Oxford University Press, 1971).
Meadows, Donella H., et al., *The Limits to Growth* (New York: Universe Books, 1972).
Wagar, W. Warren, *World Views: A Study in Comparative History* (Hinsdale, IL: Dryden Press, 1977).

Chapter 10: Apocalypses

Barkun, Michael, [review of Wagar, *Terminal Visions*], *The American Historical Review* (October, 1983), 962.

Beauchamp, Gorman, [review of *Terminal Visions*], *Michigan Quarterly Review* (Spring 1984), 299-301.

Beckett, Samuel, *Endgame* (New York: Grove, 1958).

Burgess, Anthony, "The Apocalypse and After," [review of *Terminal Visions*], *Times Literary Supplement* (March 18, 1983).

Burgess, Anthony, *A Clockwork Orange* (New York: Norton, 1963).

Burgess, Anthony, *The End of the World News: An Entertainment* (New York: McGraw-Hill, 1983).

Flint, John, "Challenging Regressive Hopes," [review of *Terminal Visions*], State University of New York, *The News* (September, 1983), F-3, F-4.

Hoban, Russell, *Riddley Walker* (New York: Summit Books, 1981).

Huxley, Aldous, *Ape and Essence* (New York: Harper, 1948).

Ionesco, Eugène, *A Stroll in the Air* [1963] (New York: Grove, 1968).

Ketterer, David, [review of *Terminal Visions*], *Canadian Review of Comparative Literature* (September, 1986), 492-495.

Lessing, Doris, *The Memoirs of a Survivor* (New York: Alfred A. Knopf, 1975).

Miller, Walter M., Jr., *A Canticle for Leibowitz* (Philadelphia: Lippincott, 1960).

Painter, Nell, "How We Died" [review of *Terminal Visions*], *The Nation* (May 7, 1983), 582-583.

Segal, Howard P., [review of *Terminal Visions*], *Technology and Culture* (October, 1984), 905-906.

Shelley, Mary, *The Last Man* [1826] (Lincoln: University of Nebraska Press, 1965).

Wagar, W. Warren, "Postscript," State University of New York, *The News* (September, 1983), F-4.

Wagar, W. Warren, ed., *The Secular Mind: Transformations of Faith in Modern Europe* (New York: Holmes & Meier, 1982).

REFERENCES

Wagar, W. Warren, *Terminal Visions: The Literature of Last Things* (Bloomington: Indiana University Press, 1982).
Wells, H.G., *The War in the Air* (New York: Macmillan, 1908).
Wells, H.G., *The World Set Free* (New York: Dutton, 1914).
Wolfe, Gary K., [review of *Terminal Visions*], *Foundation: The Review of Science Fiction* (February, 1983), 101-103.

Chapter 11: Paths to the Future

Engels, Friedrich, *Socialism: Utopian and Scientific* [1892] (New York: International Publishers, 1994).
Orwell, George, *Nineteen Eighty-Four* (New York: Harcourt, Brace, 1949).
Wagar, W. Warren, "Dreams of Reason: Bellamy, Wells, and the Positive Utopia," *Looking Backward, 1988-1888: Essays on Edward Bellamy*, ed. Daphne Patai (Amherst: University of Massachusetts Press, 1988), pp. 106-125.
Wagar, W. Warren, "George Orwell as Political Secretary of the Zeitgeist," *The Future of 1984*, ed. Ejner J. Jensen (Ann Arbor: University of Michigan Press, 1984), pp. 177-199.
Wagar, W. Warren, "H.G. Wells and the Scientific Imagination," *The Virginia Quarterly Review* (Summer, 1989), 390-400.
Wagar, W. Warren, "The Next Three Futures," *World Future Society Bulletin* (November-December 1984), 12-19; and *What I Have Learned: Thinking about the Future Then and Now*, eds. Michael Marien and Lane Jennings (New York: Greenwood Press, 1987), pp.3-21.
Wagar, W. Warren, "Profile of a Futurist: Arnold J. Toynbee and the Coming World Civilization," *Futures Research Quarterly* (Fall 1986), 61-70.
Wagar, W. Warren, "Science and the World State: Education as Utopia in the Prophetic Vision of H.G. Wells," *H.G. Wells Under Revision*, eds., Patrick Parrinder and Christopher Rolfe (London: Associated University Presses, 1990), pp. 40-53.

Chapter 12: The Human Comedy

Buck, Pearl, *The Good Earth* (New York: Harper, 1931).

Buck, Pearl, *The House of Earth* (New York: Reynal & Hitchcock, 1935).

Chatain, Robert, "Today's Tomorrows" [review of Wagar, *A Short History of the Future*], *Chicago Tribune* (December 31, 1989), 14:3.

Clarke, I.F., "And This Is the Future, Ladies and Gentlemen" [review of *A Short History of the Future*], *Futures* (July-August, 1990), 667-668.

Fowles, Jib, "Wagar's Projected Future Too Predictable, Lacks Vision" [review of *A Short History of the Future*], *The Houston Post* (January 7, 1990).

Franklin, H. Bruce, "Tales from the 2000s" [review of *A Short History of the Future*], *The Washington Post* (December 25, 1989).

Future Survey [review of *A Short History of the Future*] (November, 1989), 2.

The Futurist [review of *A Short History of the Future*] (May-June, 1990), 45.

Irwin, Robert, [review of *A Short History of the Future*], *Foundation: The Review of Science Fiction* (Spring 1990), 84-87.

Merkley, Paul, [review of *A Short History of the Future*], *The American Historical Review* (June 1991), 850.

Publishers Weekly, [review of *A Short History of the Future*], (October 13, 1989), 35.

Sargent, Lyman Tower, [review of *A Short History of the Future*], *Utopian Studies* (1990), 174.

Schwartzman, David, "A World Party: Vehicle of Global Green Left," *EcoSocialist Review* (Spring 1992), 4-5.

Stableford, Brian, and David Langford, *The Next Millennium: A History of the World, AD 2000-3000* (New York: Alfred A. Knopf, 1985).

Vehse, Ted, "A Look Back at Future Nostalgia," [review of *A Short History of the Future*], *In These Times* (January 24-30,

1990), 19.
Wagar, W. Warren, "The Day of No-Judgment," *The Magazine of Fantasy and Science Fiction* (April, 1986), 109-136.
Wagar, W. Warren, "Heart's Desire," *Isaac Asimov's Science Fiction Magazine* (July, 1984), 91-102.
Wagar, W. Warren, "Madonna of the Red Sun," *Synergy I*, ed. George Zebrowski (San Diego: Harcourt, Brace, Jovanovich, 1987), pp. 164-182.
Wagar, W. Warren, "The Night of No Joy," *The Magazine of Fantasy and Science Fiction* (June, 1987), 6-44.
Wagar, W. Warren, "The President's Worm," *The Magazine of Fantasy and Science Fiction* (September, 1986), 6-22.
Wagar, W. Warren, *A Short History of the Future* (Chicago: University of Chicago Press, 1989).
Wagar, W. Warren, "The Time of No Troubles," *The Magazine of Fantasy and Science Fiction* (December, 1988), 87-137.
Wilson, Robert N., [review of *A Short History of the Future*], *Contemporary Sociology* (January, 1991), 109.

Chapter 13: Paradigms
Hughes, Barry B., *World Futures: A Critical Analysis of Alternatives* (Baltimore: The Johns Hopkins University Press, 1985).
Polak, Fred. L., *The Image of the Future* (2 Vols., New York: Oceana Publications, 1961.)
Wagar, W. Warren, "A Funny Thing Happened on My Way to the Future, Or, The Hazards of Prophecy," *The Futurist* (May-June, 1994), 21-25.
Wagar, W. Warren, *The Next Three Futures: Paradigms of Things To Come*, (New York: Praeger; and Westport, CT: Greenwood Press, 1991; London: Adamantine Press, 1992).

Chapter 14: Second Edition
Huntington, Samuel P., *The Clash of Civilizations and the Remaking of World Order* (New York: Simon & Schuster, 1996).
Wagar, W. Warren, "Goodfood," *Journeys to the Twilight Zone*, ed.

Carol Serling (New York: DAW Books, 1993), pp. 15-32.
Wagar, W. Warren, *A Short History of the Future* (2nd ed., Chicago: University of Chicago Press, 1992; London: Adamantine Press, 1993).

Chapter 15: The World Party

Amin, Samir, "The Future of Global Polarization," *Review* (Summer 1994), 337-347.
Arrighi, Giovanni, Terence K. Hopkins, and Immanuel Wallerstein, *Antisystemic Movements* (London and New York: Verso, 1989).
Chase-Dunn, Christopher, *Global Formation: Structures of the World-Economy* (Cambridge, MA, and Oxford: Basil Blackwell, 1989).
Frank, Andre Gunder, in Samir Amin, et al., *Dynamics of Global Crisis* (New York: Monthly Review Press, 1982).
Fukuyama, Francis, *The End of History and the Last Man* (New York: Free Press, 1992).
Kaplan, Robert D., *The Coming Anarchy: Shattering the Dreams of the Post Cold War Era* (New York: Random House, 2000).
Hobsbawm, Eric J., "Some Reflections on *The Break-Up of Britain*," *New Left Review* (September-October, 1987).
Meyer, John W., "The World Polity and the Authority of the Nation-State," in George M. Thomas, et al., *Institutional Structure: Constituting State, Society, and the Individual* Beverly Hills: Sage, 1987), pp. 41-70.
Wagar, W. Warren, "Past and Future," *American Behavioral Scientist* (November-December, 1998), 365-371.
Wagar, W. Warren, *A Short History of the Future* [2nd ed., in Japanese] (Tokyo: Futami Shobo, 1995).
Wagar, W. Warren, *A Short History of the Future* (3rd ed., Chicago: University of Chicago Press, 1999).
Wagar, W. Warren, "Socialism, Nationalism, and Ecocide," *Review* (Summer 1996), 319-333.
Wagar, W. Warren, "Teaching the Future: A Memoir," *Futurevision:*

REFERENCES

Ideas, Insights, and Strategies, Howard F. Didsbury, Jr., ed. (Bethesda, MD: World Future Society, 1996), pp. 78-87.

Wagar, W. Warren, "Tomorrow and Tomorrow and Tomorrow," *Technology Review* (April, 1993), 50-59.

Wagar, W. Warren, "Toward a Praxis of World Integration" and "Response," *Journal of World-Systems Research* (June, 1996), published on-line without pagination.

Wagar, W. Warren, *The World: Coming Together or Falling Apart?* (Albany: The University at Albany, 1995).

Wallerstein, Immanuel, *The Capitalist World-Economy* (Cambridge: Cambridge University Press, 1979).

Wallerstein, Immanuel, *Geopolitics and Geoculture: Essays on the Changing World-System* (Cambridge: Cambridge University Press, 1991).

Wallerstein, Immanuel, *The Politics of the World-Economy: The States, the Movements, and the Civilizations* (Cambridge: Cambridge University Press, 1979).

Chapter 16: Doomscapes

Calvin, William H., "The Great Climate Flip-Flop," *The Atlantic Monthly* (January, 1998), 47-64.

Collins, Warwick, "Not with a Bang but a Bleep," *The Spectator* (October 8, 1994), 9-14.

Drexler, Eric, *Engines of Creation* (Garden City, NY: Anchor Press, 1986).

Joy, Bill, "Why the Future Doesn't Need Us," *Wired* (April, 2000), 238 ff.

Mueller, John, *Retreat from Doomsday: The Obsolescence of Major War* (New York: Basic Books, 1989).

Chapter 17: The Service of Being

Elgin, Duane, *Voluntary Simplicity: Toward a Way of Life That Is Outwardly Simple, Inwardly Rich* (New York: Morrow, 1981).

Huxley, T.H., and Julian Huxley, *Touchstone for Ethics* (New York:

Harper, 1947).

Lovelock, James, *Gaia: A New Look at Life on Earth* (New York: Oxford University Press, 1987).

Ward, Peter D., and Donald C. Brownlee, *Rare Earth: Why Complex Life Is Uncommon in the Universe* (New York: Springer-Verlag, 2000).

Chapter 18: Rhythms of Reason

Jaspers, Karl, *The Origin and Goal of History* [1949] (New Haven: Yale University Press, 1953).

INDEX

Africa, Thomas W., 124, 134
Albuquerque, 3, 86
Antisystemic movements, 193-196
Apocalypses, 133-138
Asimov, Isaac, 63, 159

Baltimore, 2
Baumer, Franklin Le Van, 48, 49, 53, 55, 59-60, 72, 73-74, 132, 135, 139, 171, 173
Bergonzi, Bernard, 61-62, 63
Binghamton, State University of New York at, xi, 89, 115, 118
Books in World History, 106, 116
Bowers, John Alden, 148-149
Building the City of Man: Outlines of a World Civilization, 84, 88, 90, 95-102, 103, 124, 151, 222, 227, 229
Burgess, Anthony, 135-136

Cantor, Norman F., 89-90, 105, 115, 116-117
Cattell, Hudson, 13-22, 27-30, 31-33, 35-36, 37-38, 43-48, 70, 77, 101-102, 124, 147, 160, 164-165, 173, 184, 186
Cattell, Jaques, 21, 44
Cattell, Psyche, 16, 18-21, 27, 36
Chase-Dunn, Christopher, 196, 201
City of Man, The: Prophecies of a World Civilization in Twentieth-Century Thought, 31, 44, 60, 69-72, 74, 77-82, 86, 88, 90, 95, 103, 113, 151, 153, 222
Communism, 39, 49, 53, 127-128, 179
Computer science, 217-219
Cornish, Edward, 117, 175-176

Durant, Will, 8, 10

Enlightenment, Left, 197-199, 207
Evolution, theory of, 8, 11, 26, 30

Fantasia (Walt Disney), 8, 11
First Unitarian Church (Albuquerque), 87
Fonda, Jane, ix, 94
Franklin & Marshall College, 29, 33, 37
Futures studies, x, xi, 117-121, 140, 171, 174-178

Genetic engineering, 216-217
Ginsburg, Ruth Bader, 84
Global warming, 213-214
Good Tidings: The Belief in Progress from Darwin to Marcuse, 75, 106-114
Greenwood Press, 171, 173

H.G. Wells and the World State, 60-62, 64-68, 72, 74
H.G. Wells: Journalism and Prophecy, 1893-1946, 62-64, 159
H.G. Wells Society, 146, 163
Historicism, 11
History, 36, 121
"History of the Future," xi, 96, 117-124, 140-143, 152, 163-164
Houghton Mifflin, 60, 62-64, 69, 77
Hughes, Barry B., 171, 175
Humanism, cosmic, 225-227
Huxley, T.H., 223-224

Indiana University, 38, 43-44, 48, 75-76
Indiana University Press, 106, 116, 135
Integration project, 43-53
Intellectual history, 48, 55, 74, 86, 89, 104, 130, 139, 155
Ithaca, 90, 105-106

INDEX

Joy, Bill, 219, 221

Kagarlitsky, Yuli, 163
Korean War, 31-32, 38-39

Lancaster, Pennsylvania, x, 4, 27, 37, 43, 44, 164, 170
Lititz, Pennsylvania, 5, 170

Marcuse, Herbert, 87, 107
Marien, Mary Warner, 160
Marien, Michael, 146, 150, 177
Marxism, 111, 124-129, 131, 151-152, 167, 193
McCaskey High School, 27, 29
McHale, John, 9, 117, 118
Memoirs of the Future, 184, 186
"Miss Miles," 17-22
Mitchell, Douglas C., 160, 181
"Modred," 14, 18, 22
Music, 14, 28-29, 31, 37

"The Next Three Futures," 146, 150-153, 177, 178
The Next Three Futures: Paradigms of Things To Come, 31, 171, 173, 174-178
Northrop, F.S.C., 48, 49, 56

Oil, 211-212
Orwell, George, 145, 146, 193-194

Philosophy, 8-9, 22, 23-24, 29, 30-31, 35, 65
Princeton University, 72-73, 75-76
Population, 210-211
Postmodernism, 131-132
Progress, idea of, 1, 7-11, 22-26, 30, 74-75, 103-104, 106-114

Religion, 10, 15, 23, 40, 46, 87, 212-213, 221-227

Reynolds Junior High School, 13, 29

Sargent, Pamela, 155
Schwarz, Henry, 58
Science fiction, 13, 14, 31, 155-157, 182
Segal, Howard P., 191
Service of Being, 227
Shaw, Bernard, 26, 56-57
Short History of the Future, A, 25, 31, 53, 157-163, 165-169, 179-182, 184, 187-190, 192, 196, 202-204, 207, 209, 216, 222, 227
Smith, Clark Ashton, 15

Terminal Visions: The Literature of Last Things, 135-138, 139, 155

University of Chicago Press, 160
University of Illinois, 56, 88-89
University of Massachusetts, 76
University of New Mexico, xi, 85-90, 93, 106
University of New Mexico Press, 106

Van Loon, Hendrik Willem, 10
Vietnam War, ix, 87, 94

Wagar, Bruce Alan, 63, 170
Wagar, Dorothy Bowers, 43, 44, 57, 60, 86, 87, 88, 106, 148, 159, 182, 183
Wagar, Gertrude, 4, 6, 29-30
Wagar (Lynx), Jennifer Lynne, 86, 172, 173
Wagar, John Alden, 60, 63, 164, 182-183
Wagar, Laura Stoner, x, 2, 3, 6, 29, 164, 169-170, 171-173
Wagar, Steven Lawrence, 63, 170
Wagar, Walter, x, 2-7, 170
Wagar, William, 4, 29-30
Wagar, Winnifred (aunt), 4, 6, 29-30, 159

INDEX

Wagar, Winnifred (sister), 2-5
Wallerstein, Immanuel, 118, 145, 151, 166, 177, 193, 196, 201, 202, 204, 206-207
War, end of, 214-216
Wellesley College, xi, 58-59, 72-73, 75-77, 83-85
Wells, G.P., 57
Wells, H.G., 2, 10, 25, 35, 36, 44-45, 55-68, 133, 158, 161, 176
Wells, Marjorie, 57
Womankind, 25, 83-85
World civilization, 50, 66, 74, 78-80, 95, 133, 150
World Future Society, xi, 117, 125-127, 145, 175-176
World government, 9, 17, 24-25, 40-41, 46, 51, 66-67, 80-81, 99-101
World Party, 88, 98, 166, 196-197, 202-206, 209
World Views: A Study in Comparative History, 118, 128-132. 137
"World War III," 140-145, 163-164, 191
Wylie, Craig, 62-64, 69

Yale University, 48, 59, 60
Yale University Press, 60-61

Zebrowski, George, 155, 156, 159, 160